DO NOT REMOVE
CARDS FROM POCKET

D1265543

Preparing Convicts for Law-Abiding Lives

SUNY series in
New Directions in Crime and Justice Studies
Austin T. Turk, editor

Preparing Convicts for Law-Abiding Lives

The Pioneering Penology of Richard A. McGee

Daniel Glaser

State University of New York Press

Cover photo: Richard A. McGee, believed to have been taken about 1960 (Courtesy of the California Department of Corrections)

Published by
State University of New York Press, Albany

© 1995 State University of New York

For information, address State University of New York Press, State University Plaza, Albany, NY 12246

Production by Cynthia Tenace Lassonde
Marketing by Nancy Farrell

Library of Congress Cataloging-in-Publication Data

Glaser, Daniel.
    Preparing convicts for law-abiding lives : the pioneering penology of Richard A. McGee / Daniel Glaser.
      p. cm. — (SUNY series in new directions in crime and justice studies)
    Includes bibliographical references (p.   ) and index.
    ISBN 0-7914-2695-5 (hc : alk. paper). — ISBN 0-7914-2696-3 (pbk. : alk. paper)
    1. McGee, Richard A. 2. Prison reformers—United States—Biography. 3. Prisoners—Rehabilitation—United States. 4. Prison administration—United States—Philosophy. 5. Community-based corrections—United States. 6. Parole—United States—Philosophy.
I. Title. II. Series.
HV8978.M34G53 1995
365'.66—dc20
    [B]

95-8938
CIP

10 9 8 7 6 5 4 3 2 1

Contents

Tables

Figures and Photographs

Foreword

How have governments dealt with persons convicted of crimes? How should this change? Answers to these questions are offered here in describing and assessing the career of Richard A. McGee (1897–1983), who was one of the most successful promoters of ways to control crime, yet always dissatisfied with what he achieved.

McGee's work in corrections began in 1931 as director of education in a federal prison. From 1935 to 1941 he supervised New York City penal facilities, then headed the Department of Public Institutions for the state of Washington, and from 1944 until his retirement in 1967, he directed California's state correctional programs. Throughout his years in justice agencies, and in retirement, McGee published extensively, and had numerous national and international offices and honors. This book draws much from his lucid writings.

The American Justice Institute (AJI), in an effort to keep McGee's contributions clearly in evidence as an inspiration to further improvement in corrections, recruited John P. Conrad to write a book about McGee, with whom he had worked for about thirty-five years. Following Conrad's untimely death of a heart attack in October 1992, when he had not begun this writing and left no plans for it, Lawrence A. Bennett, President of AJI, asked me to undertake this task.

Bennett provided two large boxes of McGee's writings, plus other documents, from which I have drawn greatly while writing this book. In addition, many useful anecdotes, documents, references, tapes, and suggestions were given by others who worked with McGee to varying extents, including:

David Brewer, Counselor, California Institution for Men, Chino

Robert Dickover, retired in 1994 from Research Branch, California Department of Corrections

Don M. Gottfredson, Professor of Criminal Justice, Emeritus, Rutgers University

Keith S. Griffiths, retired Director of Research, California Youth Authority

David J. Halperin, Attorney, Judicial Council of California

Norman Holt, Parole Administrator, California Department of Corrections, Sacramento

Richard A. McGee, Jr., Building Inspector, Retired Contractor, Sacramento

Sheldon Messinger, Professor Emeritus, University of California, Berkeley

E. Kim Nelson, Professor Emeritus, University of Southern California

Lloyd E. Ohlin, Professor Emeritus, Harvard University

James W. L. Park, retired Associate Superintendent, California State Correctional Facility at Soledad

Leslie T. Wilkins, Dean Emeritus, School of Criminology, University of California, Berkeley, and retired Research Statistician, British Home Office

Each quotation in this book that is extracted from a letter, note, or tape sent to me by one of the individuals on the preceding list has its source and date indicated in the notes found at the end of the book; also, each was sent to its author for review and approval before inclusion here. I am most grateful for everyone's assistance, as well as for innumerable improvements in my writing from suggestions by my wife Pearl.

Daniel Glaser

Traditional Government Reactions to Criminals

To appreciate Richard McGee's use of science and politics to achieve major changes in corrections, and to assess its utility today, one must be familiar with the history of reactions to convicted criminals before the main portion of his career began, in California in 1944. In the last two centuries, the goals most emphasized in dealing with law-breakers changed successively from revenge to restraint to reformation, but all three, and others, are often pursued simultaneously, even today. He had to cope with unfairness and corruption that have also been frequent features of correctional administration.

The Evolution of Penalties Before 1944

In Europe and America, until well into this century, vengeance for many crimes was sought by corporal or capital punishments. Death was imposed not only for murder, but often also for rape, robbery, and other offenses. Painful penalties were demanded, and still are, to avenge victims, and also in the hope of thereby deterring others from committing crimes.

Economic interests have usually influenced the choice of punishments. Offenders with resources were required to pay compensation to their victims or to the victims' families, in addition to fines; poorer law-breakers got hard labor, and corporal penalties. From ancient times until well into the twentieth century, in most parts of the world as well as in the United States, poor convicts were worked—often in chains—to quarry stone, row large coastal and river ships, build roads, and do other physical labor now done by machines (Rusche and Kirchheimer, 1939:57–58; Bramford, 1973:25–29, 317-18).

Local jails (spelled "gaols" in Britain, but pronounced as though "jails"), "workhouses," and "houses of correction," were the first widespread institutions to impose confinement for a specified period of time as a penalty, rather than merely holding accused persons until judges decided on their guilt and on physical and financial punishments. Incarceration penalties were imposed mainly on vagabonds, prostitutes, beggars, and other misdemeanants. Such institutions began in Britain in the sixteenth century, and were soon established in major American cities, when industrialization created a shortage of unskilled labor; local employers paid the government a fee to employ the inmates (Rusche and Kirchheimer:41–52; McKelvey, 1977:24–25).

Also locked up locally were persons who could not pay debts or fines, homeless individuals, psychotics, and destitute orphans for whom no other source of shelter and food was readily available. David Garland observes:

> Then, as now, penal policy was shaped by a variety of ends—such as justice, economy, vengeance, forgiveness, charity, evangelism, and so on—and had to find a way of combining rational strategies with the demands of popular sentiment and ritualistic tradition (1986:874).

A different type of confinement facility, the penitentiary, was promoted by the Quakers in Pennsylvania, who imposed solitary confinement on each offender in a large cell. A Bible or other religious book was given to every literate prisoner, and the only visitors allowed were religious counselors and preachers, who spoke through a small opening in the massive cell door. Food was also passed in through this opening, and waste removed. Work was not required; these places were supposed to be devoted only to reforming the offenders by making them penitent.

Restraint by imprisonment became the principal penalty for serious crimes in the United States and western Europe, as the Industrial Revolution reduced the market for unskilled convict labor. During economic recessions, prisoners were often idle or made to do unnecessary tasks, such as moving rocks from one side of a walled yard to the other, and then back again. With no economic incentives to keep them employed, there was much neglect of their health, and they were often starved (Rusche and Kirchheimer:ch. vi).

When prison admissions exceeded the number of cells, and new construction was opposed because of its cost, solitary confinement in penitentiaries was not feasible. Increasingly, prisoners were housed and worked in groups, but required to remain silent. When this became official policy, it was called the "Auburn system," after the New York State prison that developed it. In the nineteenth century there were widespread arguments as to the relative advantages of the Pennsylvania or "solitary" system versus the Auburn or "congregate" system of restraint. The Auburn system was generally adopted in the United States and the Pennsylvania system in western Europe.

In 1877, New York State opened a distinctive institution, for prisoners 16 to 30 years old, at Elmira and called it a "reformatory." Its prisoners were to be confined until reformed, but not confined for over five years. Soon other states and countries had similar youth prisons emphasizing academic and vocational training, with each inmate's release dependent on good conduct and learning while confined. Release from reformatory, called "parole," was conditional, as it could be revoked for post-release misconduct.

Reformatories have usually been replaced by "training schools" for juveniles. Juveniles are generally defined as children under eighteen, who are ordered confined by juvenile courts, and may be placed under state control until age twenty-one. These schools stress education, and they usually have more counseling, recreational, and social work staff per inmate than do correctional facilities for adults.

Almost all jurisdictions permit a judge, after a hearing, to decide whether an older juvenile (e.g., aged sixteen or seventeen) charged with a very heinous offense, or with repeated lesser crimes, has the criminality of an adult (usually defined as a person eighteen or older). Such youths may then be sentenced to prison as though adults. "Reformatory," where the term is still used, generally refers now to a prison for young adults, and for juveniles tried and sentenced as though adults.

Also begun, mainly in the late nineteenth century, was probation defined as a period of conditional release by the court in lieu of a confinement penalty. It resembles parole because of its good conduct requirements, and can be replaced by confinement if serious misconduct occurs before the end of the period for which it is imposed. Often courts order a combination of penalties, such as a fine, confinement in a local jail for no more than a year, and then a term of probation with some specific conduct requirements, such as doing some type of community service. All these may be included in the penalty for a single offense.

The juvenile-adult borderline became more variable under California's Youth Authority, established in 1941, and subsequently copied in several states (but elsewhere usually called "Youth Commissions"). For offenders under twenty-one years old, the duration of any sentence to be a ward of such an agency is not for a particular duration in years. Instead, parole occurs when the agency deems it appropriate, but all state control over the youngster ends at a maximum age (usually twenty-five), rather than on completion of a specified term. The offender usually receives a first parole well before that age (Barnes and Teeters, 1959:ch. 26). Most juvenile delinquents, however, are punished by local probation, or are confined in such county facilities as probation camps, group homes, or detention centers.

Political Favoritism and Corruption

In the 1940s, a widespread feature of employment in prisons, as well as parole and probation in the United States and many other nations, was its domination by politics. Especially during periods of high unemployment, applicants for correctional or other government jobs had to have sponsorship from officials of the political party in power. Whenever elections changed the party in control in a county, state, or the nation, many employees expected to lose their jobs or be demoted.

Because of the political liability of escapes or scandals in correctional facilities, however, employees who showed high competence and were not very openly partisan in politics would be retained even when the party that sponsored their initial employment lost power. The typical "professional" in corrections, who persisted in employment despite changes in the party winning elections, was a "non-partisan politician," who did favors for politically influential persons in all parties.

Often the choice of a warden for a state prison was deemed the prerogative of the legislators from the district where the prison was located. Typically, an ex-sheriff was appointed, especially in states such as Illinois where no successive terms were permitted for sheriff. Lower-level correctional jobs also had political sponsors. McGee notes:

> It was common…to hear such aphorisms as, "There's no job done by a Republican that can't be done just as well or better by a Democrat," or vice-versa. As a consequence, it had not been uncommon for an incoming administration to fire almost everybody, from auditors to janitors. This job-trading exercise was especially prevalent in times of severe unemployment….This shock to the public work forces became so critical that everybody seemed to lose. Legislators were slow to act, and even when they did, a subsequent legislature often repealed the law to make room for the party faithful (McGee, 1981:63–64).

Not until well after World War II was most such employment in the U.S. placed under civil service systems that based appointments on test results, and granted job security as long as there were no seriously unfavorable performance reports.

In addition, some prisoners procured special favors within the institutions, such as desirable assignments or even early release, by having politically important persons request them of staff. There was also much staff misuse of prison property and services, for example, having inmate auto mechanics repair their private cars or appliances (Jacobs, 1977:chs. 1 and 2).

After the Great Depression of the 1930s, when labor unions objected to inmates being employed while free citizens could find no jobs, laws were passed permitting prisons only to produce goods and services for government use. Private businesses that want to sell to the government object even to such state-use employment, so that it has usually been difficult to keep prisoners fully occupied.

When prison staff received their jobs mainly as reward for service to politicians in the community, they used various expedients to make their jobs easier. Typical strategies included delegation of authority to inmate leaders, as long as they kept the other inmates behaving satisfactorily. By this means, cliques of long-term tough inmates, the "con bosses" who had curried favor with staff, would essentially administer large segments of many prisons.

These inmate assistants to prison officials often had luxuries and freedoms not available to other prisoners, such as better food and longer hours away from the cellhouses; some even bunked in, or adjacent to, staff offices in comfortably furnished rooms, instead of being returned to their cells after their work. This was rationalized by officials partly because these inmates were on call at any hour, and also to separate them from prisoners who might pressure them for favors. In the kitchens, prime cuts of meat were selected for the officers' dining rooms and for key inmates; other prisoners complained that prison hogs had no hams and prison steers produced no steaks.

California's Pre-1944 Correctional History

California was transferred from Mexico to the United States in 1848 with the Treaty of Guadelupe Hidalgo, and gained statehood in 1850. Most of its claimed territory was in large landholdings that Mexico had granted to Catholic missions or for the haciendas of elite Mexican families. Superiors in both these types of quasi-feudal hierarchies usually dealt with the offenses of those on their lands by ordering penalties, often corporal, and requiring acts of penance. However, there were high crime rates in several areas not controlled by this system, particularly in the northern gold-prospecting region, where vigilante committees were at times the principal source of local policing and punishment. Crime also was frequent in the growing cities, notably San Francisco. Barbara Yaley reports:

> Prior to statehood there were a number of jails in California, inherited from the Mexican regime. Under an act of the new state in 1851, the jails of San Diego, Los Angeles, Santa Barbara, San Jose, and San Francisco were designated as state prisons. The location and small size of these facilities, however, made them inadequate and there were demands in the legislature for a central, large state prison. But for the first few years of statehood...its few prisoners were detained in crude barges owned by local businessmen who contracted with the government for the lease of the prisoners' labor in return for their maintenance and control (1980:58).

In 1851, the new state gave a ten-year lease to a former Mexican general, Mariano Guadlupe Vallejo, to care for approximately fifty prisoners in return for their labor, plus $137,000. He formed a partnership with a politician and former California State Militia general, James Estell (sometimes spelled "Estill"). Their first prison was an old ship, anchored in San Francisco Bay (Yaley, 1980, ch.3). Estell soon bought out Vallejo, and "formed the San Francisco Manufacturing Company, to capitalize on convict labor, and commenced accepting prisoners from... county jails throughout the state...." (Bookspan, 1987, p.23). He supplied prisoners to work for anyone who would pay for their services, including the city of San Francisco, where they graded streets while in chains.

Estell's ship was soon over-filled. Most sources say that he towed it, but it was also reported to have been washed by a storm, to nearby Point San Quentin, where he got the state to contract with him to build a prison. During the 1850s, horrible living conditions, cruel discipline, corruption, and high escape rates from the growing new institution were often reported. Many of the guards were of questionable character. Convicts whom Estell recognized as from "good families" were made trustees, and given various comforts, including some freedom to visit nearby communities. The state took over these operations temporarily on several occasions, and permanently in 1860, but continued to contract out much inmate labor. Until the supply of useful clay was used up around 1900, making bricks was the principal inmate industry at San

Quentin, California's oldest prison (McAfee, 1990b; McKenna, 1987; Bookspan, 1987:ch.2; Yaley, 1980:ch.3).

The economic recession of the 1870s increased free labor objections to competition from convicts. California's second constitution, in 1879, abolished the contract system of employing prisoners (although this provision was largely evaded for several decades). It was the first state proclaiming such abolition; the major Northeastern and Midwestern states followed in the 1880s, but some Southeastern states did not follow until the 1920s. A study in 1886 estimated that the value of all prison-made goods in the United States was only $54/100$ of one percent of the nation's total industrial output, so convict labor was not a major threat to free labor. Yet fear of its threat is readily aroused (McAfee, 1990a).

In 1889, the legislature greatly restricted the public sale of San Quentin-made goods, except for jute bags, which farmers wanted, but could only import from Asia. However, reacting to the loss of state income, in 1905 it enacted a law permitting the exchange of products among state institutions, and thus began California's state-use system of prison industry. In 1915, the state also authorized using convicts in road-construction camps in remote areas. This type of work reached its peak in the 1920s, when it employed about an eighth of the state's prisoners, who were paid by the State Highway Commission. They were then charged for their room and board, but much of their remaining income was sent to their dependents (McAfee, 1990a).

San Quentin was designed for 2,700 men, but in the 1940s held about 4,300, including psychiatric patients. It had long been customary there to put two men into cells designed for only one. Folsom, a second high-security prison, was opened in 1880, about twenty miles northwest of Sacramento, in a granite quarry from which inmates cut stones for the prison. The quarry provided work until 1947, when it was finally closed. During the 1940s, Folsom held about 2,500 men in overcrowded and somewhat dilapidated structures (Bookspan, 1987; Yaley, 1980:chs.3, 4, and 8).

A small facility for women prisoners was completed in 1931 at Tehachapi, in mountains about sixty miles west of Bakersfield. Its construction had been stalled for years, and when finally built, it was empty for over a year, due to political quarrels over its design and use. Women's club leaders wanted an unwalled women-run reformatory, modeled after the federal and Massachusetts women's prisons they had visited. San Quentin's warden, and the state's Board of Prison Directors that was appointed to make penal policy, wished to use the new prison for male first offenders, and to keep the women where they had always been, in a separate building at San Quentin. They were used there for housekeeping or sewing tasks, and some ex-prostitutes allegedly for sexual activity, with visiting legislators among their patrons. The Attorney General interpreted the law as allowing only the previously existing prisons to receive felons, but finally agreed that the women's prison could be treated as a branch of San Quentin (Morales, 1980; Bookspan, 1987:ch. 5; Yaley, 1980:243–50).

When opened in 1933, the women's prison was directed by a man designated as Deputy Warden of San Quentin. He soon built a security fence around it, but kept the women idle, never even unpacking the laundry machinery shipped there for a women's industry. Reacting to this, the Federation of Women's Clubs, the League of Women Voters, the Women's Christian Temperance Union, and others, successfully mobilized to achieve passage of a ballot initiative in 1935 that amended the state constitution to require a separately administered institution for women convicted of felonies. It was to be governed by a special Board of Trustees chosen by the legislature. Assuming control in 1936, this board promptly appointed women as the institution's director and staff (*Ibid*).

In a futile effort to curb political squabbling over a women's prison and other issues, as well as highly publicized scandals of various types, DiIulio notes:

> In 1929, the California Department of Penology was created to centralize administrative controls over the state's abuse- and corruption-ridden penal facilities. Within the year, however, it became clear that the state's Director of Penology would fail; his formal powers went no farther than calling a meeting of five division deputies once a month (1991:21). (*See also*, Yaley, 1980: 256–60).

Vested political interests had kept the autonomy of the prison wardens and the state's Board of Prison Directors largely intact. They saw to it that anyone appointed as Director of Penology was someone who supported them in lobbying the legislators.

For about sixty-five years after the 1877 opening of New York's Elmira Reformatory, there were efforts to establish such an institution in California. Finally in 1935, the legislature authorized the southern California prison to be a reformatory, but set no age limits on its inmates. Land for it was purchased at Chino, about seventy miles west of Los Angeles, but the governor objected to its being a minimum-security reformatory. Saying it would be "a prison, not a country club," he had gun towers and a high masonry wall partially constructed with funds and labor from the federal government's depression-era work relief agency, the Works Progress Administration (WPA). Then a new governor recruited as its first warden Kenyon Scudder, a federal reformatory official and former Los Angeles probation officer. He came only on agreement that it would be a minimum security institution, and that he would have no political interference with his selection of staff. It opened unfinished in 1941, as the only one of the state's three prisons for men that was in southern California, the area with a majority of the state's people (Scudder, 1952; Bookspan, 1987:ch.6).

As already noted, California in 1941 established a Youth Authority to bridge juvenile and adult corrections. There were then three state institutions for juveniles: The State Reform School for Juvenile Offenders at Whittier, in southern California, opened in 1891; Preston School of Industry, in northern California, opened in 1894; Ventura School for Girls, in southern California, opened in 1916. All were administered by a Board of Charities and Corrections, to receive from juvenile courts youngsters who "were proven to be incorrigible, vicious or beyond control, or were vagrant...[or in] danger of being brought up to lead an idle and immoral life" (Yaley, 1980:251). They became the Youth Authority's initial institutional system.

During the 1940s, California, like most other states, had prison and jail jobs determined by political connections, especially the most desirable positions. The law gave each prison's warden complete control over the hiring or firing of its employees, but the dependence of the wardens on the governor for their own appointments, and on politicians for appropriations, made them highly responsive to the personnel recommendations of politicians. Kenyon Scudder came to head Chino with a promise by then Governor Olson that he could be completely independent of politics in appointing his staff, but he reports:

When I took over Chino in 1941, I was told that prisons were out of politics, but the first thing I bumped into was that I had fifty positions to fill and that every politician in the State, I guess, had promised some guy a job at Chino, because there were twenty-three hundred of them that had been promised a job.[1]

Reducing convicts' confinement terms to reward compliant conduct, and extending them as a penalty for misconduct, are usually the easiest and cheapest ways to maintain order and security in a prison. California's "good time" laws began in 1864, and were periodically revised, to shorten prison terms by a few days for every month of good conduct while confined, with more time off for longer sentences. These benefits were presumed to motivate inmate obedience to staff (Bookspan, 1987:119).

Parole for adult prisoners was adopted in California in 1893, with release decisions made by the part-time and politically-appointed Board of Prison Directors, that also made prison policies, and were paid only for their travel expenses—no salaries. At first, parole was only used sparingly, to relieve the governor of considering many applications of prisoners for pardon or commutation of sentence due to large disparities among prison terms for the same crime. The courts had great discretion in punishment, and some judges were much more severe than others.

Later, due to economic burdens from a great increase in prison admissions, parole was granted to many more prisoners (Messinger, et al., 1985; Simon, 1990:ch. 2). In 1931, a Board of Prison Terms and Paroles was created to make decisions on parole, and a Bureau of Paroles under the Board of Prison Directors was created to supervise the parolees (Voigt, 1949).

At first, an inmate approved for parole did not leave the prison until a letter was received at the institution promising him a job if released. Parolees had to mail in monthly reports on their residence, job, and non-criminal conduct, signed by the employer and by a police officer. After 1914, parole offices, initially in San Francisco only, received the reports, sometimes checked on promises of employment, and sought homes and jobs for prospective parolees who lacked them (Simon, 1990:58–63). Parole supervision began in 1936, using an office in San Francisco with 11 field officers and one in Los Angeles with six officers, who visited parolees and inquired about their conduct (Simon, 1990:73).

The percentage of prison releases that were by parole increased from about zero in 1893 to 5.1 in 1903, 47.3 in 1913, and 73.3 in 1923 (Miller, 1980:107, 110). Parolees per 100,000 residents in California rose from 0.8 in 1901, the earliest year for which figures are available, to 14.0 in 1910, 24.5 in 1920, and 33.6 in 1940 (data unavailable for 1930) (*Ibid*:148, 228).

As use of parole expanded, the Board of Prison Directors required more staff to administer it. Parole was proclaimed an unqualified success; it reduced state costs, motivated good conduct in prison, and because of its highly selected releasees, produced few new crimes. Such support came especially from the parole administration bureaucracy (*Ibid*).

Probation was legally authorized as a court sentence in California in 1903, but its informal use by some courts occurred before then. Unlike great restrictions on the types of offenders eligible for parole initially, there were none on eligibility for probation; until 1926, it was left entirely to the judge's discretion, and included both juveniles and adults, but mostly juveniles. Juveniles were defined until 1911 as under sixteen years old, but this was changed to under eighteen in that year, a definition that has not been altered since. Probation supervision was at first only by court-approved volunteers, but the state in 1911 urged local hiring of probation officers (*Ibid*:111–17).

Probation was infrequent at first, as most judges feared criticism for leniency if they used it, but its prevalence grew as its acceptability became evident. The estimated number serving probation terms, per 100,000 California residents, rose from 160 in 1933, the earliest year for which figures are available, to a peak of 260 in 1941, and declined to 168 in wartime 1944 (*Ibid*:191, 228, 290). Meanwhile, prisoners per 100,000 population fluctuated: 143 in 1900, 82 in 1920, 125 in 1940, and only 53 in wartime 1944 (*Ibid*:376, 382).

Patronage still predominated in California prisons in January 1943 when a new state administration took office under Governor Earl Warren, later famous as Chief Justice of the U.S. Supreme Court. He knew the correctional establishment from experience as a county district attorney and as Attorney General of the state. As he puts it:

> There was no overall management of the prison system. It was supervised by a part-time Board..., with a warden often chosen for political reasons operating each prison, assisted by a small paid staff....The other people working in the prisons were the convicts themselves. They performed the clerical work, and even much of the disciplinary function....Prison records could not be relied upon because professional forgers would alter the records to show, for instance, that they were charged with one offense in the courts and convicted and sentenced for another (1977:190).

Soon after taking office, Governor Warren appointed a small committee to develop a plan for reorganizing the prison system, consulting on this with the current and prior Directors of the Federal Bureau of Prisons, plus Warden Scudder of Chino, and others. Some months later, a draft plan was completed and they expected much controversy in trying to get it enacted against political opposition.

At this point a fortuitous development occurred. The San Francisco Chief of Police phoned Warren, whom he had known since Warren's time as District Attorney in nearby Alameda County. The police chief reported reliable information about two prisoners. One prisoner was a notorious bandit, sentenced to Folsom, whom Warren had successfully prosecuted. This offender had disappeared at sea on his yacht following each of several large-scale armed robberies. The police chief learned that the two were spending weekends in San Francisco, enjoying themselves with lady friends. It seems they had become cooks at a minimum security camp that was operated by the prison for wartime harvesting of California crops, and they would sneak off to the city after Friday or Saturday bedcheck, then return early Monday morning. Warren urged that they be arrested the next time they came to the city, and with as much publicity as possible.

This arrest occurred promptly, and Governor Warren then appointed an investigating committee of legislative, law-enforcement and correctional leaders whose report detailed the deficiencies of prison operations. He then called a special session of the California legislature for January 1, 1944, to correct the problems. This legislature soon passed a Prison Reorganization Act, to go into effect May 1, 1944.

Under this Act, the prisons were to be administered by the Department of Corrections, headed by a Director, who would also chair an advisory Board of Corrections. Parole decisions would be made by another board, the Adult Authority. These boards would replace the Department of Penology, and the old Board of Prison Directors. To eliminate political influences in the appointment and promotion of employees, all prison and parole staff, other than the wardens of the already established prisons, were by January 1, 1945 to be placed under the state's civil service laws. An examination for the post of Director of Corrections was to be advertised nationally, and to be filled by May 1, 1944 (*Ibid*:191–97; Scudder, 1952:247–49; McGee, 1949).

Richard A. McGee placed first on the written examination, and was unanimously appointed after an oral examination. A new era had begun.

The Career of Richard A. McGee: An Overview

Richard McGee was born September 11, 1897 on a farm in the rural community of Wyoming, Minnesota, in Chisago County. Although one of nine children, and working first on the family farm and then as a carpenter in the construction business that his father started, he graduated high school at age sixteen. For about the next fifteen years, even when a college teacher, he worked most summers as a carpenter, and the rest of the year taught school, often while also taking college courses. Usually the carpentry work was on remote farms in Minnesota, South Dakota, or Manitoba, where construction crews received room, board, and wages.

Ten-or twelve-hour working days, 5 1/2 or 6 days per week, were then customary in rural America, but from his boyhood days of helping his father, McGee was accustomed to long hours, and greatly valued diligence. He was completely self-supporting after high school, and saved his summer earnings for his expenses in other seasons, when he was often a student.

Following high school, McGee completed a two-year program in education in five quarters at a state "normal school" in St. Cloud. At age nineteen he became an elementary school teacher in Sauk Center, Minnesota. A year later he was principal of an elementary school in South Dakota, and later of a high school. In 1918, during World War I, he enlisted in the University of Minnesota's Student Army Training Corps, electing to be in the Marine Corps unit. Following the Armistice later that year, the Corps was disbanded, but he continued at the university as a student.

In 1919, McGee left the university to attend Stout Institute at Menominee, Wisconsin, then a private institution, but now part of the state college system. Its mission was to train vocational education and home economics teachers. Approximately six months later, he became an elementary school principal in the iron mining region of northern Minnesota. He supplemented his income by also conducting evening classes in Americanization for European immigrant miners and their spouses.

In 1920, McGee returned to the University of Minnesota to study architecture, and also taught woodshop in the university's high school. A year later, he switched to the College of Education, completing a Bachelor of Science degree in education in 1923. He then taught at Stout Institute, left for a year to head the Department of Industrial Education at State Teacher's College at Minot, North Dakota, but went back to Stout for two more years.

McGee then returned to the University of Minnesota as an Instructor in the Department of Industrial Education. He also continued graduate study there. In 1926, he published *Instructional Units in Wood Finishing*, which subsequently had nine printings, the last in the 1950s.

This preparation of a manual, regularly updated, foreshadows his later custom of advocating and preparing manuals throughout his correctional career. These manuals helped to standardize performance expectations in the many types of jobs under his supervision. Some of these manuals are described in the next two chapters. His habitual initiative in task analysis is somewhat comparable to the persistence of the industrial engineers, Frank B. Gilbreth and his wife Lillian M. Gilbreth, who pioneered time-and-motion studies to get all jobs done more efficiently. This trait is described in the humorous biography about the Gilbreth's, *Cheaper by the Dozen* (Gilbreth and Carey, 1948), and in the movie from it, with Clifton Webb and Myrna Loy.

Indeed, woodworking was always McGee's hobby during his subsequent career as a government official. His son, Richard McGee, Jr. writes:[1]

> In the early 1950s, Dad drew plans for a separate shop building behind his residence on Tamarack Way. A permit was acquired and we formed, poured, and framed it. He truly enjoyed working with his tools. He once said it gave him a better perspective on all things.
>
> He was a fine craftsman. Hardwoods were collected in his travels and many relaxing hours were spent turning small and large trays, candlestick holders, etc. Staining and finishing these items was his specialty. On one occasion he produced a beautiful Hi-Fi cabinet with arched doors, lifting top, album storage, and curved inlay on door surfaces.

My eight year-old son, Richard, enjoyed visiting his grandfather. These visits developed into learning and competing in chess. One Christmas, Rich received a beautiful inlaid chess board produced by his grandfather. On the back of the board was scrolled by router, to Rich from Grandfather McGee.

McGee received a Master of Arts in Education at the University of Minnesota in 1928. While an instructor at the university, he enrolled in a doctoral program. In 1931, by competing in a national civil service examination, he became the first Supervisor of Education at the Federal Penitentiary at Leavenworth, Kansas. His main assignment was in the "Leavenworth Annex" (later the Army Disciplinary Barracks), which at the time held 1,800 inmates, 85 percent charged with narcotics offenses. Many were illiterate, and a large percentage Latinos. He had to rely on inmate teachers, but could pick from thirty-five physicians also serving sentences there. He soon learned the highly variable conduct potential of prisoners, and that many are conscientious and capable.

As Table 2.1 shows, from 1931 until his death in 1983 at age eighty-six, McGee was a leader in corrections, and in much more than education. His perspective as a teacher oriented him from the start to try to help convicts learn how to succeed in a law-abiding life. He was fond of pointing out that less than 2 percent of those entering prisons will die there. More than most others in corrections, his focus was on reducing the prospect that prison releasees would commit further crimes.

In 1932, McGee moved from Leavenworth to become Supervisor of Education at the then new Federal Penitentiary at Lewisburg, Pennsylvania. In 1935, he made a major role change when he won a national competition to become the first superintendent of the New York City Penitentiary on Rikers Island, which operated under the city's reform Director of Corrections, Austin MacCormick, a former assistant Director of Federal Prisons. The Rikers Island institution was still unfinished when it opened, and housed 145 inmates. It was so unfinished that the kitchen floor was only a dirt floor covered with ashes. It took two more years to complete, a period in which "batches" of inmates—sometimes hundreds at a time—were transferred to Rikers before facilities were ready for them.

Holding convicts with terms ranging from ten days to thirty-six months, Rikers was the main confinement place for persons sentenced for misdemeanors and lesser felonies. Rikers could be reached only by ferryboats. The boats were operated expensively by another branch of city government, and they often stalled overnight or longer due to fog,

TABLE 2.1

A Chronology of Turning Points in
the Career of Richard A. McGee

1897	Born, September 11th, in Chisago County, Minnesota.
1913-23	At various times, he was a(n) woodworker, elementary or high school teacher, in U.S. Marine Corps, elementary school principal, and university student.
1923	Bachelor of Science, University of Minnesota.
1923-26	Instructor in woodfinishing, Stout Institute, Menominee, Wisconsin; briefly Head of Dept. of Industrial Education, Teacher's College, Minot, North Dakota.
1926-31	Instructor in Vocational Education, and Ph.D. candidate, University of Minnesota.
1928	Master of Arts, University of Minnesota.
1931-32	*First* Director of Education, U.S. Penitentiary, Leavenworth, Kansas.
1932-35	*First* Director of Education, U.S. Penitentiary, Lewisburg, Pennsylvania.
1935-39	*First* Warden, New York City Penitentiary, Rikers Island.
1938-41	*First* President, National Jail Association.
1939-41	Deputy Commissioner, briefly Acting Commissioner, New York City Department of Correction.
1941-44	Director, Division of Public Institutions, State of Washington.
1943	President, American Prisons Association.
1944-61	*First* Director, California Department of Corrections.
1961-67	*First* Administrator, California Youth and Adult Correctional Agency.
1967	Retirement from State of California employment.
1959-80	*First*, Chairman, American Justice Institute,
1983	Died October 29th, in his sleep at home in Sacramento, of a heart ailment.

so that employees remained at work on overtime pay, deliveries could not be made, and visitors could not leave. (More recently, a bridge has been built to the island.) It was designed for 2,200 inmates, but was soon overcrowded. McGee quickly had to administer a much larger organization than he had ever before headed, and in a setting watched closely by the newspapers.

Rikers Penitentiary was opened under reform Mayor Fiorello LaGuardia to replace the notorious institution on Welfare Island. Under the previous mayor, the colorful Jimmy Walker, there had been repeated scandals in the city's penal operations. McGee's distinctive approach to penology, the problems he encountered, and his resourcefulness in achieving rapid change, are evident in his (1937) report on conditions at Rikers, less than two years after it was opened:

> The malcontents whom we received from Welfare Island in the summer of 1935 did not know the meaning of either orderly discipline or fair treatment without special privilege; neither were they accustomed to the hard work they were required to do on Rikers Island. The prisoners…from the Welfare Island institution have for years assumed that those with money or influence would receive desirable work assignments and that those in these assignments would eat officer's food rather than that of inmates; that they would be allowed out of their cells until late hours; that they could

Figure 2.1. Portrait of R. A. McGee, 1939, at Rikers Island

have special articles of clothing brought in from the outside; that they could cook food in their own cells; that an ordinary keeper interested in doing his duty would not be privileged to give orders to this self-appointed aristocracy of the jail. All of these abuses have been thoroughly eliminated. All inmates at Rikers Island eat on the "main line"; they all receive the same privileges as to clothing, commissary, recreation, and cell equipment. All patients in the hospital wards are there because they are sick and not because they are prison "big shots."

...the medical service...occupies a modern and completely equipped seven story hospital in addition to which are the out-patient clinics occupying the second floor of the receiving building. The outstanding clinic is that for venereal diseases in which some 600 men are under treatment continually for syphilis and gonor-rhea. The dental, the eye-ear-nose and throat, and general medical clinics treat about 750 cases per week. The medical service has a visiting staff consisting of fifty-two specialists. The resident staff is composed of a chief medical officer, four resident physicians, ten interns, forty nurses, and in addition, the necessary hospital atten-dants, technicians, dietitians, and cooks. The daily average census of the hospital itself is 180. A neuro-psychiatric clinic has been established under the direction of three visiting psychiatrists and administered by a resident psychologist....

Although the designers of the institution provided no phy-sical facilities for educational work, a building originally designed for another purpose has been converted into classroom space and there are at the present time about ninety under-educated men attending all-day classes, and 200 more are enrolled in corres-pondence courses. The vocational education program is...in abeyance pending the equipping of our shops.... There is also a very active department of recreation headed by a licensed teacher of physical education. This program includes quiet games in the cell blocks, corrective exercising, and during good weather a program of outside recreation carried out on a ten-acre recreational field. A band and orchestra of thirty pieces is also making good progress under the direction of WPA instructors. A very satisfac-tory collection of library books has been obtained through pur-chases and gifts. It now includes about 6,000 volumes. Seventy percent of the inmates make use of the library, and on a basis of those who use it, the circulation is five books per month....

With the cooperation of the WPA, a very useful and active social service unit has been established. This group is divided into two sections, an institutional unit, and a field unit. All men having indefinite penitentiary sentences, of which we receive about 225 per month, are interviewed by social workers in the institution, the family situations are investigated by the field workers, and each case is cleared through the social service exchange.

On January 1, 1936, a classification director was appointed. This employee, who has psychological training and prison experience, with the assistance of his staff develops a short case history, known as an admission summary, of each man having an indefinite sentence. This summary is used as the basis for assigning each man to work and outlining his program in the institution. Those who present unusual problems are selected out and brought before the classification board which meets every Saturday morning. Our short experience with this board has demonstrated...the desirability of bringing before it the problem cases only, rather than to attempt to make this a routine procedure for all admissions. It has further demonstrated its value in developing the morale of the institution by bringing the various specialized departments into closer contact and a better understanding of each other.

Staff was low-paid. Many from Welfare Island had welcomed gifts from the friends and family of affluent criminals, in exchange for favors, as well as money from reporters for stories about the inmates or the institution (McGee, 1981:42–45). LaGuardia gave little time to the prison. McGee had to learn quickly not only how to control it, but how to gain support from the press, and how to be a non-partisan politician, a friend of many influential persons, but obligated to none.

In 1938, McGee and others formed the National Jail Association (today the American Jail Association), to raise standards in short-term confinement. He was the president for its first three years. In 1939, he was promoted to be one of two Deputy Commissioners of the city's Department of Corrections, and briefly its Acting Commissioner; this Department ran all the city's jails and community supervision programs for pretrial and sentenced offenders. In New York, he recognized the importance of communicating to the public, and from then on, gave speeches and published extensively.

McGee married in 1931, a union that produced three children, then ended in divorce. The children usually lived with their mother in Minnesota, attending the same high school from which he had graduated, but often came to stay with him. His older daughter shared the new warden's house on Rikers Island and went by ferry to college in

New York City. Later McGee remarried.[2] His son, Richard A. McGee, Jr., wrote in an August 1993 letter to me: "Even though divorced, Dad never faltered in duty to family and love for his children." He added this recollection:

> During the summer of 1939, as a 15-year old youth, I visited my father on Rikers Island. At that time he related an incident that occurred in the Rikers Island Hospital.
>
> One day, as warden, he was called in to observe a prisoner who was hospitalized with a broken leg. The prisoner managed to rebreak his leg, after initial healing, to remain confined in the hospital.
>
> My father and the prison doctor leaned over the prisoner's leg to assess the damage. Suddenly the prisoner, with closed fist, hit my father across the jaw and sent him dazed, to the floor. The inspection continued after Warden McGee regained his composure.[3]

On December 1, 1941, McGee moved to the State of Washington to become Director of the Division of Public Institutions. This placed him over fourteen quite contrasting facilities, including not only prisons, but also mental hospitals and state schools for the blind, deaf, and retarded. Within a week, the attack on Pearl Harbor occurred, and the U.S. entered World War II. Institution populations diminished, many of their staff left for military service, and much inmate labor was directed into the war effort.

McGee's leadership qualities were manifested early. In 1943, at age forty-six, he became president of the American Prison Association (now the American Correctional Association), the leading organization of American prison personnel, and also of academics, and others interested in penology. (This was only twelve years after his first job in prisons.) In 1946 he also founded and edited its journal, *Prison World*, now *Corrections Today*. He was a leader in this organization for the rest of his life, and participated in its formulation of standards for correctional institutions and agencies. From this evolved the national program of accreditation for correctional operations (Halley, 1992; McGee, 1976).

As indicated at the close of the preceding chapter, when Earl Warren became California's governor in 1944, he soon achieved a reorganization of California's prison management, creating a Department of Corrections, and of its parole system, creating the Adult Authority as a new parole board. He appointed a three-man committee—James Bennett (then head of the Federal Bureau of Prisons), Sanford Bates (then head of

New Jersey prisons, and prior head of federal prisons), and an Associate Justice of the U.S. Court of Appeals in Washington, D.C.—to help find "the best man available" to head the new department.

The committee gave written and oral examinations to many candidates, and McGee was its first choice. According to one of Warren's aides: "The Governor had to negotiate with Governor Langlie, of Washington, to get McGee's release. It took a long time, but the Governor was willing to wait to get the best man, and finally he did get him" (Katcher, 1967:169). McGee became the first head of the Department of Corrections on July 1, 1944, and resided in Sacramento for the rest of his life.

Warren also placed a high priority to appointing a head for the state's Youth Authority. The Authority was created in 1942 by his predecessor, Governor Olson, based on an American Law Institute proposal, but it was still largely a paper organization in 1944. Warren pointed out that over 40 percent of California's serious crimes were charged against persons eighteen to twenty-one years old, and most were to be dealt with by the Youth Authority's correctional institutions, parole board, and parole supervision agents. To direct this organization, he quickly brought on Karl Holton, then head of the Los Angeles County Department of Probation.

Holton had achieved some prominence for creating forestry camps for young offenders as alternatives to jail or traditional juvenile detention centers. He brought with him his long-term deputy in Los Angeles, Heman G. Stark. When Holton returned to Los Angeles in 1952 to head its probation department for another twelve years, Stark succeeded him at the Youth Authority (Weaver, 1967:128–29). He was a close collaborator with McGee in numerous projects, not only when both held state office, but also after their retirements.

For the first seventy-seven years of the twentieth century, almost all California adult prisoners had highly indeterminate sentences, such as one-to-ten years, one-to-twenty years, or one to life (discussed further in chapter 6). The first releases under such sentences, and often some subsequent ones, were usually by parole. The dates for paroles, and decisions on penalties for reported parole violations, were made by a politically appointed board, reorganized in 1944 as the Adult Authority. There was much controversy over alleged political bias, racial bigotry, and inconsistency in the decisions of prior parole boards.

As his first Adult Authority appointee, Governor Warren picked Walter A. Gordon, who had regularly been his sparring partner in boxing when both were students at the University of California at Berkeley. Gordon, who had been an All-American football star at

Berkeley and later a part-time football coach while also practicing law, was the first African-American to hold such a high state office. Two years later, the board elected him to be its chairman. Gordon and McGee were good friends and mutually supportive. By appointment of President Eisenhower in 1955, however, Gordon became Governor of the Virgin Islands, and in 1958, a judge in Federal District Court (Warren, 1977:195; Pollack, 1979:29).

Don Gottfredson, who worked as a group counselor in the prison at Chino during 1953–55 while pursuing a Ph.D. in psychology (and later was prominent in the Department of Corrections research staff, and then as a Rutgers professor), recalls that in one of his counseling groups an "old-timer" among the inmates recalled how much worse the institutions were before McGee. This inmate drew Figure 2.2 to show his recognition of the difficulties McGee had faced in 1945.

By 1961, when the Department of Corrections had become perhaps the most advanced state organization of its type in the nation, Governor Edmund G. ("Pat") Brown, Sr. appointed McGee to a new cabinet position in the state government, Administrator of the Youth and Adult Corrections Agency. This placed him over 24,000 adult prisoners, 4,000 Youth Authority wards in custody, 10,000 adult parolees, and 10,000 Youth Authority parolees. This total of 48,000 lawbreakers under state control had increased by 11,000 in just three years (Halley, 1992:57).

During 1961–67, McGee's last years of state service, his post as Administrator of the Youth and Adult Corrections Agency decreased his direct involvement with offenders and those who interacted with them. He was now a member of the Governor's cabinet, and a participant in its discussions on many issues. Even on correctional matters, more of his time had to be devoted to courting legislators for support of policy and budget proposals. Halley (1992:57–60, 74) says, citing from McGee's writings, these years were less happy for him than his earlier ones because he became "the supporter of programs more than the instigator of them."

Kim Nelson, who took a leave from the School of Public Administration faculty at the University of Southern California during 1964–65 to be Deputy Administrator under McGee in this cabinet post, provides a similar report on McGee's frustrations in that period. He now did not have very immediate control of either the Department of Correction or the Youth Authority, as their heads had personal responsibility and autonomy in most of their decisions on their agencies, including those on budgeting and disbursement of funds. McGee's discussions with them were mainly on their long-term strategies, and on their relation-

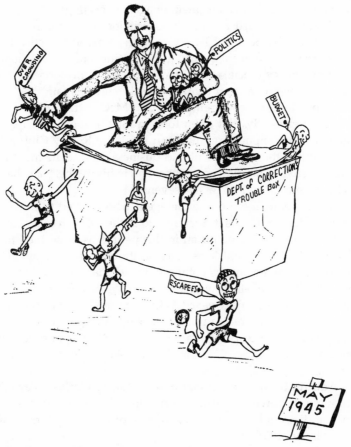

Figure 2.2. Inmate's cartoon on McGee's early problems

ships with the legislature in seeking appropriations or specific laws or authorizations. Governor Pat Brown was on good terms with McGee, but often inaccessible due to his other concerns. Also, Nelson recalls, on several occasions the governor's Legal Affairs Secretary took the initiative of giving the press statements on correctional issues, but in ways not to McGee's liking.

Observing McGee over a thirty-five-year period of either working with him for the State of California, or as a close friend when employed elsewhere, Nelson describes him as a genius in seeing long before others the theoretical, moral, and practical implications of issues and proposals being discussed. Interested in all types of new ideas, McGee invited, and sometimes hired, advocates of promising, but atypical policies. The new ideas were discussed at department or agency meetings.

Nelson concluded from their association in the cabinet post, and afterwards on the Board of Directors of the American Justice Institute, that McGee was a political genius. In promoting a proposal to legislators or funding agency officials, McGee could sense opposition at its earliest stage, and move with great charm and astuteness to gain their support. Throughout his California employment, McGee tried to know many legislators personally, and often took groups of them on trips to visit prisons. He participated regularly in the large Rotary Club in Sacramento, valuing the government and business contacts he met there. He was most active in political concerns when in his cabinet role, that ended with his retirement in 1967, at age seventy.[4]

Allen Moore, a retired parole agent who worked full time on the staff of various politicians in Sacramento in the 1950s, recalls that no one thought of McGee as a politician in this period, as he seemed too quiet and scholarly. Yet he sold legislators on the need for change in corrections so well, that he always got more money than they had expected to appropriate for him—they would say "we'll give it to you now but cut back on new money next year." When the next year came, however, McGee had planned his campaign so well, and gotten solid support successively from Republican Governors Warren and Knight and Democrat Brown, as well as from key legislators, that the process was repeated.[5]

Adding to McGee's unhappiness during his last years of state employment, however, although not impairing his talents, was his immense distress from the death of one of his daughters in an auto accident in late 1963.

At McGee's retirement dinner in 1967, U.S. Chief Justice Earl Warren, who as governor had brought McGee to California in 1944, was quoted as saying:

> In all my experience, I have never found a better administrator or one more devoted to duty and more successful in what he tried to do than Dick McGee. I didn't know him from Adam. I took him on faith and he accepted me on faith. We had an understanding. I was not to interfere and he was not to permit politics to interfere with his prison reform work (Abramson, 1983).

When Ronald Reagan won the November 1966 gubernatorial election with campaign rhetoric advocating harsh penalties, and implying that his political opponents "mollycoddled" criminals, McGee announced that he would retire June 30, 1967. Reagan, who had in his campaign asserted he would cut his cabinet from eight members to four, reappointed McGee, but said that the post of Administrator of Youth and Adult Corrections would be abolished on McGee's retirement date. Corrections, thereafter, became a responsibility of the head of the state's Health and Welfare Agency, a cabinet post to which Reagan appointed his party's unsuccessful candidate for Attorney General, who had been vehement in denouncing the state's "leniency" toward lawbreakers. In 1980, under Governor "Jerry" Brown, the son of Governor "Pat" Brown, who had established it previously, the Youth and Adult Corrections Agency was restored (but called "Correctional Agency"). It has continued to survive even under Republican governors.

Twenty-three years after he began employment in California and less than two months before his own retirement, McGee sent Reagan a 232-page monograph (co-authored with M. R. Montilla, 1967) entitled *Organization of State Correctional Services in the Control and Treatment of*

Figure 2.3. From left to right: Governor Goodwin Knight; DeWitt (Swede) Nelson, Director of Department of Conservation; Richard A. McGee; Chief Justice Earl Warren; Governor Edmund G. ("Pat") Brown; Ernest Webb, Director of Industrial Relations; September 1966

Crime and Delinquency. It began with a fifteen-page single-spaced letter of transmission from McGee to "Dear Governor Reagan." The letter predicted a large rise in the crime-prone youth population of the state. Traditionally, this rise would call for construction of more prison capacity, but McGee claimed that improvements in community corrections and social services could eliminate the need for new prisons. It shall be referred to in this book as McGee's "Farewell Address" to Reagan. There is no evidence that Reagan was influenced by it, or even read it. Halley (1992:74–77) asserts that McGee never met Reagan.

McGee did not plan a traditional retirement. As chapters 6 and 7 will indicate, he continued developing a body of profound and insightful ideas on the needs and possibilities for improvement of the criminal justice system that he set forth in important writings, before and after his retirement. He also maintained a strong interest in correctional and other criminological research, as well as in crime-preventive education.

In retirement, McGee had more time for a non-profit organization he had established in 1959 in Sacramento, the Institute for the Study of Crime and Delinquency. He chaired its Board of Directors, which included the Youth Authority's Heman Stark and a number of other California correctional leaders, plus a lawyer, John Lemmon. The institute was launched by receipt of a $105,000 "start-up" grant from the Ford Foundation, was certified in 1960 as tax-exempt, and expanded its board to include some distinguished researchers. The institute received several subsequent research, training, and education grants. To administer some of the grants, the institute established a separate but temporary non-profit organization headed by the same board of directors, but named "Center for Training in Differential Treatment."

Calling itself "a new force in the war on crime," the institute sought to accumulate an endowment of a million dollars, and gave as its purposes:

1. Expanding knowledge through research;
2. Demonstrating new programs and applications of new technology;
3. Training personnel in new methods;
4. Publishing and disseminating new knowledge to both practitioners and the general public; and
5. Providing consultation services to public and private crime control agencies.[6]

In 1971 it was renamed the American Justice Institute (McGee, 1981:144–45).

McGee was a tall and husky individual, with a ready smile and a strong, pleasant voice. Quick-witted, fond of exchanging anecdotes, a good listener as well as a good speaker, he welcomed serious discussion on any interesting topic. I first met him in 1953 at a session of the American Prisons Association, while presenting a report on my pending Ph.D. dissertation on predicting parole outcomes, prepared while I was employed in Illinois prisons for the Illinois Parole and Pardon Board. In subsequent years, when I attended Prison Association meetings, he was one of the few prison administrators interested in the small sessions of the research section. During 1958–62, when I taught at the University of Illinois and directed a large evaluation of the federal prison and parole system, funded by the Ford Foundation, McGee was a member of the project's Advisory Board.

As Table 2.1 chronology indicates, McGee was the first holder of most of his major occupational positions. He was the first Supervisor of Education in a federal penitentiary, the first head of a new New York City penitentiary, the first head of California's newly created Department of Corrections, and the first in its then new cabinet post of Administrator of Youth and Adult Correctional Agencies. He also pioneered in many of the correctional programs and policies that he introduced in California, which are described in detail in the next three chapters. In addition, as chapter 6 details, his innovative thinking extended to the entire criminal justice system.

McGee was also a founder and leader in professional organizations, and an influential speaker and writer. Throughout his career, and during his retirement, he remained inquisitive, educationally oriented, and an encourager of research. He was morally upstanding, and inspired many loyal and dedicated followers.

Governor Pat Brown, the third of four governors, from both parties, under whom McGee served in California, told a *Sacramento Bee* reporter writing an obituary for McGee:

> He was a soft-spoken individual. Cool, calm, collected. I knew him well and although he had served under my predecessor, I kept him because I admired him. I took his advice for eight years and never regretted it.

A collection of eleven short tributes were published as eulogies in *Corrections Today*, written by some of the most prominent persons in its field. John Conrad, who worked for and with McGee during most of their careers in California, wrote:

Because he lived for most of his adult life as a chief executive officer, Dick McGee was exempt from the competitive struggles that shape the outlook of civil servants. Unlike most of us, he had no need to maneuver for advancement. He devoted his entire attention to the craft of administration. There was never a question of using his power to demonstrate his superiority to those around him....Better than most of his contemporaries, he knew how far penology had to go to arrive at a state of relative decency and integrity. His long career was dedicated to making possible what was necessary (1984:81).

Figure 2.4. R. A. McGee in 1983, the year of his death (Photo by Owen Brewer, *The Sacramento Bee*)

McGee's Initiatives in California Prisons

Arriving in California as the first head of its Department of Corrections, McGee had to centralize control of scattered prisons, each with a warden who had always been highly autonomous. These quasi-feudal heads of institutions, especially at the old and large San Quentin and Folsom penitentiaries, lobbied individually with politicians for their separate budget appropriations. The politicians often expected reciprocity, for example, that their political supporters be favored when the wardens hired people or made institution purchases. Of course, each warden also wanted to prevent scandals resulting from escapes or riots that would prompt demands for new institution leadership, and each maintained press relations independently of the others.

This situation could not be changed instantly, since prisons are entrenched establishments. However, McGee's New York City and State of Washington experiences had given him the vision, tactics, and strategies to change such traditional arrangements more rapidly and securely than others in power had deemed feasible. One of his first priorities was to improve the selection and training of California's correctional employees.

Staffing Prisons

"Prisons are run by people," McGee asserted, adding:

The kind of people, the number of people, and the morale of the people are the most important considerations in determining the quality of the program. The major part of the budget of an institution is spent on salaries and wages. Unwise budgetary restrictions will be felt first and most disastrously in the personnel. However,...security of tenure, and the elimination of improper political influences in the management of personnel, are just as important as salaries. It should be accepted without argument that all...employees should be a part of a sound merit system wherein they are appointed on a basis of competitive examinations and realistic standards of qualification. Promotion through the ranks should be orderly, fair, and competitive; and personnel should be eligible for membership in a sound retirement system. Conversely, such a merit system must also make provision for the separation from service as promptly as possible of those persons found to be temperamentally or morally unfit for the work (1953a).

He deplored the lack of preparation for staffing prisons:

Since prison employees are almost never trained for their work before entering the service, it is obvious that they must learn their duties and skills while on the job. There is no field of public service in which there is more desperate need for a well-organized, well-developed program of in-service training. Such programs cost money because they take time and intelligence. On the other hand, for the amount of money spent, no other phase of prison adminis-tration pays such handsome dividends. The training and develop-ment of personnel is as important and urgent a responsibility of a prison warden as it is of a military commander or a football coach (1953a).

He stressed:

I am everlastingly amazed by the notion...in some quarters that these positions can be held by almost anyone if he is a strong personality and has the right political affiliations. The lack of administrative ability and capacity for organization in many of our institutions is appalling. I can tell you of one major institution, with several hundred employees, in which, a number of years ago, there was such complete lack of organization that 42 employees stated that they reported directly to the warden. This meant that, for all practical purposes, at least $3/4$ of them reported to nobody. It is possible to point out dozens of institutions in which there are no rules and regulations in written form constituting a body of admin-istrative law governing both employees and inmates....

Ours is a field desperately in need of aggressive, able, exper-ienced leadership. The only way that a service can obtain such leadership is to develop it from within. We must train young and able personalities who will advance through the service, with the best of them rising to the top as the years go by. It takes funds and long-term planning to provide the positions and the salary levels to implement a program of personnel development. But, conversely, able personnel will develop a program which will justify support (1953a).[1]

The fiefdoms of the long-term wardens at San Quentin, Folsom and the women's prison at Tehachapi resisted change. Duffy had been made warden of San Quentin two years earlier by Governor Olson who, in reaction to scandals and low morale in the institutions, also replaced everyone on the Board of Prison Directors. Duffy had been reared around San Quentin, where he had held several administrative posts, and his father was a guard. Reacting to rumors that McGee's reforms would include centralized control over prisons, Duffy promptly sought to maintain autonomy and raise morale by hiring a new head cook to improve the food, reducing the harshness of the notorious punishment unit, and by public relations efforts (Bookspan, 1987:240–41).

Duffy developed good relationships with the San Francisco press by allowing it ready access to interesting prisoners. Helped by a ghostwriter, he also published stories about the prison, and he started an inmate music and comedy show, "San Quentin on the Air," regularly broadcasting on a San Francisco radio station (McGee, 1976:110; 1981:9). He lobbied to preserve San Quentin's autonomy, including its separate budget.

San Quentin, especially, used inmates in key clerical jobs, a widespread custom that I saw still being done in Illinois prisons in the early 1950s. McGee relates:

> There were, if I remember right, some sixty prisoners who worked in the administration building. They were working on the records of prisoners, in the accounting office, the trust funds, in everything. They were all under the supervision of a paid employee, but it made it possible, first of all, for them to get a lot of information that ought to be regarded as confidential inside of an institution, and also to manipulate the records. I don't think I ever really convinced the legislative analyst and some of the other people that are monitoring what the state agencies do until we had an experience with a fellow at Folsom. He'd been working in the record office and was transferred to San Quentin in a routine transfer. He was at San Quentin for a few months and was released. But by that time we had set up a central record office over in the capitol.

When this list came through, and here this fellow had been discharged, somebody looked at the record and saw that he had another twenty years to do. When he was transferred from Folsom to San Quentin, he had just torn off a lot of his previous criminal record. You have these so-called rap sheets and some of these fellows have five or six sheets; he had been out on parole apparently and came back with another offense. He just destroyed that and altered the other one. San Quentin didn't know anything about all this, so when his term expired they turned him out.

When I got this information, I said this man is an escapee. We put out a warrant for his arrest, brought him back, and charged him with escape.

I went to the legislative analyst's office and said I've been telling you this for years and now here's some evidence. They assigned a young fellow to go down to San Quentin and study every position, and we finally got personnel to replace the prisoners (1976a:116).

Supported by his staff and local leaders, Warden Duffy often stalled when McGee asked him to use new procedures, but changes gradually occurred, including non-renewal of the radio show contract. McGee reports that he finally removed Duffy in 1949 by urging his appointment to the Adult Authority, then the state parole board for adult males, where "he was more comfortable...and was an excellent addition to that group" (1981:9).

McGee did not replace the heads at Folsom and Tehachapi until their retirement. Alma Holzschue had been Superintendent at Tehachapi since 1942. A former social worker and head of a girl's school, she had also worked at the famous Massachusetts Women's Reformatory at Framingham that was directed by Miriam van Waters, author of widely read books on women offenders. On her own initiative, Holzschue developed academic and vocational education at Tehachapi, established reception programs in which selected inmates helped orient newcomers, invited parolees to speak to women awaiting release, and even started work furloughs. She showed much warmth to inmates and staff, called them all "my family," and corresponded with some parolees. McGee at first overlooked her maintaining her autonomy, as he was preoccupied with the more problem-ridden men's prisons (Morales, 1980; McGee, 1976a:105–27).

In 1954, an earthquake at Tehachapi forced the temporary housing of its inmates in tents and then the hasty move to a still unfinished new women's prison being completed at Corona, adjoining Chino and near Los Angeles. Holzschue became its director. Tehachapi prison, located in a remote mountain area, was rebuilt as a light security facility for men, and in recent years has been enlarged to house over 5,000 inmates.

Although McGee described Holzschue as a strong and dedicated leader, he had problems with her. She only preferred somewhat older women, like herself, on her staff, and resisted McGee's orders to recruit younger adult women for a career service. She also tried to keep the press, and all except her supporters in influential women's clubs, from visiting the institution.

Some money from sale of prison-made goods was deposited by Holzschue into a local bank account, instead of being sent to Sacramento as the law required. She alone controlled this account, and from it she purchased drapes and other items she deemed important for the prison, rather than using it for herself. To gain her cooperation, McGee threatened to prosecute her for this illegal practice, and thereby, to make her ineligible for a state pension (McGee, 1976:105–27; 1981:10). This crude blackmail apparently worked, for she became somewhat less autonomous thereafter.

Since her appointment in 1942, Miss Holzschue had never taken a vacation, and in 1957 when McGee suggested she take one, she exclaimed "I can't do it! Who would take the responsibility?" He insisted that she depart for three months' leave, for which she had accumulated entitlement, and that she delegate more responsibilities to subordinates, including a business manager whom he sent there. After her vacation, Miss Holzschue was then retained as head of the prison until her retirement, in January 1960 (Morales, 1980:366; McGee, 1981:19).

Jim Park, Associate Warden of San Quentin during 1964–72, then with the Department of Corrections (CDC) in Sacramento for five years, and finally Associate Superintendent at Soledad, reminisced:

> McGee told of an instance when he called Duffy about one of his chief aides, who on a trip to Los Angeles allowed his bill to be paid by a notorious gangster, and accepted one dozen monogrammed shirts from the gangster. Duffy could not see anything wrong with the aide's explanation that since the shirts had his initials, it wouldn't make sense to return them, would it now? And when told his hotel bill had been paid, was he to fight the clerk and demand that he accept the money?....

An amusing period in McGee's administration is when he tried to bring Alma Holzschue, the long-time Superintendent at

Tehachapi and later at Corona, into the post-war generation. He dispatched various of his staff to Corona to discuss with her some items of administration which were to say the least, obsolete. Smith, the CDC Deputy for Business went down to demonstrate that tailor-made cigarettes were OK for the women. Alma had restricted them to roll-your-own on the notion that the hand-made cigarettes would go out if left about whereas store-bought would cause a fire. A Field Representative, a former San Quentin Captain of the Guard, was sent down to persuade her to allow tampons to be sold in the canteen. Alma didn't think they were proper and restricted the women to sanitary napkins.[2]

Very insightfully, Park noted McGee's problems:

...California prisons were in disarray, with each warden running his own show....

McGee used a beachhead technique which I always admired as a masterful piece of strategy: He took the prison system away from the old timers by establishing reception-guidance centers, first at San Quentin and then at Chino. These centers were run by Associate Superintendents appointed by McGee, and they reported to Sacramento, not to the local warden. McGee's appointees and the social worker and psychologist staff hired for the reception units, as soon as he could qualify them, went to the top of the promotional lists and became the nucleus of the new management system.[3]

Under McGee in subsequent years, when the number of California prisons increased as the state's population grew, many of those initially recruited as social workers and psychologists in such "beachheads" (including Jim Park, initially a clinical psychologist at Chino), became wardens or held other higher administrative posts. This contrasted with the tradition in most state prisons of top management consisting almost exclusively of custodial officers who had worked their way up from being guards; however, some also followed that career route in California.

Kim Nelson started in California prison work during 1951–52 at San Quentin and then Chino as a psychologist, but he was also a lawyer. He and several others were often assigned to be the "Central Office Team" from Sacramento, going to various institutions to review, and approve or change, classification and placement of inmates; he reports that the officials referred to them as "the Rover Boys." This role, he says, was "a powerful and innovative management device."[4]

In California, as in New York and Washington, McGee inherited employees who were without a system of adequate rules for salaries, promotion, overtime, sick leave, or even vacations. To establish a merit system, he developed, and negotiated with state personnel specialists and with the California Board of Corrections that he chaired, descriptions of the duties for each position, qualifications required, and salaries. He had reorganized the staffs of each of the three major prisons (San Quentin, Folsom, and Chino) to include under each warden a separate business manager, an associate warden for custody and discipline, an associate warden for education and treatment, and an industries supervisor.

McGee also ordered preparation of an *Administrative Manual* for the department, which required his review and approval prior to publication. This manual's topics included:

> duties, responsibilities, and privileges of employees;...procedures in the event of an escape, or other emergencies; regulations governing discipline and punishment, inmate councils, religious programs, educational activities, radio, library, mail, legal documents, visits, clothing, work, food, living quarters, and every detail of the prison operation (Halley, 1992:33).

Additional manuals were issued separately on other activities including inmate classification, business administration, education and vocational training, group counseling, interagency relations, and personnel administration (Himmelson, 1968:25). Most were in looseleaf binders, so that new pages could be issued periodically to replace parts that had become out-dated.

What McGee created quickly in the units of government he headed was a bureaucracy, in its most favorable connotation, as set forth in the classic writings of Max Weber (1978: ch.11). A bureaucracy is an organization that has order, continuity, and efficiency because:

(1) it consists of a hierarchy of offices with specifically described functions and powers, rather than a set of individuals linked only by ancestry or by personal obligations to each other;

(2) it has written regulations that:

    a. describe the overall structure of the organization in terms of divisions and units, and the function of each, in relationship to the purposes of the organization as a whole;

    b. state the purposes, duties, and qualifications required for each position or staff category in the organization, and their procedures in a variety of expected circumstances, as well as in some types of emergencies;

    c. include or imply an organizational chart showing which offices have authority above, below, or parallel to the others;

    d. provide procedures for reviewing the performance of incumbents in each office, and for revising the regulations;

    e. give the criteria and procedures for personnel promotion or demotion;

    f. specify quasi-judicial procedures for appealing these actions.

Bureaucracies vary in their conformity to the preceding model, and in rigidity or flexibility. Rigidity makes bureaucracies stable, despite personnel turnover. Flexibility promotes efficiency, but only if based upon continual and rigorous evaluation research; it then helps the organization adapt successfully to changes in environment, technology, and the demands made upon the system.

On upgrading prison staff, McGee reported:

A practical and continuous training program for institutional personnel was established in 1946. There is now a full-time in-service training officer at each of the major institutions under the general supervision of a Departmental Training Officer. Numerous course syllabi and manuals of instruction have been prepared. The training program of the Department of Corrections is frequently pointed to as a model for this type of personnel development.

Carefully developed organizational plans have been prepared for each institution. It is now possible for an employee to advance through the ranks following an orderly method of promotion to any position in the Department for which he can qualify. California is now recognized among the states as having more able young men in its correctional program than any other similar organization in the country (1953b).

One of the challenges that McGee dealt with, because of the period of history in which he managed California prisons, was ethnic integration. In 1944, he found that a long-established custom in California institutions was that all black and many Latino inmates were usually segregated. One exception was Chino, the new prison near Los Angeles. The superintendent, Kenyon Scudder, interviewed inmates individually at San Quentin to select a mixture of all races as the initial cohort for Chino. He then startled old prison hands when he did not segregate the prisoners in the buses (in which Scudder also rode) or at their destination. The employees at all the prisons were primarily white and had prevailing ethnic prejudices.

Even before the 1960s Civil Rights movement, McGee endeavored to reduce segregation, and he describes problems in the 1960s, when he tried to end it completely (1981:71):

> The gradual desegregation in the large cell buildings and dining rooms was not easy, partly because subordinate staff and inmates also had their own prejudices. To make matters worse, the terrorist gangs and activist groups outside carried their vendettas into prison and recruited many of their members from among prisoners. The Black Muslims were the first group to develop in California's prisons. From an early declaration that they intended to exterminate the white race, they developed into the most stable and responsible of these prison-spawned groups. Later came the Black Panthers, the Nuestra Familia, the Aryan Brotherhood, and many others.[5]

Jim Park recounts:

> A major battle that McGee fought was racial integration of the prison facilities, primarily the dining halls, and secondarily the work assignments. The halls were integrated eventually, but with much resistance from San Quentin and Folsom, Folsom being the last to integrate, well into the 1960s. He ordered Duffy [the San Quentin warden] to integrate the dining hall, which Duffy did by giving several days advance notice so that the white and Hispanic prisoners had ample time to stir up a riot.
>
> The long-time warden at Folsom stalled for years, citing the problems at San Quentin. Incidentally, Lou Nelson as Associate Warden Custody [at San Quentin] integrated with no problem. The announcement was made just the afternoon before, and all staff, and presumably inmate informants were told to listen for whites who were mouthing off about it. Guess what? None of the anti-integration leaders got unlocked for breakfast that morning, and once the ice was broken, there was little more resistance.[6]

McGee also pointed out:

As a matter of historical fact, religion was the very root of the concept of prison reforms 150 to 200 years ago. In spite of this, the religious programs of penal institutions during my own lifetime have, with a few notable exceptions, been sporadic, half-hearted, and often inept. In California, we have attempted to rescue our religious programs from the doldrums into which they had fallen by securing the interest of outstanding church leaders in the State. To this end, we have appointed a committee of seven members made up of recognized church leaders in all the major branches of the Catholic, Protestant, and Jewish faiths. This Committee on Institutional Religion has helped to formulate an overall policy which has been adopted by the administration. This has resulted in raising the standards for chaplains, providing for their training in penology, and in the construction of special and appropriate places of worship within the institutions (1951).

On another critical factor in institutional morale, McGee reported:

Food has been the source of numerous scandals and disturbances in California's prisons in the past. A new system, based on sound and scientific principles, has been developed. A Departmental Food Administrator has been added to the central office staff to provide professional supervision over the institutional culinary services (1953b).

The record system for keeping track of inmates was also reorganized and centralized, as it became evident that the institution-based systems were defective; inmates listed at San Quentin as on parole were sometimes found to be confined under a new sentence at Folsom. McGee promoted the development of a state Bureau of Criminal Statistics in 1947 in the California Department of Justice, under Ronald Beattie. It prepared reports for the Department of Corrections on the number of prisoners and parolees, their characteristics, and their movement.

McGee could assert in 1953:

Data on more than 25,000 prisoners have been collected, classified, and analyzed. The plans for the development of the Department are now based upon factual material, rather than upon whimsy and crystal gazing (1953b; *see also* McGee, 1981:136–37).

From the information collected, in relationship to demographic and crime trends, McGee convinced the governor and the legislature of the need for additional prisons.

McGee repeatedly obtained higher salaries for prison staff, and in a few years, arranged for them to have peace officer status.

John Conrad, who during 1947–67 worked for McGee in many capacities, as social worker at San Quentin and as CDC's Chief of Research, remarked on "what it was like" to work for him:

> I arrived on this scene three years after his appointment as California's first Director of Corrections. I was one of the new young men...assigned the job of assembling the clinical and criminal histories of new prisoners at San Quentin, conducting group counseling, and spending long hours of deliberation on classification committees. Echelons of superiors stretched up the ladder between me and the summit in Sacramento where the Director was to be found.
>
> At my level, I found colleagues who were...fearful of a new master who was said to be willing and able to discipline severely and even to fire employees of long, if not unblemished, service. I heard often that unreasonable things were expected, things that had never been done at San Quentin or anywhere else. In spite of all these forebodings, new and better principles of prison management emerged. Civilian employees were hired to keep orderly and confidential records. Case histories were written, and psychological tests were administered by professionals rather than by prisoner autodidacts. Convict bosses were replaced by qualified foremen. Work and program assignments were made by classification committees, not by the captain and his prisoner clerks. In spite of all the grumbling, San Quentin visibly changed from a structure based on patronage and manipulation to one of increasing efficiency.
>
> ...As the years went by, I moved up...,eventually...to become acquainted with the man whose handiwork had brought about the collaboration of the San Quentin old guard with the newly minted correctional professionals....I began to learn how the transformation had been accomplished.
>
> It is hard to recapture the excitement of those days. We worked for a restless perpetually dissatisfied leader who exacted superior performances from his subordinates. His intellectual curiosity swept in ideas from every point of the compass; our job was to translate these ideas into programs. It was inconceivable

that a year could pass without a new experiment..., a new study, or a new program to train people to do more than they had previously thought possible....It is an exhilarating experience to engage in an enterprise in which all participants are convinced that they are leading the world to great improvements....We knew that that was the case; we could see the improvements and their effects, and we heard the acclaim from travelers who came from all over the world to see for themselves. The grumblers changed their tunes.

...Not much could have been tried or done without McGee's pragmatic concern about...administration. His staff soon learned that...to survive in Sacramento, they had to act on verified facts, for which opinions and assumptions were not...substitutes. There had to be a flow of information into the director's office...he had to know what was going on....

In most prison systems, the only excitement in humdrum routines occurs when something goes seriously wrong: an escape from maximum custody, a riot, the taking of hostages. For those of us who worked with McGee, the excitement was of a different quality—a new program that proved its worth, new legislation to solve an old problem, or a new procedure that simplifed operations. There were mistakes and disappointments, but it was unthinkable that we could be allowed subside into the management of drift.... Even our failures during McGee's regime had at least the benefit that something important was under trial; there was hope for a system in which optimists were in control.

That was what it was like to work for McGee, a man who could stimulate the best in his subordinates and maintain their loyalty to him by virtue of his own loyalty to those who served him well....

For too many people in public life, administration is...an opportunity to demonstrate superior virility by bending the wills of others to their own. For McGee, public service has always been public service; the interest of the people had to be discovered and served. For administrators..., this record demonstrates how politics and a competent bureaucracy can work in successful partnership for the public interest in even so unpromising an arena as the American prison (1981a).

McGee, an inspiring taskmaster to bright and dedicated staff, could also be stern when he felt that they "let him down," according to "off the record" tales. He was said to be generally soft-spoken, but to have a "ferocious temper" at times, and to be feared by many for what was called his "ass chewing." One such story is when McGee had a psychiatrist, who had been employed at San Quentin since the 1930s, come to Sacramento in order to "call him on the carpet." The psychiatrist remained impassive, then tapped McGee's chest with his forefinger and said: "Mr. McGee, a man of your age should not demonstrate this much emotion. It is bad for the heart."

Lawrence Bennett, who succeeded Conrad as Director of Research, reports that McGee did indeed have a heart attack around 1956, but this was not generally known by his staff. Bennett adds:

> Part of McGee's genius was to select and promote people with high qualifications. He was constantly winnowing his staff to find people with promise, and he recruited people who offered potential for contributing to the department. When he came in, he brought several psychiatrists from the State of Washington. While they may have had personality quirks (one of them was nicknamed "Prince Hell," because of his drunken escapades), they were very highly qualified professionally and helped lead the department toward professionalism.[7]

McGee sought and welcomed advice from others to a degree that was remarkable for a government official, and when the advice seemed to have some possible utility, he considered it carefully. But he also had definite ideas about the need for clear and unquestioned authority in a prison system:

> The director's office should be organized on a line-and-staff model, an old concept in the administration of large, complex organizations. The line of direct authority implies the flow of orders through a so-called chain of command. Because prisons are crisis-prone organizations, all employees should know just who can give orders as opposed to advice. Line personnel give and receive orders. Staff personnel give advice and technical assistance. As such they have influence but not authority. If authority is required to implement a staff recommendation, the staff person should bring the matter to a line superior, who will decide to issue or not to issue the order. Unless this system is adhered to, an institution head may find his subordinates getting orders from the director's staff that he knows nothing about, or even with which he

disagrees for reasons not apparent to the visiting expert from the state office. If bad relationships develop between the state director's office and institutional managements, it will usually have its basis in this lack of understanding of the protocol of the line and staff relationships. Unless both the director and his principal deputy monitor this relationship constantly, human carelessness or perversity will short-circuit the system.

Another source of misunderstanding...is the difference between the flow of orders and advice..., and the flow of information. Information can come from any source and can travel over the lines of least resistance without regard to the rigidities of the line-and-staff protocol. The example of the supervising cook who heard about an escape plot but thought it none of her business and failed to report it illustrates the point. Conversely the executive who plants subordinate employees and inmates throughout the institution as privileged informers can be more destructive to morale than the damage from having missed some bit of information that is often only distorted gossip anyway (1981:79).

With bureaucratization, continuous attention to employee training, recruitment of exceptional administrators and staff, as well as good line-and-staff relationships, many California correctional personnel became highly oriented to inmate reformation in addition to maintaining secure custody. Yet there remained some resistance from "old timers." Norman Holt, who worked successively in institutions, on research, and as parole administrator in the Department, recounts:

When I came in December 1966 (when Reagan had been elected Governor), there were two Departments of Correction, divided by the Tehachapi Mountains. There was a perennial tug-of-war for power between the southern "prisoners-are-people" and the northern "freeze-'em-and-drive-'em-in-the-ground" group. The "nice guys" had been in the saddle awhile under Walter Dunbar, who went to New York after Reagan was inaugurated. Staff from the North considered it an insult to be called "Correctional Officer," the official term initiated under McGee. They preferred "Guard," or better yet, "Bull."[8]

It has probably always been true everywhere that, as Messinger asserts for California, "the over-riding concern of prison personnel was with prison discipline—with managing relations among inmates and between inmates and staff" (Messinger, 1969:9). He elaborates, "the workaday world confronted by prison officials at all levels moves their attention persistently to the issue of *control of inmates*" (*Ibid*:289). The strategies of control, however, vary from one institution to another, and McGee, to a great extent, reduced their interference with reformation efforts.

Inmate Employment and Training

As soon as McGee began to head prison systems in New York City, the distinctive teaching orientation that he brought to correctional work became highly evident when he pointed out in systematic detail how jails and prisons can maximize on-the-job vocational education even without formal classes:

Prison inmates required to mop the same floor day after day or to sit in idleness listening to the obscene boastings of their companions or watching the imponderable doings of a cockroach are no doubt learning, but the outcomes of that learning are of doubtful value either to themselves or to society. There is a multiplicity of necessary tasks which must be performed by the inmates. These tasks, whether they be in...routine maintenance...or manufacturing are usually determined on a purely utilitarian basis....An effort should be made, nevertheless, to organize as much of the prison work program as possible...to develop its educational possibilities....

...for the inmates to develop useful skills, and to acquire related information and attitudes in performing these necessary tasks, there are a number of...requirements which must be met....

First, there must be as extensive an opportunity to do planned and purposeful work as possible. This presupposes a sincere effort to eliminate idleness and make-believe work activities.

Second, the work performed must have a purpose which has significance to the doer. Unless the work...has a practical value for which the worker can have a certain degree of respect, the educational results...will probably be negligible.

Third, the work...must have a close similarity to work done outside...and for which there are employment possibilities in free society.

Fourth, the organization of the activities...must have conscious instructional...as well as production objectives. For example, in a shop where there is a variety of specialized jobs and specialized machines the maximum production will probably be obtained if each worker is required to specialize upon some very narrow task, but the instructional objectives will not be achieved unless the learner is shifted from task to task...to broaden the base of his knowledge. Then, when his knowledge and skill have reached a certain general level, he should be allowed to specialize to a higher degree in one or more limited phases of the process.

Fifth, the work must be done under skilled guidance. It is naive to assume that a man can learn plumbing from an employee who is not a plumber. He may not learn the trade even then, unless the employee in charge has some knowledge and capacity in...teaching. This is often the weakest point in a program of vocational training which is conceived as only incidental to the production process.

...there must also be an educational officer in charge of the whole training program who has a thorough knowledge of techniques of vocational training...in the preparation of trade analysis, instruction sheets, organization of subject matter, the development of related information courses, and other forms of organization work.

Sixth, there must be an opportunity for the worker to learn the related subject matter.... For example, an electrician's helper might develop a high degree of manual skill in such operations as wire splicing, installation of conduits, testing circuits, and so forth, but unless there is some...instruction in the theory of electricity he cannot hope to become a skilled craftsman.

Seventh, there must be a desire on the part of the worker to improve his knowledge and skill in the work performed. Therefore, an effort should be made to assign a man to work from which he is expected to obtain educational result, to take into consideration his interests as well as his capacities. But...spurious interests should be guarded against: a man's interests in learning to become a waiter are sometimes more closely connected with his desire to obtain a better grade of food than with his vocational ambitions. [Inmate are often waiters in officer's dining halls-dg].

...the experienced and conservative prison administrator who knows the shortcomings of his inmates, the inadequacies of his staff, and the abnormal nature of many prison work activities, is all too often unable or unwilling to see the few opportunities for training that do exist.... In truth, however, there are probably fewer opportunities for training than the professional educator supposes and more than the prison administrator appreciates.

As a matter of principle every opportunity for vocational training in the maintenance and industrial activities of an institution should be given its maximum use (1939).[9]

McGee continued the above with detailed instructions on analyzing the institution's work program for educational ends by listing all work activities, making trade analyses of each, considering the employment opportunities for ex-convicts in these trades, taking into account in work assignments the safety concerns of the institution, surveying instructional literature in each trade, maintaining progress records on the training in each shop, establishing quotas of trainees for each trade, and careful testing and interviewing to select for each type of trade training those men most likely to benefit from it.

However, during the Great Depression of the 1930s, both business and labor, objecting to convicts working when so many non-criminals were unemployed, got federal laws enacted to ban interstate commerce of prison-made goods. McGee found it difficult to keep all inmates well occupied, and lamented:

The enforced idleness of a substantial percentage of able-bodied men and women in our prisons...militates against every constructive objective of a prison program. It is one of the direct causes of the tensions which burst forth in riot and disorder. About forty percent of the prisoners in an unselected prison population will be completely idle insofar as constructive work is concerned unless there are provisions for their employment in the production of agricultural and industrial goods. In years past there have been abuses of prison labor such as its use in chain gangs, and in sweatshop industrial activities. In eliminating these evils, we have come close to eliminating all kinds of prison labor—good as well as bad. The opposition of pressure groups, attempting by every means possible to eliminate even the slightest competition, has resulted in restrictive legislation, both state and federal, which has reacted against the public interest by forcing us to maintain prisoners in idleness while they deteriorate physically, mentally and morally. Prisoners who spend their days in enforced idleness also constitute a heavy and unnecessary financial burden on the taxpayer. Productive labor wisely employed can substantially reduce prison costs.

Even more important than the immediate costs of idleness in prison are the incalculable costs of future crimes committed by men who leave prison, after years of deterioration in enforced idleness, with neither the ability nor the will to earn an honest living. The deterioration of idle prisoners, moreover, is not always a slow and quiet process. Students of mental health have always recognized the importance of interesting and satisfying work as a basic factor in maintaining emotional stability. When agitators strike the spark that starts a riot, prisoners surfeited by monotony flare into revolt as dry and crumbling tinder bursts into flame. The most striking characteristic of the great majority of our prisons during the past generation has been an atmosphere of dry rot and a certain purposeless passage of time.

...Taxpayer groups deplore the cost of prisons and then prevent them from doing the only thing that might reduce costs— namely, permit the prisoner to pay for his own keep by his own labor. Organized industry and labor must begin to assume some active responsibility for assisting government with this difficult and persistent problem (1953a).

Although prisons always must employ some inmates to feed the others, keep the institution clean, and for maintenance and repair work, this is generally not enough work to keep everyone adequately occupied. Therefore, in California prisons in the past half century, as in Illinois prisons when I was employed by them between 1950–54, and at most other penal institutions today, many inmates have as their full-time daily work assignments tasks that could be done in a few hours. For example, one inmate is assigned as janitor for a hundred feet of hallway inclusive of the six or eoght offices or other rooms adjacent to the hallway. The area may be dusted and swept or even mopped daily, and rubbish baskets emptied, but this still does not fill most of even a four-or-five-hour workday. Thus, inmates become habituated to slow work and short work days, unlike the demands of outside jobs.

When McGee came to California in 1944, it was one of the few states in which prisoners did not make state vehicle license plates. In 1947, backed by the governor and the Department of Motor Vehicles, McGee established a plant at Folsom to make them. The president of the California Manufacturer's Association headed a firm that previously made these plates, and the association lobbied vigorously, but unsuccessfully, to stop these prison operations. This plant became the largest prison industry in the nation. At Chino and Soledad, McGee opened factories to manufacture school chairs and desks, but private firms lobbied successfully to drastically limit the variety of furniture that could be made there. However, the prisons also developed: furniture repair and refinishing services for schools and government offices; shops to manufacture easels, building blocks, and other school supplies; a cotton textile mill, and for the women's prison, a sewing project (McGee, 1953a, 1953b).

For many prisoners considered low-security risks, McGee developed outdoor jobs including clearing trails, constructing campgrounds, and performing a variety of nature conservation work in state and national forests and parks. The prisoners were also used to fight forest fires, and to clear snow. He reported:

...one of the most popular developments in the prison system... was the...network of forestry camps. When I retired from the State on June 30, 1967, there were about forty of these in addition to several youth camps and three medium sized installations known as Conservation Centers. The normal strength of each camp was 80 inmates.

These camps probably constituted the largest and best organized wild land fire fighting force in the world. In addition..., a great deal of fire prevention, reforestation, stream clearance, and work of that sort was also done....With the recent drop in the prison population..., and fewer minimum security prisoners, the program has been reduced (1976a:187–88).

Describing such camp programs, McGee said:

The appropriate cooperating agency supervises the work; custody and control of the inmates is the responsibility of correctional personnel. Besides the permanent camps, the Department, in conjunction with the United States Forest Service, operates summer forest camps from April or May until October....

...The work benefits the State and the community, and also the inmates. While a prisoner is out working he pays for his own keep and is able to accumulate some funds to assist in the support of his family, if any, and to start him out in community life when he goes on parole. The work of these inmate crews on fire lines brings many expressions of gratitude and praise (1953b).

McGee reported in 1953:

We have accepted the principle that prisoners should be engaged during their waking hours in constructive and useful activities. We also accept the thesis that prison labor should not interfere unduly with private enterprise....Within the framework of these two somewhat conflicting objectives, the Legislature established a Correctional Industries Commission in 1947. The Governor appoints representatives from organized labor, industry, agriculture, and the general public, to this commission. The Director of Corrections serves as chairman. It is the Commission's duty to find and authorize constructive work projects for prison inmates....

The products of the Correctional Industries' manufacturing operations at the prisons can be sold only to and used by institutions within the Department of Corrections or other tax-supported public agencies, such as schools and mental hospitals. There is no direct competition with private industry. Operation of farms at five of the institutions is another part of the work program. Surplus...is sold...within the Department, or to other State agencies.

...the Legislature has authorized a small wage for prisoners engaged in productive enterprises. On June 20, 1953, there were 50 industrial and agricultural enterprises in operation within the Department, employing 2,089 inmates. In this fiscal year there were produced goods and services with a sales value of $3,185,800 as compared with a production of goods and services valued at $850,000 for the fiscal year ending June 30, 1946 (1953b; *see also* 1954).

Unfortunately, these efforts never sufficed to keep most of California's inmates well occupied and paid in prison. Much of the Correctional Industries Commission's concern, especially of its business and labor representatives, was to minimize use of prisoners to produce items that private firms wished to sell to the state. This resistance began in the state legislature, and as one historian indicates:

With legislative authorization to create new "correctional industries" in 1945, ample opportunities apparently opened for convict labor. However, no real reform occurred, for the 1947 legislation establishing the Correctional Industries Commission set low statutory annual maximum production levels for every prison enterprise. The act stated: "No industrial enterprise which involves a gross annual production of more than twenty-five thousand dollars ($25,000) value shall be established unless and until a hearing concerning the enterprise has been had before the Correctional Industries Commission." Any expansion of annual production worth $25,000 also required a public hearing, and a statutory and annual production ceiling of $175,000 was placed on each prison industry except for the license plate factory at Folsom.

Due to monetary inflation, this legislation was altered in 1982 to require special hearings only for annual production increases valued at $50,000. This subsequent act also removed the absolute production ceiling required in the 1947 act. Nevertheless, the overall effect of both laws insured that California's prison industries would not effectively tap the huge state-use market....

Sadly, the "treatment ethic" of the rehabilitators provided the intellectual justification for maintaining unrealistic work environment in California's prisons. In 1959, the Family Counseling Project of the Department of Corrections argued that continuously watching television helped prepare the inmate for release into an increasingly leisure-oriented society. Together with playing cards, chess and checkers, watching television supposedly helped establish leisure-time habits so that the released convict would not return to a life of crime. In an Orwellian manner, the Department of Corrections recast the atrophying of California's prison industries into a blessing of increased leisure time activities supposedly crucial to the inmate's rehabilitation.

...By the mid-fifties California had eleven permanent convict conservation camps, ten seasonal conservation camps and only three permanent road camps. About 1,000 inmates were then involved. Governor Brown proposed to double this figure. He succeeded in 1959, for new conservation camps were less expensive than the new prison facilities that otherwise would have been required to house California's growing convict population. Nevertheless, this reform had a rider: The camps were put under the authority of the Correctional Industries Commission.

...in 1965 the legislature authorized "work furlough" for state prisoners. This program supposedly tested a convicts' readiness for parole. Prisoners in the program worked in the community for a wage. During their leisure hours, they stayed in a "half-way house" or a residential custodial facility. Part of their wages paid for room and board costs....(McAfee, 1990)

In addition, for each industry at a prison, McGee had the warden try to establish a Trade Advisory Committee of local employers and union officials for every field of inmate labor. By 1955, there were thirty-eight such committees. Each committee counseled on its type of work, recommended equipment and supplies and, formulated standards to give inmates the abilities and attitudes needed for outside employment. The committees also visited the institutions at regular intervals to assess their achievements, and helped procure post-release employment for qualified prisoners about to be released. The committees created a public interest in the institution's goal of increasing legitimate employability of inmates (Halley, 1992:47–48).

Kim Nelson recalls that McGee often expressed the hope that, by giving business and labor officials in such committees personal contacts with prisoners as persons, they would recognize inmate abilities and character, and would become less resistant to employing ex-convicts. McGee hired Wes Asch to visit institutions to establish and assist such committees, as Asch was exceptionally talented and had many useful labor and business contacts for this task.[10]

McGee concluded on prison labor:

...most of the productive capacity of men and women in state prisons and county jails remains untapped. Everyone is the poorer for it. Strong opposition to prison labor by those in private enterprise generally is based on simplistic notions, almost none of which has any valid economic or technical basis. One commonly hears such phrases as, "unlimited supply of cheap labor," "you don't have to pay taxes," and "unlimited capital furnished by the taxpayers."...

Cheap-Labor Issue

...prison labor is far from cheap. No operation...will operate without management, supervisory, and custodial personnel, who work forty hours a week. Thus although the prisoners are available and most...would be glad to work six eight-hour days a week, their workday is seldom longer than six hours and often as short as four and a half or five. Start-up time, lunch, and closing down all must be fitted into the working hours of civilian and custodial employees. In addition, the workday of individual prisoners is frequently interrupted by competing activities such as visits, special interviews, and disciplinary or parole board hearings....

Because of these interruptions and...an oversupply of inmates, to say nothing of turnover due to transfers and releases, the factory manager tends to keep on the job from 25 to 100 percent more workers than are needed. This...results in inefficiency and a waste of capital, since buildings, machines and inventories stand idle almost half of the daytime hours and all of the time (with rare exceptions) during the other two shifts....

Price versus Cost Issue

Most state-use statutes require that prison-made goods not be sold at less than the prevailing market price. It is sometimes difficult to tell what that price is, especially for goods that in the free market vary widely in quality and where overstocked items frequently are dumped.... The purchasing division often bought up stocks from bankrupt dealers or accepted the lowest public bid with little regard to quality....

Capital-Investment Issue

Those who think that unlimited funds are available to buy land, buildings, machines, and talented management for prison industries are mistaken. Such money must come either from bond issues approved by the voters which is virtually impossible, or from legislative appropriations. All...such appropriations must compete with more-appealing needs for schools, hospitals, bridges, roads, and sewers....

Another factor...is that technological change is so rapid and widespread that there is a constant need for new capital investment to keep plants and equipment up to date....

The state-use system, which was intended to protect prisoners from exploitation and guarantee a share of the state market for their products, is a failure. If prison labor ever was a threat to free enterprise, that time has long since passed (1981:99–102).

McGee sought in vain to have inmate labor opportunities comparable to those of the U.S. Bureau of Prisons, which established a non-profit corporation (now called UNICOR) to run prison industries; it is permitted to fill portions of federal purchase contracts, with its payments set at the price received by the lowest corporate bidders, using production equipment and procedures like those of such corporations (Keve, 1991). California was not one of the seven states selected by the Justice Department in 1979–88, under special legislation, for "joint ventures" of prisons and private firms in trial deviations from the ban on interstate sale of prison-made goods (Dwyer and McNally, 1993; Auerbach, 1993).

Inmate Schooling

As a former teacher, McGee was especially interested in improving the education of prisoners. In 1955, 26 percent of California's inmates had less than a sixth-grade education. The U.S. Bureau of the Census in 1974 completed a *Survey of Inmates of State Correctional Institutions*, covering a representative 191,000 inmates. It found that 23 percent had never been in the 9th grade, and an additional 45 percent had never been in the 12th grade, which was interpreted as showing that at least 68 percent were undereducated for today's society (Petersilia, 1979). Most probably had poor school achievement records in whatever classes they had completed, for poor school work is one of the best predictors of a juvenile's arrest, and juvenile arrestees have high risks of imprisonment as adults.

It should be noted that prisons formerly, and many still today, provided most of their academic education for prisoners by assigning their more educated inmates as instructors, who had little or no training in pedagogy. Also, inmates with skilled trade experience are not only job foremen at institution work assignments, but also classroom vocational instructors. Usually, one or two of the employees of each institution are licensed and experienced teachers, and they are made the supervisors of education, as McGee was at Leavenworth and Lewisburg. Monitoring by staff, especially of tests, is needed with such arrangements to prevent inmate students from corrupting the education procedures by using bribes, threats, or violence to shape the conduct of their inmate teachers (Glaser, 1964:268–71, 1969:180–83; Leopold, 1958).

In California, McGee quickly got most prisoners enrolled in day or night classes, usually taught by licensed public-school teachers who worked in the prison on a part-time basis while holding full-time employment in a public school system. In addition, it was often possible to place the prison school partly under the supervision of the public school board of the district in which the institution was located. This allowed the prisoners to receive credits and diplomas from the public school system. McGee astutely noted:

> We have given over the responsibility for education in our institutions to the public school system, instead of trying to do it ourselves, because as soon as we try to do it ourselves we get the failures of the school system as teachers....(McGee, 1947a)

He could assert in 1953:

Educational programs are now offered at all seven institutions of the Department of Corrections. Education, and especially vocational education, is one of the foremost positive factors in preparing men and women for return to society. Approximately 6,000 inmates are registered today in one or more courses each in our institutions. During the past four or five years...enrollment in job training classes has increased more than five-fold. These classes are administered as part of the adult education program of the State Department of Education. Accomplishment in these classes is recognized by labor unions and employers on the same basis as comparable work in the public schools. Through the assistance of local high school districts and junior colleges, plus services of teachers employed directly by the Department of Corrections, instruction is offered in more than 40 subjects at the seven institutions. Trade advisory committees, consisting of employers and union leaders, have been of great assistance in developing this program. Upon their release, inmates, trained under competent instructors, are finding ready employment in skilled and semi-skilled fields of industry (1953b).

The California Department of Corrections published in 1971 a survey of the post-release job experience of 729 inmates who were paroled during 1967–69, after at least two hundred hours of vocational training in prison with grades of C or better. It found that:

1. About 35 percent got their first jobs on parole in the trade in which they were trained, and about the same percentage were employed in these trades at six months and 12 months after their release.
2. The percentage employed in this trade increased with their hours and their grades in this training.
3. The percentage employed in their trades also increased the closer their termination of training was to the date of their release.
4. Interviews with 107 of these parolees, of whom twelve had been returned to prison, but the rest were still on parole, revealed that most had experienced much job turnover, and over 60 percent complained that their earnings were below what they expected.
5. Parole agents were credited by only 17 percent of the parolees with getting jobs for them, the rest being procured by their own efforts, and with help from friends and relatives, as well as from state employment agencies.

6. Interviews with 106 parole agents elicited a variety of explanations for parolee employment problems, particularly that they were inadequately trained or trained in inappropriate trades.
7. Interviews with thirty-three employers, or their representatives, revealed that over 80 percent regarded their prison-trained employees as about as well or better prepared for their jobs as their average entering employee who claimed prior training or experience.
8. The principal employer complaint about parolee employees was absenteeism, much of it ascribed to drink or drugs (Dickover et al., 1971).

McGee had noted earlier:

> It is relatively easy to develop the skill and the technical knowledge required to do efficient work in a specific job....But we have not available...techniques...to develop, with comparable satisfactory results, the human behavior that enables the individual to get along with others....This ability...is more important than skill and technical knowledge in determining the success of the worker on any job. Studies show that of every 100 discharged workers, 75 lose their jobs because they lack the ability to get along with others; ....Only 25 are released for not having enough skill and technical knowledge to do satisfactory work (1953c).

He also asserted:

> ...institutions for convicted offenders must do everything possible to prevent the return of men to criminal behavior after release. It takes 25% of the Department's budget just to feed the prisoners. It takes 35% just to guard them. We are probably spending less than 15% of the entire budget on positive programs designed to influence attitudes and behavior. We need to spend more, not less, money in this category. These institutions must, in fact, be treatment and training centers, not places of punishment for punishment's sake alone (1953b).

Incentives and pressures were greatly used to get inmates to attend school and perform satisfactorily there. Good performance was a requirement in some prisons to obtain housing in the "honor units." These units had somewhat more freedom or comfort than regular units, and staff emphasized that honor unit housing would favorably impress members of the parole boards. Also, as Messinger details, it was a strategy for controlling inmates, not only by the threat that misconduct could cause their removal from school, but also to keep them occupied and "out of the yard" where they were more likely to get into conflict or rule violations with other inmates (Messinger, 1969).

Prison Architecture

McGee, coming to California in 1944, entered the nation's most rapidly growing state, which always had a high crime rate, hence many prisoners. He anticipated the need for more prisons, but did not want large ones. As he put it:

> Institutions for adult prisoners, in most of the more populous states, have been allowed to become much too large. Any such institution, operating as a single unit, becomes increasingly inefficient and unsafe as its population exceeds 1,200. The ideal size for a prison for adults has been held to be one of 800 to 1,000 capacity—some say as small as 500.
>
> A large prison, built for 2,000 to 5,000 prisoners, is a dangerous and stupid mistake at the outset. But, to make this even worse, both large and small institutions frequently have from 10% to 100% more prisoners in them than they were built and equipped to handle. This is accomplished by putting two beds in cells built for one; crowding one hundred beds into a dormitory built for sixty; serving meals in the dining rooms in shifts; and, in fact, overloading all the facilities of the institution, overworking the personnel, and failing, generally, to meet the most elementary requirements for segregation of types and the maintenance of decent standards of moral behavior. Such a prison is not only unsafe, it provides within itself the chief obstacle to its own corrective functions....
>
> The most striking and consistent characteristic of history's long account of vile and unsavory prison conditions is to be found in the excessive crowding of large numbers of prisoners into old, inadequate buildings under sub-standard conditions. The irritations and frustrations of such conditions encourage the prisoners to riot and weaken the ability of the management to control them (1953a).

He was able to open a new prison for men at Soledad in 1946, but in its early years it had to house inmates in sheet-metal buildings made from war surplus materials. It was designed for only 350 inmates, but the overcrowding in the other institutions soon forced it to house 700. Permanent prison buildings at Soledad were not opened until December 1951 (Halley, 1992:36).

The original California Institution for Women at Tehachapi, at an isolated mountain site in Kern County, was designed to hold 150 women in cottages instead of cell blocks, with each unit having its own sleeping quarters, kitchen, and dining room. After 1949, it averaged 300 prisoners, and by 1952 had over 400. The new California Institution for Women opened in 1954 at Corona, adjacent to Chino, and was architecturally similar to that at Tehachapi but much larger. Since residents of the town of Corona objected to being identified with a prison, a new post office called "Frontera" was created for this institution, but until recently it was generally referred to as "at Corona." A second prison for women was not opened until 1987 (Halley, 1992:16–17).

In 1946 a former Air Corps flight academy near Lancaster, in Los Angeles County, was converted to the California Vocational Institution, for the youngest of the male prisoners. Meanwhile, buildings for an institution were being constructed at a more permanently satisfactory site about seventy miles east of San Francisco. It was opened in 1953, and was renamed the "Deuel Vocational Institution." It provides secure custody and rehabilitation services for youthful felons (Halley, 1992:41).

In 1950, the state leased from the U.S. Navy some hospital facilities on Terminal Island, at San Pedro, to create the California Medical Facility for housing inmates who were psychotic, tubercular, or sexually deviant. In 1955, the medical facility was moved to a larger set of buildings that the state constructed at Vacaville. Later, a Reception-Guidance Center was also established there to receive all new prisoners from the northern part of the state. The prisoners stayed about sixty days of physical examinations, testing, orientation, classification, and then assignment to another institution. A similar facility had already been established adjoining Chino to receive all new prison admissions from southern California (Halley, 1992:39–40; McGee, 1953b).

During 1944–68, as new specialized institutions were built for the growing number of prisoners, Messinger points out that "each prison tended to develop a view of its special competence," and the Department of Corrections evolved from "a 'congerie of prisons' to a 'prison system'" (Messinger, 1969:13, 21).

McGee found that political and administrative problems in getting new prison sites approved and purchased prevented his trying to scatter small institutions across the state. Instead, it was usually expedient to build a new facility adjacent to an old one, on land the state already owned.

The new structures were given a type of non-penal nomenclature initiated at Chino under Scudder, whereby that place ceased to be called a "prison," and was instead called "California Institution for Men." The head was called "Superintendent," rather than warden. The "California State Prison at Soledad" was renamed "The California Correctional Training Facility." Other names not suggesting a prison were used at all new institutions, such as the "California Men's Colony" near San Luis Obispo, where McGee got the small institutions he desired by compartmentalizing a larger edifice into several identical smaller units adjacent to each other. The units shared some common walls and services, but each had its own housing, dining, and recreational facilities, and was managed as though separate and autonomous; however, movement to work, school, or other services often permits contacts between inmates from different components.

The rationale for classification of prisoners into types, and for the segregation of different types in different institutions, was well stated by McGee:

In order to conduct a constructive program of training and rehabilitation for prisoners, it is not enough that the troublemakers be segregated on the one hand, and that the young, impressionable, inexperienced first offenders be segregated on the other. The process of study and segregation must be, in theory, at least an individual proposition. Therefore, we believe that no modern prison program can be successful without what we call a good classification system which must provide for a corps of personnel, professionally trained and experienced, to study the personality pattern of each individual prisoner. In California we have more than one-third of our 13,000 prisoners in unwalled camps and institutions. We believe that this would be wholly impossible if it were not for the careful classification studies that we make of our men and women (1952).

McGee continually encouraged research to reduce classification decisions based on the subjective impressions or bias of staff, and to increase their grounding in scientific data on what kinds of facilities are best for what types of offenders (Glaser, 1982; Gottfredson and Gottfredson, 1982; N. Holt, et al., 1982; Baird and Austin, 1985; Spindler, 1986).

Although the Youth Authority found that wards assigned to forestry camps had lower recidivism rates than those sent to more traditional correctional institutions, a controlled experiment that assigned youths randomly to camps or institutions found no significant difference in their recidivism rates (Molof, 1967). Apparently, the classification system's selection of lower risk offenders for the camps fully accounted for their better post-release conduct.

Smaller living units are advantageous in training schools for delinquents, a Youth Authority study concluded, because:

(1) they increase the proportion of staff-inmate relationships that can be intimate or close;
(2) they increase the time available per resident for desirable activities;
(3) behavior problems in them are more readily managed, and disturb fewer other persons, than those in large groups;
(4) their methods of control can be less rigid;
(5) residents misunderstand staff less readily in them than in larger units, and mistakes are corrected more quickly when they do occur;
(6) they make it easier for staff to reward desirable inmate conduct (Knight, 1971).

The Youth Authority tested these conclusions at Fricot School for Boys by randomly assigning youths to regular and smaller-sized housing units. Of those in the larger units, 52 percent violated their paroles during their first year out, while boys who had been housed in the smaller units had a 37 percent violation rate for their first year on parole (Jessness, 1972).

Later it retested these conclusions by experimentally changing the number of residents and staff in dormitories at Preston School of Industry, which holds advanced delinquents. Of two dormitories that normally averaged forty-seven wards and had five staff, one had its staff increased to six but kept its forty-seven wards, and the other kept only five staff but reduced its wards to thirty-eight. After fifteen months, these resident-and-staff numbers were reversed. In both cases, the staff-resident ratio was about one to ten, but with nine fewer beds the conduct records of wards and their learning achievements improved enough for their average release dates to occur much earlier. The net savings by earlier release equaled, on average, the cost of seventeen beds; it was profitable to have fewer in a dormitory (California Youth Authority, 1980).

As shown in Table 3.1, California's prison population declined during the 1940–45 World War II years, when the total prisoner population in the U.S. was also dropping. But after the war, from 1945 to 1978, the state's prisoner population increased more rapidly than it did in the rest of the nation, as both the state's population and its crime rates was rising. The relative decline in prisoners for several years thereafter was due largely to McGee's promotion of more use of parole and probation, the latter through the Probation Subsidy Program, discussed in chapter 4.

In the 1960s, when McGee was in his Cabinet, Governor "Pat" Brown is reported by Norman Holt to have:

...vowed not to build any new prisons, but built three conservation centers and camps instead. By 1972 almost one-third of the prisoners (5,000) were in them. The main reasons camps were finally cut back was that the forestry department later cut a bunch of

TABLE 3.1

Sentenced Prisoners in California, and in
Total U.S. State and Federal Prisons, 1925–90[1]

Year	California	Total U.S.	% in California
1925	5,285	91,669	5.8
1930	7,116	129,453	5.5
1935	8,578	144,180	5.9
1940	8,182	173,706	4.7
1945	6,628	133,649	5.0
1950	11,056	166,165	6.7
1955	15,230	185,780	8.2
1960	21,660	212,953	10.2
1965	26,325	210,895	12.5
1970	25,033	196,441	12.7
1975	17,296	240,593	7.2
1980	23,264	304,692	7.6
1985	48,326	465,236	10.4
1990	97,309	774,375	12.6

1. P. A. Langan, J. V. Fundis, L. A. Greenfeld, and V. W. Schneider. *Historical Statistics on Prisoners in State and Federal Institutions, Yearend 1925-86*. U.S. Department of Justice Report No. NCJ-111098. Washington, D.C.: Bureau of Justice Statistics, May 1988; U. S. Department of Justice, Bureau of Justice Statistics. *Correctional Population in the United States, 1990*. NCJ-135946 (Washington, D.C.: U.S. Govt. Printing Office, 1992, Table 5.6.

forestry foremen (the inmate supervisors) from their budget to finance an enhanced retirement package.[11]

When there were conservative state governors after McGee's 1967 retirement and his death in 1983, concern with prisoner reformation was often derogated as "leniency." After 1983, under Governor Deukmejian, a prison construction boom occurred that used new, cheap mass-production building methods and designs, oriented to economical control rather than to rehabilitation. Deukmejian could boast in his 1990 "State of the State Address":

> In 1983, California had just twelve prisons. Since then, we have built fourteen new prisons. That has enabled us to remove 52,000 convicted criminals from neighborhoods to send them to state prison (quoted in Simon, 1990:3).

Included in the construction during this period was the maximum security prison at Pelican Bay, to be "California's Alcatraz." Its inmates, intractable at other institutions, were placed in solitary confinement, under continuous electronic surveillance, and fed in their cells. They left their cells only when shackled. In 1993, this led to a much publicized law suit charging the state with cruel and unusual punishment in violation of the 8th Amendment to the U.S. Constitution (DeWitt, 1986). Meanwhile, California's crime rates were spurred by population growth and the "war on drugs," plus increased poverty and homelessness. Its unemployment rates and economic inequality reached their highest levels since the Great Depression, and were among the highest in the nation.

Coping with Criminogenic Chemical Addictions

Throughout history, most arrestees in the United States have had criminal conduct involving, or ascribed to, their use of behavior-altering chemicals. Until about 1950, this almost always meant alcohol. Increasingly since World War II, the chemicals have also been various non-alcoholic illegal drugs, such as marijuana, opiates, and cocaine. Since alcohol is dealt with differently from the non-alcoholic illegal drugs in our daily lives, and in the law, the penological implications of these two types of chemicals should be considered separately.

Alcoholism and Drunkenness

As warden of Rikers Island Penitentiary for the City of New York during the 1930s, McGee had to cope with the main source of jail inmates at that time—public drunkenness. Arrests, fines, and short confinement terms were then the standard punishments in the United States to those who seemed to be drunk in a public area, especially in the "skid row" sections of our largest cities. These sections are slums near central business areas where "flophouses" for poor transients and day laborers are concentrated. Police used "paddy wagon" vans as well as patrol cars to round up anyone who appeared to stagger or collapse from drunkenness in public places.

Speaking at a UCLA symposium on "Public Aspects of Alcoholism" in 1947, McGee graphically described this problem:

> The recognition of alcoholism as a symptom of disease has been slow in emerging. On the other hand, the recognition of the alcoholic as a public responsibility, if not a public nuisance, has been reluctantly accepted for generations. However,...the means of treatment...have consisted of the night stick, the patrol wagon, and the jail. The "morning after" they are brought in bedraggled lines before a judge who has neither the knowledge nor the facilities to deal with the miscreants before him. In any event, the public has provided him with limited courses of action: fine (but the man has no money); probation (but there are no probation officers to supervise him); discharge (only to get him back in a few hours or days); "float" him out of town (only to have him replaced by another "floated" out of a neighboring town); or jail for a few days or weeks in an institution so poorly supported that medical attention is provided only upon the display of symptoms of acute distress and the dietary allowances are barely above the maintenance level. Eighty percent of these institutions do not even meet sanitary standards demanded by common decency. In passing, I should say that I have rarely ever seen a jailer who did not want to run a jail which would deal with his problems on a better basis, but his legislative body and the public have been willing only rarely to supply the needed funds (1947b).

These were called "revolving door arrests," as the subjects were usually rearrested on the same charge a few days or weeks after their release. McGee anticipated later orientations to public drunkenness as he continued:

> ...The practicing criminologist has learned that he can deal successfully with his subjects only on one basis...individual case

work. This can only be accomplished by the establishment of adequately staffed clinics and institutions....Large numbers of alcoholics can be referred directly to the clinics without passing through the courts. Each court should have an adequate staff of probation officers specially trained in this field, who would check on the intake and advise the judge on the most appropriate disposition. Field supervision by trained workers will be essential (*Ibid*).

Today public drunkenness is no longer a crime because courts hold chronic alcoholism to be a sickness. The public increasingly views alcoholism as a mental illness rather than as sin, in sharp contrast to the perspectives that led to the Prohibition era. Drunken persons on the street are usually either left alone or transported by the police, or by various public and private social work agencies, to detoxification centers. The many who are instead arrested must be charged with some offense other than intoxication, such as the catch-all charge of "disorderly conduct."

Nevertheless, the law holds drinkers responsible for knowing when they have consumed too much alcohol for tasks such as driving, that make them a danger to the public. People are arrested and given jail terms for "DUI" or "DWI"—"driving under the influence of an intoxicating substance," "...while intoxicated," or "...when impaired." During the past twenty years, the number of such arrests has risen at over five times the rate of increase in licensed drivers, due in large part to the lobbying of "MADD"—"Mothers Against Drunken Driving." These arrest rates are highest among young drivers, peaking in 1989 at one arrest annually for every forty-six licensed drivers 21-to-24 years old; skid-row arrestees tended to be somewhat older. Rates of such arrests have declined since 1980 for those under twenty (Cohen. 1992). Less than 3 percent of DUI or DWI arrests are ascribed to drugs other than alcohol.

In addition, half or more of the assaults, rapes, and homicides for which prison sentences are imposed, are found by investigators to have been committed while the offender, and usually the victim as well, were drunk. Also, most small-scale check forgery is committed by chronic alcoholics seeking funds to continue drinking (Lemert, 1967, ch. 7). However, such serious property crimes such as burglary, robbery, and large-scale forgery or fraud are usually not associated with drunkenness.

A 1974 survey found that 44 percent of state prison inmates said that they had been drinking at the time of their offense, and half of these, that they had been drinking heavily. Of this 22 percent, only 19 percent were in prison treatment programs, and they were disproportionately the older white prisoners (Petersilia, 1979). Recently, these percentages have declined as illegal drug use increased. Thus, in 1991, 18 percent of prisoners said that at the time of their offense they were under the influence of alcohol only, 14 percent of alcohol and drugs, and 17 percent of drugs only; 18 percent of all drinkers in prison had joined alcohol treatment programs while in prison (Bureau of Justice Statistics, 1993a).

McGee's viewpoints on alcoholism remain appropriate today, for he emphasized public education and research to combat it, without much confidence in efforts to prohibit or to treat it:

> ...alcohol is an essential industrial material and its use as a beverage in moderate quantities is demanded by so large a proportion of the population that the prohibition of its manufacture, sale or use as a beverage could not be enforced.
>
> Since we must have alcohol, and since it is widely abused, controls must be instituted upon its production, sale, and use. There are only two approaches to this type of control. One is... placing social taboos upon the misuse of alcohol as a beverage. This can be accomplished only very gradually by...public education,...and there will always be a small percentage of people who will ignore the conventional standards of their society. While this process is going on, an immediate remedy is the exercise of political controls. It is here that we run into our greatest difficulty. The temperate drinker objects to having his personal liberties curtailed too much because of the few who abuse those liberties. The industrial and commercial interests with huge capital investments and many thousands of employees resort to every political expedient to protect their selfish interests.
>
> ...If the controls are loose, the abuses become rampant with the inevitable result of a wave of public revulsion. If the controls are too strict, the law will be widely violated and ignored with a resultant corruption of public officials and the development of a rich and powerful group of racketeers. So far, America has no satisfactory solution to the political control of the alcohol problem....
>
> Committing alcoholics to institutions should be limited to a small percentage of cases in which intensive medical and psychiatric treatment are needed, or in which long-term physical regeneration is indicated. An additional value of a few institutions for alcoholics lies in the possibilities for research....
>
> If the day ever comes when we can identify the potential alcoholic before he takes his first drink, and as strong a social taboo

is established against permitting the susceptible person to drink as now exists against giving whisky to babies, alcoholism will be under control (1947b).

Today, courts and parole agencies that deal with felons whose crimes are ascribed to alcoholism, often threaten or impose punishments for further drinking, and recommend or even coerce participation in Alcoholics Anonymous (AA) or other therapy. But these measures usually fail to end further drunkenness. The effort to end alcoholism must be voluntary to have much prospect of success, although it can be aided by ex-alcoholics who help themselves by helping others; Alcoholics Anonymous seems to have the best long-term success record of any voluntary program of treatment for this ailment (Vaillant, 1983).

Unfortunately, entry into AA or other programs, or simply abstaining forever on one's own initiative without formal programs, is usually prompted by "hitting bottom" through suffering "the last straw" in distress from drunkenness. But this last straw varies greatly for different people; for many, only death from drinking too much is alcoholism's final stage.

A 1987 Gallup Poll found that about a quarter of American homes reported having someone with an alcohol problem. This was the highest incidence since their first such survey, in 1950. Possibly the increase was not the number of people who drink, but the number of people willing to define drinking as a problem. This was suggested by impressions that heavy drinking is more common among poorer people, but the poll found that reporting an alcohol problem in the home is most common among the affluent and the college educated.

Heavy lobbying by victims of drunk driving accidents and their sympathizers has resulted in laws that mandate jail terms for drunk driving offenses. Drivers stopped by the police that are suspected of driving while intoxicated must submit to breath or even blood alcohol tests. However, rigorous studies, compiled over many years and various locations, show that:

(1) recidivism rates are not affected by any traditional type of penalty;
(2) it is the publicity about the penalty risk, not the penalty itself, that causes any local decline in rates of this offense following stricter laws, but publicity and enforcement campaigns soon decline, and offense rates rise again (Ross, 1992; Jacobs, 1989;).

Studies show that pressures to prosecute drunk driving not only have no appreciable effects on rates of this offense, but by overburdening courts, jails, and probation offices, greatly reduce the time these agencies could give to other types of offenders (Kinkade, et al., 1992). One half of all American adults polled admit that they have driven after they "had too much to drink," 37 percent admitted that it was in the past six months (Gilbert, 1988).

Despite laws in Arizona mandating jail terms for all drunken drivers, about 99 percent of those convicted of this offense in the Phoenix area were not jailed. Where laws mandated jail on the second conviction, 45 percent in New Mexico and 70 percent in Indiana were at least briefly confined. Judges often ignore such laws, and sometimes sheriffs do not impose the penalties even when the courts order them to (Ross, 1992). A 1981 California law permitting murder charges to be brought against those who kill someone while driving drunk was in its first decade applied to only about 3 percent of such cases. H. Laurence Ross (1992) implies that such failures to enforce laws against drunk driving occur because it is a "folk crime," an offense by law, but not regarded as a crime in the prevailing popular culture. John Braithwaite (1989:166) argues that these laws are ineffective simply because our society does not shame drunk drivers adequately. This also was McGee's theme, quoted earlier, that called public education the only way to curb alcoholism problems more adequately.

There is evidence that educational efforts have now made some progress. Polls show that 90 percent of high school seniors in the U.S. have at some time consumed alcoholic beverages, but also indicate a decline in the percentage who report that they had done so in the past month. Drinking by pregnant women has also declined since it has been shown to produce babies with "fetal alcohol syndrome." This syndrome is characterized by mental retardation and other birth defects, and is especially prevalent among Native Americans (Dorris, 1989).

Alcoholic beverage containers, as well as bars and liquor stores, must now display warnings about the risk of alcohol to pregnant women. There has also been an increase in the proportion of beverages with low or no alcohol sold or consumed where alcoholic drinks are dispensed, as well as in the proportion of "designated drivers." These drivers refrain altogether from drink at gatherings so that they can drive others home safely. Furthermore, increased "sin taxes" on beverages with high alcohol content have reduced overall sales.

Mandating that drunk driving be punished as a felony has been shown to result in police making fewer arrests for this offense, ignoring less extreme cases that previously would be prosecuted as misdemeanors (Kinkade and Leone, 1992). Yet some new types of penalties appear to reduce rates of recurrent alcoholic misconduct more than past punishments. One is the "day fine," long used in much of Europe for various offenses, and now increasing in the U.S.: instead of one sum as penalty for everyone, offenders are fined a specified number of days' earnings, less deductions for dependents and for minimum sustenance. The number of days' earnings that comprise the fine are increased on each repetition of the offense. Even ordinary fines are demonstrably more deterrent than confinement or ordinary probation penalties, but day fines are more uniformly deterrent and equitable if offenders differ greatly in earnings (Hillsman, 1990; Glaser and Gordon, 1990; Gordon and Glaser, 1991).

The newest special penalty for drunken driving is a period of probation with a condition that the probationer only drive an automobile where an interlock device has been installed on the ignition. The engine will not start unless the driver first breathes into this device with a breath free of the prohibited percentage of alcohol. In California, since July 1, 1993, this has been the mandated penalty for the second and subsequent drunken driving convictions. The interlock device has been shown elsewhere to reduce recidivism rates more effectively than license suspension (Morse and Elliott, 1992).

Addictions to Other Psychoactive Drugs

After World War II, prisons in California and the rest of the United States had a growing number of inmates who were addicted to narcotics, especially to heroin. Their sentences were usually for possession or sale of illegal drugs, or for other crimes committed to obtain funds for purchasing drugs. During the 1950s, addicts became a major portion of felony prosecutees in many areas. Penalties for drug crimes escalated, but this did not seem to reduce their prevalence.

Meanwhile, a movement developed to treat addiction and resulting law violations, not as crimes, but as expressions of an illness. The claim that when committing a crime mental illness causes the illegal behavior is a much used legal defense that, when successful, makes the perpetrator not guilty (discussed further in a later section of this chapter). This defense is used mostly in assault, rape, or murder cases. If the court accepts this defense, however, it may make the accused subject to state control and involuntary treatment for the illness.

In the controversial 1925 *Linder* case, and more clearly in the 1962 *Robinson* case, the U.S. Supreme Court ruled it cruel and unusual punishment, in violation of the Eighth Amendment to the U.S. Constitution, to imprison someone for the illness of drug addiction (Lindesmith, 1965; Bakalar and Grinspoon, 1984). This made illegal some state penalties that could be imposed simply for being under the influence of drugs, but in most cases other crimes, such as illegal possession, sale, or intent to sell (inferred from the amount possessed) were charged.

Despite the therapeutic perspective of these court decisions, hysteria developed from mass-media claims that drugs made persons violent criminals, and some politicians proposed extreme penalties for drug offenses. Indeed, in 1958 the Elks organization in California obtained over a million signatures on a petition demanding a mandatory thirty-year sentence for narcotics peddling (Himelson, 1968:12; Simon, 1990:109).

Lawrence Bennett, former Director of Research in the Department of Corrections, reports:

> At one point in this stage of history, the penalties were five years of mandatory incarceration without parole for first-time drug sales, 10 years without parole for second offenders, and 15 years on the third offense. Examination of cases so sentenced found that these were often Mexican laborers who did not realize the kind of difficulty they were getting into. The law was subsequently modified, and sentences were reduced through special appeals, but conservatives in the legislature demanded even more severe penalties.
>
> McGee, in an attempt to head off such insanity, asked whether drug addiction causes crime or criminals become drug addicts. He put some of us to work reviewing cases, but the results (never published) were inconclusive: they suggested that about half those sentenced to the Department of Corrections were involved in drug use incidental to their criminal life style, and the other half got into crime to support their drug habit.[12]

Bennett adds that it was an illustration of "McGee's ability to turn serious assaults on the criminal justice system into improved and advantageous programs," when California enacted legislation in 1961 to permit treatment of addiction as an illness. It provided that persons convicted of a misdemeanor or a felony, and who were addicted to narcotics, or "in imminent danger of becoming addicted to narcotics," could have criminal procedures suspended prior to imposition of sentence, and be given a civil commitment for treatment. This commitment could be ordered only by civil court hearings like those required to confine someone for mental illness.

Bennett reports that McGee's original conception of civil commitment for addiction was "for a very short period of incarceration (six–nine months), followed by intensive outpatient supervision, with the idea that slippage could result in short term return for additional treatment." He notes, however, that at first the legislature imposed a term of seven years, and later of either five or ten years, of involuntary treatment at a rehabilitation center, and in the community.

The therapy during confinement consisted mainly of physical conditioning, counseling, and labor. Release of civilly committed addicts to "outpatient status" (the civil equivalent of parole, and generally called "parole"), could occur after as little as six months in confinement. Early discharge from the commitment could occur after three drug-free years (McGee, 1965).

Treatment of addicts was at first done in several prison structures, but in 1962 was shifted to a former naval hospital at Norco, near Chino, called the California Rehabilitation Center (CRC). Later, a center for northern California was created, adjoining San Quentin. Addicts paroled from the centers to Los Angeles or San Francisco, who lacked adequate housing and employment arrangements, were first released to halfway houses, modelled on those already used for state prisoners.

The addict "outpatients" were assigned to supervision officers who gave them periodic Nalline tests, a since-abandoned procedure in which:

(1) the diameter of a subject's eye pupils were measured by a physician in a location with standard lighting (as opiates make the pupils widen);

(2) the physician then injected the opiate-antagonist Nalline (N-allylnormorphine) under the person's skin;

(3) in a few minutes, the pupils are measured again. If their width contracts, the person's bloodstream had a significant amount of opiates during the preceding forty-eight hours.

Those found to have used opiates again could be returned to the centers for up to ninety days of treatment without being declared parole violators. At first, the parole agents had much discretion on return, but after a year of police and political protest over non-confinement following positive tests for drugs, reconfinement was made mandatory (Himelson, 1968, chapters 6 and 7). One study that followed releasees for up to five years concluded that discharge was so rare, and the releasees' reconfinements to CRC or to prisons were so prompt and frequent due to tests showing renewed drug use or new drug crimes, that the program was not justifiable as treatment (Kramer and Bass, 1969).

Nalline test results for the same person were reported to vary greatly from one tester to the next. The tests agreed only about 70 percent of the time when their results were compared to the presumably more accurate, but then more expensive and time-consuming, urine analyses tests for opiates. Nalline testing ceased in the 1980s because urine testing became quicker and cheaper with the Enzyme Multiplying Immunossay Technique (EMIT), a urinalysis test done with portable electronic equipment and not requiring a physician. Even now, drug testing is still legally controversial (Visher and McFadden, 1991; L. Glaser, 1992).

An appreciable proportion of the first civilly committed addicts were soon released on writs because appellate courts found the commitment procedures illegal. The procedures were then changed to make them legally acceptable. This permitted follow-up studies that compared the post-release behavior of addicts released early on writ, with the conduct of those retained at the CRC for treatment. The findings showed that those discharged early by writ had much higher rates of subsequent reconfinement or death from drugs than those held for treatment until paroled (Anglin, 1988).

This conclusion, based on follow ups for only a few years, was validated by a later study that followed the subjects for twenty-four years (Hser, et al., 1993). The study showed that most of those who seem at first to be "cured" eventually relapse to severe alcoholism or recurrent addictions to opiates and other drugs.[13] Robert Dickover, Chief of Research for the Department of Corrections, suggests that the higher survival rates of those committed for treatment may well be due not so much to the prison therapeutic programs, as to the control of outpatients by frequent testing, and the return of the addicts to the institution when not conforming.[14]

Civil commitment of addicts for treatment in an institution was gradually replaced by the 1970s with treatment at residential centers or as outpatients in the community, Dickover reports. But he adds that imprisonments of addicts on criminal sentences for drug crimes or other offenses also increased, so that the state now has almost as many addicted prisoners as ever.[15] Bennett says that this abandonment of the CRC program was due to:

> ...the misguided view of some legislators and perhaps some correctional administrators that the program had not demonstrated any capacity to "cure" addicts. Of course, no thinking person ever expected such outcome. Rather, the intent was to achieve more control of the problem, and in a less costly manner.[16]

The California history is consistent with the history reported in other states. In 1967, New York State was estimated to have half the nation's then 500,000 heroin addicts. The state established a Narcotics Addiction Control Commission that in five years spent a billion dollars. The commission subsidized almost every type of addiction therapy, much of it imposed involuntarily in the commission's own confinement places. Addicts convicted of crimes could elect to have their sentence set aside and receive about three years of commission treatment; they usually did this if the alternative was to be a longer prison term.

But heroin use in New York still increased, so in 1973 the state reversed the policy by enacting what was called "the nation's toughest drug law." The law mandated long prison terms for possession or sale of any illegal drug, expanded the number of police and courts available to prosecute these cases, and made it easier to grant lower penalties to addicts for informing on others. Yet in three years, it was concluded that "heroin use was as widespread in mid-1976 as it had been when the 1973 [law] revision took place" (Joint Commission, 1977; *see also*, Griset, 1991:62–68). The law was modified in 1979 to reduce penalties for possession of small amounts of drugs, and permitted more flexibility in sentencing, changes that already prevailed through plea bargaining.

Of course, a large variety of illegal drugs other than heroin—especially marijuana—were widely used, particularly in the 1960s and thereafter. During the 1980s, "crack," a relatively cheap smokable form of cocaine, replaced heroin as the illegal drug most associated with persistent property crimes.

Drugs remain the nemesis of the criminal justice system, in California as elsewhere. There are growing movements for partial legalization of drug use, with government licensed distribution, medical supervision of "hard-drug" users, rehabilitation efforts, and low publicity. Such practices are now well established in the Netherlands and Switzerland. Great Britain long had successful programs minimizing crimes associated with opiate use by using a medical approach; physicians prescribed heroin for addicts and then gradually tried to taper down their dosage and switch them to morphine, then methadone, then abstinence, but did not insist on any change in drug use. Under Britain's conservative government in the 1960s, it imitated U.S. policies of treating drug use as crime, but this has proved to be a costly and unsuccessful mistake.

British criminologist Leslie T. Wilkins reported in 1993:

Of course, punitive legislation resulted in a tremendous increase in the street price of drugs and made it worthwhile for organized crime to move in.[17]

However, concern about achieving greater control of the spread of AIDS has promoted free, clean needle distribution to addicts in much of Europe, and after much resistance at first, the program is growing in the United States, and together with intensive anti-drug education efforts, is apparently growing in effectiveness. Under the Clinton administration, there is a movement to divert addicts to treatment clinics and educational programs, but with strict surveillance and testing procedures. This program was pioneered by Miami's "Drug Court" when Attorney General Janet Reno was the prosecutor there (Finn and Newlyn, 1993).

Increasing and Improving Visits to Inmates

Typically, delinquents or criminals have deficient personal bonds with law-abiding persons in the community. Yet despite prior conflict in the relationships inmates had with their parents, absence while incarcerated usually makes hearts grow fonder, and visitors are treasured by most prisoners. Their initial post-release housing, and other assistance, is usually with parents or other relatives. However, for married inmates, absence tends to make spousal and offspring relationships indifferent; they drift into bonds with others, especially if the marriage was brief or troubled, and if the spouse is young.

Visits to inmates can be a major factor in repairing these relationships. But because so many prisons are distant from the homes of their inmates, visiting is often difficult for the many family members who are poor. In addition, many prisoners have few non-criminal friends or relatives who wish to see them.

Department of Corrections research has shown that of inmates having no contact with family members while confined, only 50 percent completed their first year on parole without arrest, and 12 percent were reimprisoned in this period. Of those with three visitors, 70 percent were free of arrests in their first year out, and only 2 percent were reimprisoned. When prisoners were grouped by estimates of their risk of recidivism, based mainly on their prior criminal records, the worst post-release criminal records in all risk groups occurred for those with no visits while in prison. However, visiting rates were not significantly related to prison conduct records (Holt and Miller, 1972).

Several ways of improving the relationships of inmates to outsiders were pursued under McGee's leadership. Both the Department of Corrections and the Youth Authority, with limited success at first, recruited volunteers to visit inmates, and to assist them on parole. This was the "M-2 Program," which sought to match two persons, one incarcerated and one free.

A research project to determine the optimum matching of these volunteers with Youth Authority (YA) wards, and to expand the supply of such volunteers, was initiated in 1971. It found that wards with M-2 visitors had better outcome rates at twelve, eighteen and twenty-four months after parole, than similar wards paroled without sponsors, although this difference was only large enough to be statistically significant at twelve months. The volunteers associated with the highest success rates were thirty years old or older, employed, and veterans of military service. The wards most successful in this program were under twenty-one, sent to the YA by a juvenile court, without prior YA or other confinement, and without escape history. Over 80 percent of both wards and sponsors in the program said that they were "very satisfied" with it. The project succeeded in recruiting more volunteers, and eventually had more volunteers available than there were inmates for whom a sponsor was sought (Lewis, 1976).

McGee endorsed another innovation, conjugal visits to married prisoners by their spouses, in private rooms, with sexual intimacy permitted. This practice had long existed in several European countries, and in the Mississippi prisons, but McGee thought it was not politically feasible in California. However, it was initiated gradually during the 1970s, after his retirement. At first, it was only for inmates in low-security units, such as honor farms, but it has since been expanded to all segments of most prisons. Residences that include kitchen and other facilities, as well as hotel-like bedrooms, are used for these visits. These visits are scheduled for all day or even overnight. Jim Park reports:

> An interesting sidelight on conjugal visiting was that Governor Reagan was the prime mover for this program. The suggestion that we try it came from his office. I always thought that Nancy couldn't stand the idea of men getting it on with each other, and she thought if wives could visit, homosexuality would be eliminated.
>
> We had talked for years about this program, but felt that the public would never stand for it. But with a conservative governor willing to take the heat, we set up a pilot program at Tehachapi, by then converted to hold only male prisoners. Tehachapi was totally unknown to the news media, and most people thought it was still a woman's prison. The six-month pilot program worked without incident, as we knew it would, and the program was extended, with Governor Reagan's blessing.
>
> What derailed the Family Visiting Program, as it was officially called, was the Prisoner Bill of Rights, PC2600, that allowed

prisoners to marry whoever they chose. So the conjugal visits, instead of cementing existing marriages and relationships, became a program of convenience where willing young women married convicts simply to provide sexual experience. This may be good or bad, depending on one's philosophy, but it did not change the focus. Incidentally, some 40 percent of Family Visits are not spouses, but are parents and other relatives.[18]

All accounts indicate that conjugal visiting has worked very well in California, as it has in other nations where it is a long-standing practice, and in other states that have the program. Lawrence Bennett reports:

It was initiated at Tehachapi where press coverage would be minimal, and only after it developed a stable and successful operation was it expanded to the other institutions. While initially in minimum security settings, it soon also included maximum security places such as San Quentin and Folsom.

A study of the Family Visiting Program, initiated by the Department, found that some 95% of the inmates approved of it although only about 30 to 40% could take advantage of it. The rest either were not married or their family lived out of state. Staff members also endorsed the program at about a 90% level. These pilot response rates probably represent a unique high in correctional programming.[19]

A 1993 bill to curtail conjugal visits failed in the California legislature, but not only because of much emotional testimony against it by wives of convicts. The Department of Correction reported that of 26,000 family visits to prisoners in 1992, only 18 had known misconduct incidents, most of which were attempts to smuggle drugs, alcohol or other forbidden items to the prisoner (*Los Angeles Times*, May 19, 1993).

Apart from sponsors and conjugal visits, the Department of Corrections encouraged visits to inmates by representatives of a large variety of organizations believed to have a reformative influence. These included all bona fide religious organizations, as well as Alcoholics Anonymous and other groups concerned with a specific type of problem. One group, Centerforce, has been especially devoted to facilitating visits to prisoners. Aided by state funding, it established and operates centers for visitors at all prisons. Most of the centers have playgrounds for children, and other pleasurable amenities. Centerforce provides some assistance in transportation for would-be visitors who need it, and recruits visitors for inmates who desire them.

Another way to expand prisoners' contact with outsiders is to allow inmates to leave the institution for temporary furloughs. The temporary furlough usually occurs when the parole date is near, and is now mainly for family emergencies, but formerly was a way for some inmates to find jobs. These brief leaves, as well as work furlough centers that reduce the need for them, are discussed in the next chapter.

Expanding Inmate Counseling Programs

Since many parolees return to crime even after they receive education and work experience in prison, McGee tried to provide inmates with psychological treatment as an additional contribution to their reformation. Two broad and diverse types of treatment were attempted; group counseling and individual counseling.

Group Counseling

Speaking before California's State Personnel Board in a 1957 effort to get more and better staff for psychological treatment of prisoners, McGee admitted that:

> You couldn't hire enough psychiatrists and psychologists to make a drop in the bucket in dealing with this mass of people.

Therefore, he said, he was trying to convert all penal institutions into "therapeutic communities" by making each employee part of a treatment team. More specifically, he asserted:

> Every employee, we don't care what his classification...has a responsibility to deal with the emotional and personal problems of the people...under his supervision...He has the responsibility of creating an atmosphere within the institution in which people can grow and develop, rather than be oppressed and made more bitter than they were when we got them.
>
> We have established a program which we call group counseling, lay group counseling....This is not group psychotherapy, because these people are not qualified therapists. But they are under the direction of therapists. We, on a voluntary basis, involve...our employees...in meeting with groups of inmates once a week to discuss their problems. This is putting a demand on such a person that sitting in a guard tower or even being a foreman of a work crew never put on him before, because he's being questioned.

He's being challenged. At the present time 8,000 of our 16,000 inmates are engaged in it...and nearly half of our employees.... Now this is something that has...actually taken fire only in the last three years. Much remains to be done to refine it, develop it, test its effects, and that sort of thing (1957).

Staff at all institutions, were encouraged to volunteer to lead counseling groups of inmates and they were trained for this by prison psychologists and social workers. These efforts were directed from the Department of Corrections in Sacramento by senior psychologist, Dr. Norman Fenton, who was made "Deputy Director for Care and Treatment." Counseling was non-directive; the inmates in the groups were encouraged to initiate any topic for discussion, and when any of them asked questions, staff leaders were to address questions to the group to try to get the inmates collective participation in arriving at consensus on answers. The issues considered seemed most often to be problems of institutional life, and of relationships among the prisoners, rather than relationships with staff or anticipations of postrelease life.

Fenton, a friend of Scudder from their pre-prison days, especially emphasized the group counseling at Chino, bringing as consultant there for about two months the British psychologist Maxwell Jones, whose book *Therapeutic Communities* (1953) had inspired many such programs in mental hospitals. E. J. Oberhauser, who was on the initial staff at Chino's opening in 1941, and rose through the ranks to become super-intendent a few years after Scudder's retirement, recalls that officers were at first uncomfortable sitting in a circle of chairs with inmates as though equals, instead of being in front of a rectangular block of chairs as if presiding in a classroom. They soon got used to the new arrange-ment as Scudder had trained them to chat with prisoners in a friendly manner, but officers at San Quentin and Folsom who were known to be customarily impersonal and authoritarian with prisoners, strongly opposed group counseling. Oberhauser says he retained this program at Chino even after McGee's time—when the Department no longer encouraged it—because it helped staff get to know inmates, and it made inmates more concerned with each other rather than only with "doing their own time."[20]

McGee remarked:

The old-time wardens resisted group counseling because it made the officers too friendly with the prisoners, so that people won-dered 'Whose side are they on?' They saw every group session as a small riot that just disturbed the institution. I never expected it to create any miracles,but lots of people did, and it seemed worth trying.[21]

In 1961, after sitting in on seven groups at three different institutions, and talking with prison staff and department researchers, I concluded:

> The evaluation of such intra-institution communication has lagged far behind the actual communication efforts....I think there can be no doubt that this program has improved relationships between staff and inmates, as well as helped inmates to get along with each other. I am sure that this has been a major factor in the virtual absence of riots in this large correctional system, a calm which is especially striking to me because it is my impression that there is more overcrowdedness and consequent idleness in California prisons than I have observed in Federal and in Illinois prisons. Whether improved communication in the institutions also reduces the extent to which inmates return to crime upon release is another matter (Glaser, 1961).

A Department of Corrections study reported in 1964, based on 8,000 parolees, provided suggestive data on this issue:

> The statistically significant findings show that men who had group counseling at the institution of release did better on parole than those who had no group counseling. Men who had a "stable" group counseling experience of over a year with one leader generally did much better on parole than those who had "unstable" group counseling.
> Men with group counseling did 5.1 percent better on parole within 12 months and 2.5 percent better within 24 months than those with no group counseling.... Men with stable group counseling did 6.3 percent better on parole within 12 months and 9.5 percent better within 24 months than men with unstable group counseling.
> ...Low inmate member turnover in groups, part of the original concept of stability, was not included in this definition [of stability] because data on member turnover was mostly unavailable.
> ..."Community living" at Tehachapi consisted of small counseling groups in the living units four times a week plus a larger

group meeting once a week. Although the 1960 releases favored men with only once-a-week group experience, the 1961 releases had parole outcomes which significantly favored...the five-time-a-week groups (Harrison and Mueller, 1964).

A key question in assessing the preceding data is whether, at places with less than 100 percent in group counseling were the inmates in these programs better parole risks in the first place than those without such counseling? The ideal method for resolving this issue is to have a controlled experiment, with cases randomly divided into a treatment group that receives the counseling and a control group that does not. Since this is often administratively and even legally infeasible, Leslie Wilkins, a British statistician in criminological research who was a consultant to the California Department of Corrections, and Don Gottfredson of the department, devised what Gottfredson called the "Base Expectancy" method of evaluation as an alternative to experimental design.

In this statistical research method, inmates are divided into risk groups determined by the items of information available when they enter prison that prior statistical analysis has shown will best predict subsequent parole outcome. The best predictors are usually the extent of their recent criminal record, and how young they were when first arrested. Forecasts can also be made more accurate with data compiled from their pre-prison school and work records, family status, and alcohol or drug use. Prison programs are then evaluated by comparing the post-release outcome rates *for releasees of the same risk group* who received different prison programs; often programs have different success rates for low, medium, or high-risk cases. In the study previously reported, aptly called "Clue Hunting About Group Counseling and Parole Outcome," the researchers only determined that the average base expectancy risk scores were about the same for inmates in or not in group counseling, or in stable or unstable counseling groups.

To produce a more conclusive and rigorous assessment of inmate group counseling, by independent researchers outside of the Department of Corrections, the National Institute of Mental Health of the U.S. Public Health Service funded an experimental evaluation directed by UCLA sociologists. This evaluation was initiated at the California Men's Colony in 1962 when the prison was still being completed. This institution had four physically adjacent identical units (called "quadrants") operated as though they were separate prisons (already described in this chapter's section on prison architecture).

Inmates were selected for this experiment if they were eligible for parole within six months, and were neither elderly nor classified in advance as probable "troublemakers"; those excluded on any of these grounds were housed in a separate quadrant. The remaining inmates were assigned to mandatory counseling if their serial numbers were divisible by two, and to voluntary counseling if they had odd serial numbers. There were five alternative conditions of group counseling:

1. *Voluntary Small Groups* (10 to 12 men) met weekly for an hour, with counselors recruited and trained from all components of staff;
2. *Voluntary Controls* were the inmates declining to participate in voluntary small groups;
3. *Mandatory Small Groups* had two one-hour meetings per week;
4. *Mandatory Large Groups* required all inmates in each of three fifty-man sections of one quadrant to meet for an hour on four days as large groups, and on the fifth day in three smaller groups with different leaders
5. *Mandatory Controls* were all the approximately six hundred excluded inmates in one separate quadrant. As in the "Clue-hunting" study described, average base expectancy risk scores on admission were about the same for all groups compared.

The disturbing finding of this experiment was that all these counseling groups, mandatory or voluntary, despite the variations in size and frequency of sessions, had about the same parole outcome rates. Inmates classified into various types by personality tests, or base expectancies, also had about the same parole outcome rates whether they were in one of the counseling categories or in the control groups. The researchers ascribed the low impact of counseling primarily to the strong influence of the inmate subculture. They also reported little enthusiasm for the non-directive counseling by either the inmates or the staff's newly trained group leaders. Some suggestion of inmate attitudes to counseling, and of the inmate subculture, is provided by lines selected from the poem of a semi-literate inmate that is quoted at the beginning of the researchers' book (Kassebaum et al., 1971:v–vi):

The object of this meeting is as far as I can see.
Is to squeel on each other.
The biggest fink goes free.
Thers one now telling his life as a boy according to him it was all
Sorrow no joy....
We are all hear to gether regardless of our crime

And you can bet your cottin picking ass were going to do some
time.
So lets knock off this shit of talking to the Man, and let him figure
It out for him self the best way he can

In an article scathingly attacking any conclusion from this study,
Herbert Quay pointed out that no treatment should be expected to be
effective unless the treating personnel, the treatment, and the persons
treated, are all appropriate to the theory and purpose of the treatment.
None of these prerequisites existed in this California Men's Colony
experiment with group counseling, he pointed out, because:

1. Two-thirds of the prison's group counselors were reported not
   to expect the program to affect recidivism rates;
2. By professional psychology's standards, few of the counselors
   were qualified for their counseling role;
3. The training given the counselors did not provide them with
   specific counseling techniques appropriate for offenders;
4. There was poor attendance at counselor training sessions;
5. All of this training preceded the beginning of the counseling
   program, instead of continuing while the program was in
   progress;
6. The counselors seldom consulted the counseling coordinator;
7. In most of the groups, inmate participation was involuntary,
   participants included extremely deviant prisoners, and the
   inmates rated the content and structure of the counseling
   sessions as poor;
8. Staff let many counseling sessions be taken over by a few
   talkative inmates, and in others, the counselor allowed the
   whole group to be completely silent for an hour, instead of
   addressing questions to it (Quay, 1977).

Jim Park, who was a California prison administrator under McGee,
concludes that the failure of the group counseling program, despite
psychologist Fenton's brilliance and dedication in trying to have a great
impact from it, "was due to some scholarly misreading of the prison
employees blue collar culture."[22]
The gradually established and then long-term counseling programs assessed in the "Clue-hunting" report, especially those with stable
leadership, probably affected post-release conduct of inmates more than
did this poorly-run experimental program that was set up hastily at

California Men's Colony when that institution was getting its first occupants.

Since the primary focus of non-directive group counseling sessions that I visited in California and elsewhere, was on relieving tension in the institution, I expected that the effects of these group discussions would be to improve social relationships in these establishments. Indeed, rigorous experimental evaluations of group counseling in California Youth Authority institutions, one evaluation with the median age of inmates 16.7 and one 19.1, found no impact on parole outcomes, but those in the counseling groups had significantly fewer misconduct reports while confined than control cases without group sessions (Seckel, 1965).

Anyone who has spent significant time in daily interaction with inmates in a prison knows that the inmates are very preoccupied with minimizing their victimization by other prisoners, and maximizing the small comforts and pleasures available to them, and that they are unlikely to focus much realistic attention on post-release prospects. This was emphasized in Hans Toch's (1977) research finding that inmates are primarily concerned with finding a secure and comfortable niche in their prison housing and work, often at the expense of their long-term interests.

In the 1960s, a research project at Deuel Vocational Center was specifically focused on raising the morality of relationships among inmates in one housing unit, holding over two hundred prisoners. University researchers sought for nearly two years to promote discussions among inmates, as well as between inmates and staff, to resolve administrative problems, and to organize recreational activities in a non-bureaucratic manner. They were not aiming to change the personalities of individual prisoners in this fashion, but to resocialize the inmates as a group, so that the inmates would internalize more consideration for others and more ethical values. The research yielded anecdotes and some questionnaire findings indicating that such an impact occurred, but it was not a rigorous assessment. Also, they claimed that what they accomplished was largely destroyed in the end by the staff's bureaucratic administrative orientation (Studt et al., 1968).

Individual Counseling

In the cited "clue-hunting" studies of group counseling and parole outcome you will recall that benefits of counseling are somewhat greater when the same staff member always leads the group, rather than different persons. This finding suggests that it may not be the interaction among inmates that improves parole outcomes, but their interaction with this single staff member. If so, individual counseling by staff may reduce recidivism rates more than did the non-directive counseling by prisoner groups. When inmate groups alone discuss life outside of prison, they rationalize their failures at both legitimate and criminal pursuits, and derogate those who disagree with them—the blind lead the blind; in individual counseling of one prisoner by one staff member, the inmate is usually relating to a more mature person who has successfully led a non-criminal life. Of course, communication may be hampered because each inmate comes from quite contrasting economic, social, and cultural conditions, yet some influence is often feasible.

One controlled experiment with individual counseling that used clinical staff was begun in 1955 at the Deuel Vocational Institution. About 1,600 youths, average age twenty, sentenced by the courts to be wards of the Youth Authority, but held in this Department of Corrections prison for adults, were assigned to a "Pilot Intensive Counseling Organization," or "PICO." A clinical team of psychologists, sociologists, or social workers classified all newly admitted Youth Authority wards as either "Amenable" or "Non-amenable" to individual counseling. Instructions described Amenables as bright, verbal, and anxious to change, and Non-amenables as more dull, less verbal, and resistant to change. The two groups from this dichotomy were of almost equal size.

Independent of their amenability classification, these prisoners were also divided randomly into a treatment and a control group. The treatment group was assigned to units for which individual counseling was provided by clinical psychologists and psychiatric caseworkers, who had counseling caseloads of about twenty-five per therapist; the control cases were in units with no counseling services.

Post-release results of the PICO experiment for 1,200 offenders paroled over thirty months showed dramatically less reconfinement for the individually counseled Amenable cases than for Amenable cases in the control group. As of thirty-three months after release, the intensively counseled Amenables averaged 2 3/4 months less time back in custody (in jail or prison) than did the Amenables in the control group who had received no counseling. Conservatively estimating government costs of confinement as $150 per month at that time, individual counseling saved a total of $412 per case for Amenables. Since the average duration of counseling was nine months, and each counselor maintained a twenty-five-inmate caseload, the results indicated that each therapist saved $13,500 of reconfinement costs by counseling Amenable inmates.

These savings were then considerably more than the average counselor's salary. Also, evidence for Amenable cases released longer than thirty-three months suggested that the savings from lower reconfinement rates were cumulative, growing as more post-release time elapsed. These estimates do not take into account the savings in police, court, and jail costs for those not returned for new crimes, and most important, the public benefit from fewer crimes committed..

Contrastingly, for prisoners deemed Non-amenable at admission, counseling seemed to make little difference in rates of reconfinement. For Amenables, after thirty-three months on parole, 6.2 percent of the counseled but 14.5 percent of the non-counseled were locked up again; however, for Non-amenables after thirty-three months on parole, the locked-up figures were 14.6 percent for counseled and 16.7 percent for non-counseled (Adams, 1962).

Managing Mentally Ill Offenders

Criminal justice agencies have no authority to control persons when the courts grant the plea of insanity, thereby declaring them not legally responsible for their lawbreaking. Such a defense against criminal charges, in its most widely accepted formulation in the United States, is that:

A person is not responsible for criminal conduct if at the time of such conduct, as a result of mental disease or defect, he lacks substantial capacity either to appreciate the criminality of his conduct or to conform his conduct to the requirements of the law.

It adds, however, that:

...the terms "mental disease or defect" do not include an abnormality manifested only by repeated criminal or otherwise antisocial conduct (Goldstein, 1983).[23]

Unfortunately, courts are not always clear and consistent in distinguising between legal insanity from mental illness and legal sanity. One dramatic example was Edmund Emil Kemper, III, a 6' 9", three hundred pound, nineteen year-old from Santa Cruz, California. He was released from a mental hospital in 1969 after five years of confinement, due to insanity, for killing his grandparents. In the year after his release he killed eight women, including his mother, by shooting, stabbing, and strangling them. He also attempted to rape them, cut off their limbs, and eat parts of their bodies. He decapitated his mother and removed her larynx, which he discarded in the garbage disposal. He then drove off. He was charged with killing six hitch-hikers after calling the police from Colorado to express fear that he might kill again. In these offenses, he was declared legally sane.[24]

McGee gained familiarity with attributes and treatment of the mentally ill not only from his prison work, but from supervising both prisons and mental hospitals during his several years in the State of Washington. On persons who are assaultive and dangerous, and may be deemed either criminally insane or sane but mentally ill, McGee said:

> The broad question...is...how can government devise programs which, on the one hand, protect the public and on the other, safe-guard the offender's rights and best interests? Most of the laws... have placed their major emphasis upon the protection of the public at the time the danger becomes visible and apparent. These laws... place a disproportionate emphasis upon...punishment and banish-ment. More and more we are coming to realize the sharp limi-tations of...punitive measures...for the control of antisocial behavior. In the administration of the criminal law, the...failure is most obvious in dealing with...offenders who are mentally dis-ordered, socially maladjusted, and culturally deprived....
>
> ...The bizarre, acting-out adolescent with a serious person-ality disorder is not only often dangerous but often regarded by mental hospital authorities as untreatable and...as unsuitable for reeducation and training in correctional schools.... As a conse-quence, many of these cases are passed from agency to agency, each of which feels that the problem is better handled by someone else, with the result that many...get no treatment...and are continually... returned to the juvenile court.... The history of many of our hazardous mentally disordered persons will reveal... truancy, expulsion from school, thievery, assault, sexual mis-conduct...interrupted by intermittent trips to the courts and to mental hospitals for 90-day observation, placement on probation, and referral to welfare workers, both public and private, all...as a kind of...delaying action in hopes that the child will mature and will eventually grow up to be a responsible adult. Instead,...the result is a hostile, alienated person who under sufficient stress may eventually do serious damage to others....
>
> In...California, we came to the conclusion...that we could no longer permit this group to fall through the cracks...between the numerous...agencies....Accordingly, we have set up several

specially staffed psychiatric units...of the California Youth Authority...within...five different state institutions. These are small units...for...different age groups and sexes....The post-institutional period of supervision also still needs much attention because...these individuals should be put back into the normal community as soon as possible. But lacking adequate natural homes, it is necessary to find foster homes. Foster home care for this class of individual is difficult to find, and even more difficult to maintain.

...On the question of whether corrections or mental hygiene should handle the socially hazardous mentally ill offender, my answer is that corrections should. If...convicted of a crime...and sent to a correctional facility,...these persons, with rare exceptions, should be provided for within the correctional system. This avoids the frequent shuttling of difficult cases back and forth between correctional institutions and mental hospitals. It strengthens the psychiatrically-oriented programs within the corrections depart- ment so that these services may address themselves to related types of cases which would not ordinarily be considered eligible for transfer to a mental hospital but who nevertheless, can profit by psychiatric treatment. And the correctional institution...is much less likely to mishandle some of these cases if they are...under psychiatric care.

Our Medical Facility at Vacaville...was conceived in 1945 on this basic...idea. Our conviction that this is the best way...to handle the problem has been reinforced by...years of successful experience.[25] We have attempted to deal partially with the post-institutional problem with adults by providing psychiatric out-patient clinics attached to the parole division—one in Los Angeles and one in San Francisco. These clinics provide...direct treatment of a limited number of cases who have been paroled. They also provide a consultative service to the parole agents...who have cases which call for special professional knowledge and skill. Many inmates have been released successfully to this...out-patient service who otherwise would have been retained in the institution ...much longer....

Because of the...relaxed regimens of mental hospitals, it has become increasingly difficult for these institutions to control a few of the unresponsive, violent patients committed under civil proce- dures. In 1961 our Legislature authorized the Department of Mental Hygiene to enter into a contract with the Department of

Corrections to provide care, custody, and treatment for persons too recalcitrant and dangerous to be held safely in a mental hospital. This law grew out of a single case, one Robert Cathey, who committed a first murder in Arizona. Because he had California citizenship, he was...transferred...to the mental hospital at Atascadero, California, from which he was released as sufficiently improved to be...in out-patient status. Shortly afterward he killed three more people in a barroom brawl. He was again found not guilty by reason of insanity and returned to Atascadero where he subsequently organized an escape effort which resulted in the murder of a hospital attendant. Following this, as a measure of safety he was transferred to Vacaville where he promptly engaged an attorney and filed a writ of habeas corpus on grounds that he was... illegally...in a State prison. The District Court upheld the transfer of the patient, but...the appellate court...ordered his return to the Department of Mental Hygiene institution. However, before the court order was carried out, an emergency act was passed by the Legislature authorizing the contractual arrangement....While at Vacaville he was kept under the closest confinement and constant observation...But in spite of this, he engaged in a series of assaults..., both on other patients and on staff. A few months ago he died peacefully in his bed of a coronary occlusion.

Finally, a word should be said about the need for...research and experimentation...to better understand how these destructive careers are developed and...how to treat and manage the persons involved.... We will most certainly not increase our knowledge by trying to hide the problem in the back wards of our institutions (1964a).

Prisoners deemed mentally disturbed were transferred to the California Medical Facility at Vacaville, where most received individual or group psychotherapy or both. A follow up completed on 735 of the prisoners, who were released during 1965–68 after an average of twenty months of group psychotherapy, found that after six months, 6 percent had been reimprisoned, compared to 11 percent for a control group without psychotherapy that was matched on variables predictive of parole outcome. This difference in return rates diminished with more time out of prison, and was no longer statistically significant two years after release. The spread between reimprisonment rates for the two groups was greatest for older inmates with few prior commitments sentenced for homicide or sex crimes; the high return rates for young offenders with drug, robbery, and assault charges and much prior criminality seemed to be unaffected by group psychotherapy (Jew et al., 1975).

McGee recognized psychiatry's limitations in "curing" advanced offenders of criminality. As he put it:

> These sociopaths are very often better at manipulating the doctor than the doctor is at manipulating them. About the only thing we know to do about those people really is to let them get older; they're infantile or immature and eventually they develop some emotional maturity or they just get tired and slow down (1976a:175).

McGee's dedication to serving the public rather than worrying about bureaucratic jurisdictions, and his agility in pursuing such service, is well illustrated in the following account by Lawrence Bennett:

> ...his administrative and philosophical points of view were illustrated by an early incident at the Napa State Hospital when some convicted sex offenders, placed there by formal proceedings, were alleged to be planning a riot. Although this was highly unlikely, it caused great consternation to the hospital administration. McGee accepted the hospital assessment that it was a serious problem, and immediately had the sex offenders moved to San Quentin, although he had no legal authority to do so. However, after things calmed down, he moved them back to Napa. A crisis was averted and he proved to be a hero, although he probably had to do some adroit negotiating to legalize this maneuver. His point of view, as he stated it, was "in a crisis you *act*. You *do* something."[26]

McGee's initiatives in the care for mentally ill lawbreakers, like so much of his other pioneering, were oriented to integrating the functions of different agencies to improve their total service to the public, both in institutions and in the community. This contrasted with continual efforts of many officials in this field to pass responsibility for problem cases to others.

By 1993, however, after McGee's time, both state mental hospitals and county programs for community care in boarding homes, nursing homes, or families, had been drastically cut. Consequently, over a tenth of those sent from mental hospitals to county care were homeless within six months, and 5,000 mentally ill prisoners were in the Los Angeles County Jail, making it one of the largest "mental hospitals" in the nation

(Liberman et al.,1993). Meanwhile, many allegedly mentally ill prisoners were held without treatment in California's post-McGee Pelican Bay prison, for continuous solitary confinement of intractable inmates, although psychiatrists considered them amenable to treatment. Also, a law suit alleged, many were rendered mentally ill from their solitary confinement at Pelican Bay.

Summary and Conclusion

McGee's first and most persistent emphasis in directing California's correctional systems was to improve the selection and training of its personnel. This began by "beachhead" strategies to replace the top officials he inherited who had been installed and maintained by political patronage. He developed a set of manuals for an efficient organization with clear divisions of line and staff functions. His enthusiasm, dedication, and diligence in pioneering efforts inspired much enthusiastic imitation by his deputies.

McGee asserted that 85 percent of the cost of running prisons is for holding the inmates securely and keeping them alive, with only 15 percent of the cost for trying to improve the inmates. He believed everyone should see how best to use the 15 percent to keep the inmates from returning.[27] He sought inmate work, as well as academic and vocational training, relevant to their post-release job possibilities. Much expansion of prison industries was achieved under his leadership, but private businesses continually used political influence to limit employment of inmates. However, prisoner education services grew tremendously. The services were linked to local school systems to provide transferable credits and standard diplomas.

Meanwhile, the number of prisoners committed to the California Department of Corrections rose rapidly, overcrowding prisons, and requiring construction of new ones. McGee sought smaller institutions that research demonstrated were more reformative. When stymied by resistance to prisons in new locations, he achieved "smallness" by building compartmentalized larger edifices and operating each segment as though autonomous.

The use of alcohol or drugs are associated with most crimes resulting in prison or jail terms, as well as with many offenses getting probation. McGee pointed out persistent failure of efforts to prohibit these vices purely by criminal penalties; he promoted treatment and education as primary countermeasures.

McGee initiated measures to increase visits to prisoners by law-abiding persons. He regarded conjugal visits for married prisoners, with sexual contact, as desirable but not politically feasible. However, after his retirement, such visits were initiated and grew to sizable numbers during and since the otherwise conservative governorship of Ronald Reagan.

Efforts to convert California prisons into "therapeutic communities" by extensive group counseling for inmates usually failed to reduce recidivism rates. Small gains in reformation by such programs were limited to groups with little turnover in staff leadership, suggesting that it was the staff's development of personal relationships to inmates, rather than the inmate group, that had the most reformative impact. Experiments with individual counseling showed that significant reductions in parole violations occurred only for those inmates rated in advance as "amenable" to counseling because they were "bright, verbal, and anxious to change."

That mental illness causes a defendant to commit a crime is the legal rationale of insanity which may make a person immune from a prison sentence, but subject to confinement in a mental hospital. Many such culprits, however, prove too intractable for safe custody in these hospitals, while many prisoners exhibit mental disturbances requiring psychiatric care. To cope with such problems, McGee got legislative permission for appropriate transfers of persons from mental hospitals to correctional facilities, or vice-versa. He also expanded psychiatric services for prisoners and parolees. Unfortunately, care for the mentally ill in California has deteriorated drastically, with many of them today either homeless or held in county jails.

McGee's Initiatives in California Community Corrections

The most extensive and rigorously collected information on the life histories of offenders was compiled by the Gluecks, who in the 1930s probed intensively into the rearing and conduct of five hundred Boston male delinquents and five hundred non-delinquents of similar background. They followed the lives of these youths for a subsequent fifteen to twenty-five years. Recent reanalysis of their data shows that the offenders who reformed did so mainly by obtaining secure jobs, developing lifestyles compatible with such employment, and having strong bonds with conventional persons, especially wives (Sampson and Laub, 1993; Laub and Sampson, 1993). Most of these resources, their "social capital," had to be secured *in the community*, and only after release could a lawbreaker's reformation be demonstrated.

McGee always advocated more and better correctional efforts in the community, rather than trying to reform criminals only when they are locked up. After 1961, when his cabinet post placed him over all California state correctonal agencies, his responsibilities included both Department of Corrections and Youth Authority parolees. He also promoted expansion and improvement of county probation, although in California as in most other states then, it was not a state function.

Increasing Both Aid and Control for Parolees

From 1945 to 1957, the Adult Authority not only decided when male prisoners should be paroled, and when their parole should be revoked, but also administered their supervision in the community. Authority over parole was sought by McGee, Sheldon Messinger asserts, for "prison officials had a considerable stake in influencing sentence setting and paroling policy" (Messinger, 1969:15). This involved, "first, creating discretion over prison terms so that they can be used as punishments and rewards for conduct in prisons; and second, lodging such discretion in the hands of those responsible for operating the prisons" (*Ibid*:30). Such desires underlay the original introduction of parole at Elmira Reformatory in 1877, and before that of similar "tickets of leave" in Australia and Ireland, where institution administrators used their control over the date of conditional release to encourage work and study achievements by inmates.

Messinger also reports that prison officials objected to the overcrowding of their institutions by what they deemed were unwarranted denials or revocations of parole, and that in an informal conversation, McGee expressed a wish to be over the Adult Authority as well as the Department of Corrections (*Ibid*).

In 1957, the offices and agents for parole supervision were placed under the Department of Corrections; the Adult Authority remained responsible only for individual case decisions on parole or its revocation. McGee thus acquired the task of improving the selection and training of parole agents. He placed Milton Burdman, one of his long-term associates in prison administration, in charge of the Parole Division of the Department of Corrections, under which were all the supervision offices formerly under the Adult Authority. Burdman's first tasks included retraining the supervision personnel, and changing the Adult Authority's staff directives into a Department of Corrections Parole Manual.

Parole agents were under civil service, so that even if it were desirable to replace them, this could not be readily done. They were organized in entrenched hierarchies, were long in office, and had habits that could only slowly be changed. Jim Park notes that not only did McGee inherit the feudal fiefdoms at San Quentin and Folsom prisons, but:

> ...the parole offices were headed by similarly feudal lords. San Francisco was noted for the "Irish Gang" who did as they pleased regardless of directives from Sacramento, and were utterly ruthless in destroying anyone who opposed them. In the 1960s, Milt Burdman wanted me to accept the post of Regional Administrator for the San Francisco office. I declined, telling Milt that since I had no parole experience, the Irish Gang would dispose of me in no time, even to the extent of framing me or planting some illegal substance on or about my person. I was that convinced that they played for keeps.[1]

McGee asserted in 1958:

I believe in the principle of parole. I believe in the desirability and the efficacy of supervising most men and women and juveniles for at least two years after release and in some cases much longer. We are faced here with an area of public misunderstanding due to the confused and inadequate manner in which parole is administered. As an important phase of the correctional process, we have a nationwide problem, not because a few parole boards have made occasional mistakes in judgment in individual cases, but because we have no consistent policy throughout the country; we have no clear-cut standards of release criteria, or caseload size, or of supervision techniques (1958).

In 1962, he told a State Senate Committee:

Parole is not leniency. It is not...the old system of giving time off from fixed sentences for good behavior. It is the scientific way to release a man.
...I think...our caseloads are unrealistically high. We may be able to partially overcome this handicap by differential distribution of cases. That is, give one agent a large number of cases with a high potential for success and another agent a much lower number of the difficult cases. But what we really ought to capitalize on is that the cost of the most intensive sort of parole is far less than the cost of imprisonment.
It would be nice to say that intensive supervision will let all the parolees out of prison, and thus save a lot of money....But it will also uncover behavior of some that will cause their return. This is a plus dividend in public protection. This saves money as well as grief by returning the parolee before he commits a serious new crime with a long minimum term. Tied together...is the advantage of relatively short reconfinement instead of...for 18 months or more. In the narcotics program...this short-term confinement—a sort of refresher course—has proved very effective (1962).

In the 1960s and thereafter, opiate and other types of drug addiction, or chronic alcoholism, became characteristic of most California prisoners. In the 1980s and early 1990s, the state's rates of unemployment and homelessness rose. Therefore, it became increasingly difficult to find jobs for parolees. Drug testing was required for most urban parolees, and the test appointments, rather than visits to parolee homes were the agents' main source of contact with them.

Most parolees were unemployed or on welfare, were black or Latino, and were members of the socio-economic "underclass" living in urban ghettos or barrios. They could be returned to prison as parole violators if they tested positive for drugs, missed their testing appointments, or had arrest warrants for absconding issued because of thirty or more days of non-contact with the parole staff, even if they committed no new felonies (see Simon, 1990).

Furthermore, from the beginning of California's parole administration under its indeterminate sentence system, once a parolee was returned to prison:

> ...the term could be reset to anything within the maximum. Typically, upon revocation the Adult Authority...would reset the term to the maximum and delay a new parole date and term for a year or two. Thus, in the most extreme cases, a parolee, within months of completing the term initially set by the Adult Authority, could be released, revoked, and begin a new term of life imprisonment all without being convicted of committing a new offense (Simon, 1990:155–56).

Since the late 1960s, a third to one half of California prison admissions have generally been for revocation of parole.

By the 1970s, as chapter 6 details, McGee was rather discouraged with the indeterminate sentence, and with letting traditional parole boards decide when inmates should be released. But he advocated a period of conditional release under supervision in the community for all prisoners, rather than a sentence that ends at completion of the term of confinement. This became the practice under California's revised Penal Code, summarized in chapter 6, which took effect July 1st, 1977, a decade after McGee's retirement. He also wanted more assistance for released ex-prisoners who needed it, as well as closer surveillance, to arrest those who reverted to crime.

In his 1967 retirement "Farewell Address," McGee proposed (in vain) to newly elected Governor Reagan that the state:

> ...approve community-based correctional industries, including contracts or agreements with existing non-profit corporations, for the provision of sheltered workshop training of parolees; provide

authority to extend agreements to serve county probationers (McGee and Montilla, 1967:12–13).

Because of his dissatisfaction with the available knowledge about optimum parole supervision, McGee encouraged experiments in community correction. One innovation, after his cabinet-level appointment, was the Youth Authority's Community Treatment Project. Because the project was so different from traditional parole, it will be discussed separately. Other parole experiments will be reviewed collectively.

The Community Treatment Project

The "Community Treatment Project" (CTP) was conducted by the Youth Authority (YA) during 1961–69 in Sacramento and Stockton; after 1965, it was also in San Francisco. Over a thousand thirteen-to-nineteen year-olds (one-fifth of which were female) were designated by juvenile courts as eligible for CTP on their first YA committment. They averaged 5.8 prior contacts with law-enforcment agencies for arrests, local detention, or probation. Burglary and auto theft were their most frequent charges; those held for violent crimes were excluded. Their proportions in different ethnic groups were similar to those of other YA wards, and they comprised about three-fourths of first-time commitments to YA from these three cities.

YA is authorized to have custody of its wards until they reach age twenty-one or twenty-five, depending on their age and offense when sent to YA. The YA first sends them for four to six weeks to a reception center and clinic for routine medical and dental work if needed, plus testing and orientation. They are then usually confined in an institution from which most first-timers are paroled in a few months. If they behave well on parole, they are likely to be discharged before the maximum age for their YA term.

In this experiment, a randomly selected 686 youths eligible for CTP were sent directly from the reception center and clinic to a special program of intensive supervision in the community; the remaining 328 were a control group, processed in the traditional YA program that usually begins with confinement.

CTP parolees were in caseloads not exceeding twelve per officer, while control cases were in traditional caseloads several times as large. CTP officers made a commitment to be available many hours, including evenings and weekends, to contact parolees or be contacted by them. Much attention was given to where and with whom each youth would reside, using foster homes and group homes when deemed appropriate.

A CTP "community center" building in each city had not only the staff's offices, but accredited remedial school programs and tutoring for those wards needing these programs, as well as individual and group psychological treatment. There were also recreational activities for CTP wards and officers at the center and group field trips to diverse places.

Based on intensive initial interviews and staff conferences, all eligible CTP youths were classified into types at the reception center before their random division into experimental and control cases. For each experimental, a treatment plan was developed that depended largely on the youth's classification, with each officer's caseload limited to only some of the following types:

> *Neurotics* were 53 percent,[2] and were of two subtypes. "The first...attempts to deny—to himself and others—his conscious feelings of inadequacy, rejection, or self-condemnation....by verbally attacking *others* and/or by the use of boisterous distractions plus a variety of 'games.' The second... often shows various symptoms of emotional disturbance— e.g., chronic or intense depression, or psychosomatic complaints. His tensions and conscious fears usually result from conflicts produced by feelings of failure, inadequacy, or underlying guilt." These two types are often referred to as "neurotic acting out" and "neurotic anxious" (and the whole category was later called "conflicted" in CTP publications). Controls classified as neurotic were arrested 2.7 times as often as experimentals, excluding arrests for minor misconduct such as non-injurious traffic accidents, running away, or incorrigibility, for which the controls' arrest rate was only 1.3 times that of the others.
>
> *Power Oriented* were 21 percent, and they were also of two types. "The first...likes to think of himself as delinquent and tough. He is often more than willing to 'go along' with others, or with a gang...to earn...status and acceptance, and to later maintain his 'reputation'." The second "often attempts to undermine or circumvent the efforts and directions of authority figures. Typically, he does not wish to conform to peers or adults; and not infrequently he will attempt to assume a leading 'power role' for himself." These two subtypes were often called "cultural conformists" and "manipulators." Of eligibles deemed power oriented, those in the control group (with traditional YA programs) had fewer arrests than the ones in the CTP program.
>
> *Passive Conformists* were 14 percent. They usually comply to peers and adults whom they think "have the 'upper hand' at the

moment, or who seem more adequate and assertive" generally; they consider themselves "lacking in social 'know-how'" and expect to be rejected by others despite trying to please them. They were also called "immature conformists." They had a slightly better post-release record if in the experimental rather than the control group.

Relatively Rare Types of Youths were the remaining 12 percent that included "asocialized passive," "situational emotional reaction," and "cultural identifiers." The first of these types did somewhat better if in CTP, the last better in regular YA, and the middle one about the same in either.

Girls seemed to perform about as well in the traditional YA programs as in CTP, regardless of their classification type. Also, the language defining CTP types, although derived from established concepts in clinical psychology, included so many vague and subjective terms that it created doubts about the reliability of these designations. Humans are so extremely diverse, vary by such fine gradations on so many continuous personality variables, and are so often inconsistent in their behavior and thought, that the more we study individuals, the more many of them seem to be mixed or borderline cases in any set of types. The more types one differentiates, the more borderlines there are. Almost always, one must gloss over many differences to designate numerous persons as of the same type.

Costs of both the regular YA program and CTP rose rapidly due to inflation, salary raises, and program enhancements. For those paroled to Sacramento-Stockton during 1961–69 and discharged no later than March 1, 1973, the YA "career costs," from admission to discharge, rose for control cases from $5,734 at the beginning of this period to $14,327 at the end; for CTP cases they rose from $7,180 to $14,580. The cost of collecting, analyzing, and reporting the evaluation research data was paid by a grant from the National Institute of Mental Health (NIMH).

Overall, this research found that nearly two-thirds of first admissions to YA could appropriately be paroled immediately to CTP after their initial study and classification at the reception center. On the other hand, one-third did not benefit from CTP, or were more likely to engage in crime, if not first confined in the traditional manner.

On the basis of these findings, during 1969–74, NIMH attempted to divide CTP-eligible youths into: "Status 1" cases, described as "the most troubled and troubling," for whom initial institution programs would precede parole to the intensive CTP supervision and assistance; the rest were "Status 2" cases, who were paroled directly to CTP. The original CTP personnel, including its parole agents, participated in the new institution program for Status 1 cases; the agents were assigned those wards at the institution whom they would later have for parole supervision. This new institution was a dormitory for twenty-five CTP cases in the reception center and clinic that served the Sacramento-Stockton area.

In addition, CTP eligibility was broadened to include all first admissions to YA from Sacramento County regardless of offense, rather than barring those convicted for violent crimes. It also included both juvenile and adult court commitments to YA, rather than the juvenile court cases only. After these cases were classified at the reception center as Status 1 (46 percent) or Status 2 (54 percent), each group was randomly divided, thus forming four categories as follows:

A. "Appropriately-placed Status 1 cases," who were initially placed in the CTP dormitory;
B. "Inappropriately-placed Status 1 cases," who were immediately paroled directly to CTP supervision in the community;
C. "Appropriately-placed Status 2 cases," who were immediately paroled to CTP in the community;
D. "Inappropriately-placed Status 2 cases, who were initially placed in the CTP dormitory.

The results favored initial use of the dormitory for "troublesome" youth, the Status 1 cases: 94 percent of the inappropriately placed Status 1 cases, who were paroled immediately, had one or more offenses in their first 1 $^1/_2$ years on parole, as against 58 percent for those appropriately confined first in the dormitory. Status 2 cases had slightly lower arrest rates if paroled immediately, than if first confined; these differences were too small for statistical significance, but suggest that the cost of confinement for them was unnecessary.

Apparently, only the Status 1 cases had post-release benefits from the intensive counseling, and the contact with their future parole agents, given while they were confined. Also, locking them up initially protected the public from immediate crime enough to more than pay for the higher cost of confinement.

The preceding classification of cases had some variation of terminology in YA publications. Also, the classifications worked in conjunction with a seven-level Scale of Interpersonal Maturity (called "I-level") that was routinely applied to all YA cases. The scale begins with infantilism as Level 1, rates most delinquents as levels 2, 3, or 4, and more interpersonally mature youths and adults at higher levels, but only an ideal person was rated at Level 7 (Sullivan, et al., 1957; Wedge, et al., 1980). Yet it was shown that the YA's classification of wards into I-levels, determined by results of questionnaires, could be nearly duplicated from intelligence test scores and questions on moral issues (Austin, 1975).

Because CTP parole agents initiated most arrests of their wards, but could place a parolee in custody briefly without declaring that subject a parole violator, the validity of CTP's outcome statistics was questioned (Lerman, 1968). Yet lower failure rates in CTP than in regular programs for Neurotic cases (later called "Conflicted") occurred even with outcome assessed only from arrests by police initiative, excluding arrests made by, or at the request of, parole agents (Wedge, et al., 1957).

Most offenders eventually become largely law-abiding. Changes in their success or failure at legitimate and illegitimate pursuits, and changes in the persons with whom they associate and identify, seem necessary to assure their reform. But the changes in CTP youths could have resulted from their doing better in school or work as a result of CTP assistance, as much as from the personal influence of CTP staff; the relative impact of different components of the CTP program on various types of offenders is uncertain.

CTP's effectiveness in the community seems to be appreciable only for the approximate half of the cases classified as Conflicted (originally, "Neurotic") or Status 2. Note the similarity of this finding to that in the PICO project on intensive individual counseling in institutions, which was only clearly effective for those classified as "Amenables." Most Amenables, Conflicted, and Status 2 youths seem to share in common their dissatisfaction with their delinquent or criminal lifestyles. In studies summarized in previous sections on alcoholism and drug addiction also, only those who voluntarily sought help to control their cravings proved likely to succeed; those involuntarily assigned to counseling or psychotherapy usually failed.

The Status I cases, the troublesome youngsters generally non-Amenable, had better post-release records if confined before release, held in facilities where they had contact with their subsequent parole agents, and had access to remedial education, medical, and counseling services. Possibly their separation from undesirable associates in the community, and these other contacts while confined, increased their amenability.

Some Other Parole Innovations

McGee notes that around 1950:

...a parole agent carried a caseload of about 150 parolees. We argued that working forty hours a week, an agent could give a parolee only sixteen minutes per week; with travel time, vacation, sick leave, and report writing, this average time per case per week actually was five or ten minutes. Thus a parolee was unlikely to receive any attention at all, except for the initial interview, unless he was in trouble and, more often than not, in the local jail....

...to rehabilitate offenders and prevent further crime, caseloads had to be reduced.

...A staff analyst of the legislative...office,...to recommend cost cuts...,suggested that we parole some men three months early and use the money saved to pay the added costs of the experimental caseloads (1981:142).

Thus began, in 1953, the most rigorous series of parole studies.

Controlled Experiments in Parole Supervision

The first phase of the "Special Intensive Parole Unit" (SIPU) accepted for two years a pool of male prisoners soon eligible for parole, excluding about 20 percent who were hardened drug addicts, psychotics, mentally defective, non-English speaking, or inmates going either out of the state or to relatively inaccessible areas of California. The Adult Authority gave this pool early parole hearings. Of those it granted parole, a randomly selected one half were released ninety days earlier than normal, and assigned to supervision in these ninety days to agents with only fifteen-man caseloads. They then shifted to standard caseloads, averaging ninety men per agent, to which control cases went on their regular parole dates. This SIPU 1 study found that post-release arrest rates were not significantly different between the two groups (Reimer and Warren, 1957; Burkhart, 1977).

SIPU 2 accepted cases for eighteen months, with inmates randomly selected for release three months early assigned to agent with a thirty-man caseload for the first six months of parole. Narcotic addicts were no longer excluded. Again, there were no significant differences in new offense rates between SIPU parolees and controls in regular caseloads (Havel and Sulka, 1962; Burkhart, 1977).

SIPU 3 accepted cases for two years, and classified them by risk level, using a well-tested base-expectancy score. It assigned randomly selected experimental parolees *for the duration of their parole supervision* to caseloads that averaged thirty-five parolees per agent; the remaining parolees, the control group, were to get regular supervision in caseloads that averaged seventy-two parolees. In actual practice, however, man-power shortages prevented maintaining the reduced caseloads for experimentals for the full parole period; after six months to one year out on parole, most were transferred to another parole agent with a larger caseload.

In this two-year effort, the experimentals classified in *the middle range of base-expectancy scores* had fewer arrests than the control cases of the same risk levels. Such differences were especially marked for major arrests in a twenty-four-month follow-up period. For the worst and best risk parolees, however, outcome rates were about the same for experi-mentals and controls (*Ibid*).

SIPU 4 tested hypotheses for the optimum matching of parolees with parole agents and caseloads. Four agent positions were given small (fifteen-man) caseloads, eight had medium (thirty-man) caseloads, and six had large (seventy-man) caseloads. Parolees were accepted for two years and were classified as "Low Maturity" or "High Maturity," using the I-level rating system employed by the Youth Authority (previously described in the discussion of the Community Treatment Program). Parole agents were differentiated by researchers as "Internal" or "External" in their orientation to their work, according to whether they focused on the internal feelings and thoughts of parolees, or on the parolees' performance at jobs and other activities. The hypotheses were:

1. Low-maturity parolees do better with external than with internal parole agents, and high-maturity parolees do better with internal than with external agents.
2. These differences would be most marked in the small caseloads, and least in the large caseloads.

Neither hypothesis proved valid, but for all parolees, *if there was no change in parole agent*, the smaller the caseload, the lower the arrest rates. Also, base expectancy score was a good predictor of parole outcome (Havel, 1965; Burkhart, 1977).

The Summary Parole study selected 627 males who were con-sidered the safest 32 percent of those paroled from prison in the last eight months of 1976. This assessment on safety was based on their having the lowest risk by base expectancy scores, but regardless of score, it excluded those serving sentences for first degree murder or for sex crimes. They were randomly divided whereby 310 cases received only summary supervision, and 317 received regular supervision. For the summary cases, parole agents were to make no routine contacts with the parolees, but to initiate contacts if return to criminal activity was known or suspected, or if the parolee requested assistance.

Records indicated that summary cases received an average of five contacts during their first six months on parole, and regular cases averaged ten contacts. Only a randomly selected one third in each group were followed up for twelve months, but there were no significant differences in any type of outcome rates for the two groups in either follow-up period. Summary parole for these cases was thus shown to be a justifiable economy (Star, 1979).

High-control parole supervision focused on control, rather than assistance, and only on parolees whom agents selected as higher risk cases. It placed primary emphasis on investigations through monitoring the parolees or contacting persons who would know about them. Two types of high-control supervision were tested. The *Investigative Model* used parole agents to make short-term inquiries and observations to check on parolees suspected of involvement in crime, to apprehend these parolees if necessary, and to work toward a successful prosecution. The *Intensive Supervision Model* used parole agents in a more traditional manner, but with smaller caseloads, to deter parolees with serious prior criminality by closely monitoring them.

High-control supervision was tested for twenty-eight months during 1977–80 at four parole offices in medium-sized cities, two using only the investigation model, one only the intensive supervision model, and one both. The test was quasi-experimental; the records of the specially supervised cases were compared to those of similar cases receiving regular supervision. High-control agents selected 243 parolees as high risk from a total of 1,027 received in these four offices; those selected most often had a narcotics history and a prison record prior to the sentence from which they were being paroled.

Investigation Model agents sought information from police or prior supervision agents, primarily on whether the parolees were suspected of either assaultive or narcotics activities. They made investigations lasting an average of sixty days, employing direct surveillance, questioning associates or possible witnesses, and checking police or other records. A much higher proportion of their cases were returned to confinement than those of the comparison cases, but the difference was primarily in rates of parole revocation rather than in new sentences. Of those convicted of new crimes, there were severer penalties, more recovery of illegal goods or funds, and more assistance of the prosecution by the parole agents, than in regular supervision cases receiving new convictions.

Intensive Supervision Model agents only were assigned ten to fifteen cases at a time. The agents averaged ten actions on a parolee per thirty day period. Ninety percent of their actions were direct personal contacts with the parolee, and the remaining contacts were with others presumably informed about the parolee. Regular supervision of the comparison cases only averaged about one third as many actions. Intensive supervision, however, apparently resulted in more detection than deterrence of criminal activity. In both six-month and twelve-month followups, their cases had higher proportions returned to custody, including more with serious new criminal sentences.

Overall, the main contribution of high-control supervision was not reformation of offenders, but more and quicker returns of high-risk parolees to prison for proven or suspected relapses of lawbreaking. This is a greater immediate government expense, but a long-term reduction in society's costs from parolee crimes (Star, 1981). Meanwhile, lower risk cases can be beneficially released to appropriate and less costly early supervision.

Table 4.1 summarizes California's parole experiments.

Work-Unit Studies

What was called the "Parole Work-Unit Experiment" was actually a series of trials of various methods of caseload assignment and some surveys, none of which proved to be a controlled experiment. However, they were quite instructive for parole administration.

These studies began as a continuation of the SIPU experiments, and divided about 10,000 adult parolees, deemed non-aggressive, into an experimental and a control group. The experimental parolees were each designated as requiring a specific number of supervision work units, the number being proportional to the amount of supervision time they were deemed to require. The number of units could be reduced when the parolee seemed well-adjusted, and raised when more supervision time was indicated.

Parole officers for the experimental half of the cases were each assigned a caseload totalling 120 work units, so that they had smaller caseloads if they had many high work-unit cases, and larger ones if the average work units of their cases was low; they averaged thirty-two parolees per officer. The control group had regular supervision, in caseloads averaging about eighty. In addition, all cases with high-aggression histories were placed in work-unit caseloads and assigned a high number of work-units, but since none were in the control group, the relative effectiveness of the experimental and control conditions in reducing recidivism rates cannot be well evaluated.

TABLE 4.1

Major California Parole Supervision Experiments

Experiments	Subjects	Variables Tested	Conclusions
Community Treatment Program, First Project	13-19 yr.olds on first commit-ment to YA from Juvenile Court.	Community treat-ment, rich, and varied by typology of parolees.	Reduces arrest rates for cases classified in advance as "conflicted."
Community Treatment Program, Second Project	Above; divided Status I (worst cases) and Status 2 (best cases).	Above from start, or after 3 months lockup with parole agent visits, rem-edial education.	Worst cases best if first confined; best cases better if not confined.
SIPU 1	80 percent of adult male parolees (omits mostly drug addicts).	90-day early re-lease to 15-man caseloads for these 90 days.	No effect on out-come; saved money by early release.
SIPU 2	Almost all adult male parolees (including addicts).	40-day early re-lease to 30-man caseloads for these 40 days.	Same as SIPU 1.
SIPU 3	All adult male parolees divided by base expect-ancy levels.	35-man caseloads for first 6 months to 1 year paroled.	Middle-risk exper-imentals had fewer arrests than such control cases; no difference for others.
SIPU 4	All adult male parolees divided by maturity (I-level).	"Internal" or "External" agents; small or large caseloads.	No difference by type of agent or case's maturity; smaller caseloads did best.
Summary Parole	Lowest third in risk,minus First Degree murder or sex crime cases.	No parole agent contact unless requested or need is indicated.	Same arrest rate as controls with regular agent
High-Control	Highest fourth in risk by agent judgment.	Low caseloads with much checking on crimes by parolees and regular or more home visits.	High revocation rates without more new convictions, but new sentences more severe.

The Legislative Analyst's office and the Department of Finance authorized an increase of one hundred parole agents for this experiment for one year to see if its net effect reduced correctional costs, although correctional officials questioned whether one year permitted an adequate test. But in the first six months there were higher rates of both technical violations leading to parole revocation and of new felony convictions in the experimentals than in the controls. Such differences prevailed for all base-expectancy risk categories of parolees.

In reaction to these initial findings, however, during the second six-month period the practice of reimprisoning a parolee for lesser rule violations was eliminated. The results were striking, as Lawrence Bennett, one of the research staff on this project reports:

> When information on the initially very high rate of technical returns to prison was fed back to parole administrators via rapid progress reports on the research, it was emphasized that return to prison was the *last* resort for dealing with a parolee's problems. All community-based alternatives should be exhausted before return to prison would be suggested for a technical violation. The results were a precipitous drop in returns to prison. The recidivism rate dropped from around 50% down to about 24%, and the most startling aspect of this was that while technical violations were a great portion of this drop, *those returned with new felony convictions also dropped.*[3]

During the Work-Unit Project's first year, a study was made on variation among parole agents in urging parole revocation. The agents had autonomy in writing reports and recommendations on parolee misconduct to the Adult Authority; that agency followed about 80 percent of agent recommendations against revocation, and 90 percent of those for revocation. It was found that parole office rates of urging return to prison varied inversely with the length of local jail terms imposed for misdemeanors, and with the availability of local jail space in which parolees could be held (for misdemeanors, or pending investigation of alleged rule violations) (Robison and Takagi, 1968:4).

All Department of Corrections parole agents, and their supervisors, were also given a questionnaire in the Work-Unit Study that asked them to make recommendations on ten hypothetical parolee misconduct cases, based on actual cases that differed greatly in nature of the violation, as well as in attributes and prior record of the alleged violator. Willingness to continue alleged violators on parole, rather than return them to prison, varied directly with rank of the respondent in the parole supervision hierarchy. Apparently, the field-level personnel directly contacting parolees were most rigid about the rules.

There was little difference among the five parole administrative regions in percentage recommending "continue," but there was much variation among the thirty-eight parole offices in these regions. A comparison of the office with the highest rate and that with the lowest rate of such recommendations showed that both supervisors and subordinates in each of these offices tended to conform to their office's distinct pattern. Statewide, officers with college training in social work had by far the highest rate of "continue" recommendations, and those with prior law-enforcement experience the lowest. There was no clear relationship between an office's "continue" recommendation rate and whether it had work-unit or conventional caseloads. This survey's initial findings strengthened the department's campaign against excessive rates of return to prison, which soon resulted in their decline (Robison and Takagi, 1968:6–29).

According to Robert Dickover, longtime researcher in the Department of Corrections, the reduction in rates of new felony commitments was slightly larger for the work-unit cases than for the control group's larger conventional caseloads, because most parolees with histories of highly aggressive crime were assigned to work-unit caseloads. The fact that such offenders normally have lower than average reimprisonment rates probably accounted for the small differences in favor of work-unit cases.[4]

Burkhart claimed that the lower than expected reimprisonment rates for work unit cases more than paid for their smaller caseloads (Burkhart, 1969, 1977), but this is open to challenge, Dickover asserts, because of the likelihood that reimprisonment rates for such lower-risk parolees would also have been lower without the work unit program.[5] Dickover finds support for this conclusion in:

(1) the fact that reimprisonment rates dropped for the control as well as the work-unit caseloads;
(2) the evidence from the work-unit experience, which suggests that *revocation and court commitment policies* for parolees are more significant than caseload size in determining revocation rates.[6]

Other Parole-Supervision Research

A 1965 California Penal Code amendment required that the cases of all adult felons on parole for two years, without major violation, be reviewed to permit discharge from parole of those who seemed to be rehabilitated. The review process was begun by the supervising parole agent, and continued through higher supervisory officials before decision by the Adult Authority, which accepted 99 percent of the discharge recommendations. When the review process began there was a large backlog of cases and discharge was urged for about two-thirds of the cases, but there was much variation among agents and regions in recommendations. Rates of recommendation for discharge diminished thereafter, and became less diverse, perhaps because agents learned what advice was most likely to be accepted. Initial follow up showed that within one year, only 1.3 percent of those discharged were recommitted to prison, but this rate was 2.6 percent for the 73 percent of eligible cases who were reviewed and not discharged. This result suggests that two years is a fairly safe duration for parole (Robison, et al., 1971).

The foregoing studies were exclusively with male prisoners paroled by the Adult Authority. A follow up of women paroled from California's Correctional Institution for Women by the Women's Board of Terms and Parole during the same period found that male parolees were more often returned to prison for new offenses, but less often reimprisoned for rule violations. These differences, which gave women a higher overall return rate than men, increased with each succeeding year of parole's duration. Such differences appeared to be from administration, rather than from gender-related conduct: the Women's Board was less tolerant of parolee involvement in non-felonious misconduct or drug use than was the Adult Authority, especially after the latter's Work-Unit and other research (Spencer and Berecochea, 1972).

Recently, in the 1990s, Norman Holt advises, return of parolees to prison for rule violations is still a problem, but it has been greatly reduced without increasing the rates of arrest for new crimes. During 1990–91:

> ...overcrowded jails began refusing to hold parolees for hearing, court orders were issued requiring faster processing of revocations, there were massive increases in parolees and parole agents, but there was a lack of administrative focus on parole's mission of providing a transition from prison. By new directives on rule violations, the return rate dropped from 58 percent to 36 percent in 1991–93. This translates to about 1,000 fewer returns to prison per month, using 3,000 fewer prison beds, and annual savings of $30 million.

Who are the parolees not being returned? They are mostly people who are alcohol or drug dependent and who have violated either a non-criminal condition of parole (such as not reporting) or committed a minor misdemeanor, which is unlikely to be brought to trial. We still return over 2,000 each month that we consider a serious threat. We have the highest rate of successful discharge we have had in some years, and new felony returns have held steady for several years at about 20 per 100 parolees.[7]

Unfortunately, one cannot now rigorously determine which revocation practices reduce crime most. The McGee years of scientific evaluations by controlled experiments have ended in California.

Halfway Houses and Community Centers

Another way to increase assistance and control of released offenders is to make their transition from confinement to freedom a graduated process. This began in California with the transfer of state prisoners to jails in San Francisco, and other large cities, to join programs that selected inmates, close to their release dates, to work outside jobs daily, and return to jail at night. The state paid the counties to include state prisoners in this work release.

In the 1960s, these programs developed into state Work Furlough Centers, often called "halfway houses." California's first ones were in harvesting areas where inmates picked fruit or did other farm labor, and some of these were on the grounds of prisons, at Chino and Deuel.[8] Later the state centers were in small apartment buildings, hotels, or rooming houses in the state's larger cities, notably the Central City Correctional Center near the University of Southern California in Los Angeles.

Persons still technically prison inmates can be moved into these Work Furlough Centers a few months before their parole dates. Food, shelter, and supervision are provided. Residents can depart daily to seek work or to hold jobs if they have them, but must return on schedule, and not be intoxicated. When their parole dates are near, those with good conduct records, especially if planning to move to a family home, are allowed to move there early, but must check in regularly at the center. In the 1980s and thereafter, selected elderly prisoners on Social Security, pensions, or both would reside in these centers for most of their sentences.

In addition to being cheaper than imprisonment, halfway houses protect the public by often allowing officers prompter information than is normally available with ordinary parole, on any releasees who flee, get drunk, use drugs, or seem to have illegal incomes. Those who misbehave can be returned to prison and get their parole date deferred, and those who flee can be prosecuted for the crime of escape from prison, and receive a new sentence for the escape, just as would occur if they broke out of a regular prison. There was some early evidence that the average duration of imprisonment was longer for halfway house inmates than for those paroled directly from prison because of the number penalized with parole deferrals, or even new sentences, occurring when inmates went carousing instead of returning promptly from work (Bass, 1975).

Also used since the 1970s is a three-day "Temporary Community Release" whereby inmates scheduled for parole or even discharge in a few weeks, can leave the prison for up to seventy-two hours to make job and living arrangements and then return to the institution.

The Youth Authority's community center in Stockton, opened first for parolees in the CTP program, has already been described. Several similar centers for parolees were opened later, including four in Los Angeles, two in San Francisco, and one in Oakland. All were in high delinquency areas where there were many YA parolees. In addition to the parole agent offices, the centers provide school tutoring, counseling, and hot lunches for parolees. Parole agents had caseloads of only about twenty-five wards in the community, plus about eight from the center's neighborhood, whom they contacted in YA institutions before parole. These YA community centers also involved in their activities the parents and others in the neighborhood who affected the wards. Some centers had special treatment programs, such as behavior modification or trans-actional analysis therapy, Outward Bound activities, and service in state and national parks and forests.

A research project found that in their first two years of operation, the Youth Authority's parole centers had a violation rate for their wards during the first year on parole of 29 percent, compared to a statewide YA rate of 39 percent. Almost two-thirds of center parolees had been visited by their parole agent when in a YA institution, before their parole, and about 11 percent were paroled directly from YA Reception Centers without confinement in an institution. The rates of success of parole were higher when agents contacted the ward's families, out-of-home residential places, or employers, prior to the ward's release from the institution (Seckel et al., 1973).

Probation Subsidy

Quite early in his California experience, McGee was impressed by how counties varied in their use of probation as a penalty, and therefore, how often one county would send offenders to the Youth Authority or to prison and another county would place the offenders on probation. One factor in this variation was economic: the counties paid for probation supervision, but avoided this expense if they sent a potential probationer to a state institution.

Lawrence Bennett recalls the vital role played by research in laying the groundwork for pioneering in probation policy:

> McGee got chief probation officers together, asked them to define clearly what they saw as the criteria for selecting people for probation versus prison, and found that over 30 percent of the admissions to California prisons fit the criteria for supervision in the community.[9]

Several compilations by the Youth Authority and the Department of Corrections on overlap of probation and prison admissions, and on advantages of community over institutional programs for many offenders, had similar conclusions: that the state could save money, enhance crime prevention, and increase uniformity in penalites, if it paid the counties for the costs of improving and expanding local probation services (Youth and Adult Corrections Agency, 1965).

Don Gottfredson recalls that getting probation subsidy enacted as law was a seventeen-year effort, and "a good example of McGee's adroit management, involving a substantial number of different agencies with diverse missions, and finally achieving consensus."[10] He notes that passage of the first version of this law through the California Senate failed because its hearing before the Finance Committee was scheduled for the day when the Giants baseball team played their first game after moving from New York to San Francisco, and too many supportive senators went to the game! He and Leslie Wilkins prepared Figure 4.1 to show the intricacies of this effort, which after the first bill failed required a decade of new studies and recruitment of support from women's clubs, PTAs, County Boards of Supervisors, and others.

The resulting Probation Subsidy Act of 1965, taking effect July 1, 1966, in its first decade allocated $160 million to pay counties up to $4,000 for each serious offender not sent to a state correctional institution. It thereby kept over 43,000 juvenile and adult offenders out of state-imposed confinement, and saved the state $120 million (Feeney, 1978). The counties, instead, were to give these cases intensified probation supervision, with caseloads of not over fifty probationers per officer. McGee said:

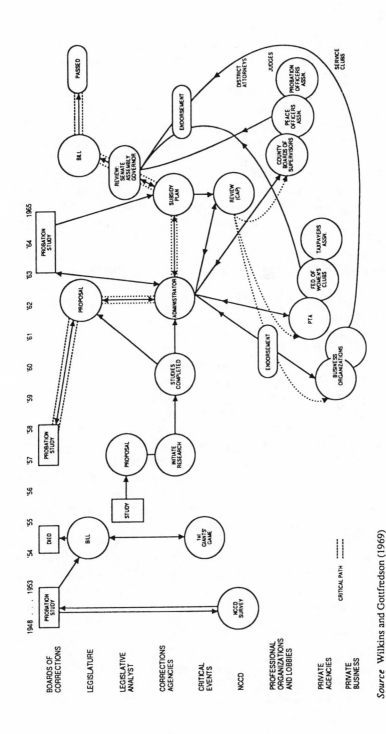

Source Wilkins and Gottfredson (1969)

Figure 4.1. Evolution of the 1965 Probation Subsidy Act

My idea was to have a system so that counties can't play games with us. Some sent 14 percent and some 68 percent of their convicted felons to us.[11]

Supervision of the subsidy program's administration in the counties, for both juveniles and adults, was done by the Youth Authority. The process began complexly by assigning each county, as a "base commitment rate," the number of offenders per 100,000 population that it sent to state institutions during 1959–63 or 1962–63, whichever was higher in annual average commitments. This counted only the newly convicted; not persons sent for parole violation, civil commitment for narcotics use, or presentence diagnosis. Base rates averaged 60.4 probationers per county, but ranged from 21.8 to 119.3 for different counties. Payments was made for reduction to an "expected" rate, with the maximum $4,000 per case paid for a full reduction. Thus, a county previously sending few offenders to the state did not have to cut its rate much to get this full stipend, but one with high prior rates had to cut drastically (Lemert and Dill, 1978:24–25).

Marked changes in incarceration rates followed. At prisons for adults, admissions per 100,000 California population dropped from 38.9 in 1965 to 25.1 in 1970, but civil commitment of addicts to the California Rehabilitation Center rose from 4.7 to 9.5. During the same period, commitments to the Youth Authority per 100,000 population dropped only from 10.3 to 9.4. One should note, however, that total population in the state was rising rapidly then, especially in high-crime-rate teenagers born during the post-World War II baby boom.

Offenders sent to state agencies by Juvenile Courts can go only to the Youth Authority (YA); those from Superior Courts can go either to the YA (if under twenty-one years old and not deemed advanced in criminality) or to the Department of Corrections (DC). Between 1966 and 1972, Juvenile Court commitments to the YA dropped 48 percent, while Superior Court commitments rose by 17 percent to the YA, and 23 percent to the DC (Lemert and Dill, 1978:60). One might conclude from these contrasts that probation subsidy worked only in the juvenile courts, but Lemert and Dill, after interviewing many judges, prosecutors, and probation officers in all the larger counties, offer the following explanations for the court differences:

(1) Although Superior Court commitments to YA and DC were constant, they would have risen greatly without the subsidy program because of higher penalty laws in this period, particularly for drug crimes.

(2) Juvenile Court penalty decisions are less affected than those of Superior Courts by plea bargaining, in which traditions on the appropriateness of probation, shared by the lawyers involved, change slowly.

(3) Juvenile Courts have a large range of alternative local placements for probationers (e.g., foster homes, county probation camps, and special schools), but Superior Courts have only jails, that they can use in "split sentences" that start probation with a term in jail. Use of the alternatives for juveniles was expanded with subsidy as most of these alternative programs were administered by the juvenile court's own probation department; in many counties, when such facilities became full, the number that the court sent to them was not cut but stays in them were shortened. Jails, however, were administered by politically active sheriffs, who resisted increased commitments to their already overcrowded facilities.

(4) More basically:

For adults, the key link to social structure is employment. Juveniles, on the other hand, are not subject to the adult norm of self-maintenance but are instead linked to social structure by a variety of familial, quasi-familial, and institutional arrangements. The much broader range of sentencing alternatives for juvenile offenders reflects this difference. Consequently, the development of resources for community treatment of adult offenders faces special obstacles even if unfavorable community attitudes could be overcome (Lemert and Dill, 1978:63).

Allegations were made that probation subsidy "widened the net" of the criminal justice system by putting persons on probation who previously would have been released without penalty. Miller's intensive analysis of California statistics on this issue concluded:

New alternatives to incarceration will tend to draw most of their clientele from other alternatives to incarceration and not from institutions (Miller, 1980:326).

Yet the primary impact of probation subsidy seems to have been in reducing rates of confinement for lesser crimes, especially for juveniles. The increase since the 1965 Probation Subsidy Act in the total proportion of the California population under control by governments (either by confinement, probation, or parole supervision), reflects mainly the increased illegal conduct associated with more urbanization, particularly illegal drug use, and more government efforts to "crack down on it."

The reduction of caseloads required for counties to receive subsidy payments was not without problems. Officers with the subsidized smaller caseloads often were resented by their co-workers who were assigned more cases. But subsidized low-caseload officers were often given extra tasks, such as drug-testing, which they resented. Yet the entire program affected only about 10 percent of the state's probationers, and it saved state funds by reducing state institution populations. It also cut, by about 40 percent, the range of probation use by different counties (Smith, 1972; Johns et al., 1974; Conrad, 1977).

In the 1980s, probation subsidies to the counties were repeatedly cut. Also, Dickover reports, "the later state subsidies to local correctonal systems moved from the strict performance criteria of the original subsidy law to less strict to virtually none. They became detached from formulas for reductions in prison commitments."[12] Finally, they were renamed "Delinquency Subvention Funds," and restrictions on their use were largely eliminated. In the 1993–94 budget, the only item of this type retained was $33 million for county probation camps, restored after much controversy on its proposed deletion.[13]

A quite different approach to reducing disparity between counties in use of probation, introduced under McGee, was to permit courts to send convicted, but unsentenced, felons to state prisons for pre-sentence diagnostic observation. The prison then sent an advisory report on sentencing to the judge. This option was used for only small percentages of convicted felons, and to a diverse extent by different counties, but it probably made a slight contribution to statewide uniformity of sentencing. Some judges claimed that short imprisonment for pre-sentence study was a deterrent, making the offenders better risks for probation (Dickover and Durkee, 1974).

Summary and Conclusion

Research under McGee in California showed that recidivism rates for the better risk majority of youngsters were reduced by their prompt release to intensive community treatment; those who had strong ties with law-abiding persons, and good school or work records tended to lose this "social capital" with long confinement, and to become criminalized by incarceration. However, confinement of the "most troubled and troublesome" youthful offenders, plus remedial education and contact with their future parole agent while confined, produced distinctly less recidivism than occurred if they were immediately paroled, even to an intensive community supervision program. Unless separated for a while, they apparently went back to their old social circles with other lawbreakers.

For adults, smaller supervision caseloads reduced recidivism rates for middle-risk parolees, but did not alter the low rates of new crimes by the least criminalized, or the high frequency of parole failures for advanced offenders. Yet intensive surveillance of the high-risk adults was justifiable if it focused on criminal investigation, because it yielded earlier detection and more effective prosecution of those who returned to crime. Early release of low-risk cases proved profitable, as their recidivism rates were low, and confining them was much more expensive than their supervision on parole. Two years of parole supervision seemed to suffice for recidivism prevention; very few of those not in violation within two years violated thereafter. In summary, no type or timing of community supervision proved best for all kinds of cases.

Work furloughs and halfway houses that graduate transition from incarceration to freedom were other major developments in prison services under McGee. These guarantee economic sustenance for offenders who try to begin employment and rebuild family ties in the community, and they also protect the public by increased surveillance of those releasees who recidivate in this period.

McGee also promoted payment of state funds to counties to subsidize use of well-supervised probation in lieu of state confinement for many lawbreakers. This was especially effective in cutting juvenile court commitments to state institutions. Probation permits offenders to retain any desirable home and job resources available to them. Juveniles may get remedial education or other assistance through probation placements if needed, as well as continued surveillance. But when non-criminal rule violations or only petty misdemeanors, rather than new felonies, lead to long incarceration for probation or parole violation, total government costs for corrections rise without cutting serious crime rates. Also, when caseloads are as immense as they generally are, both assistance and control by supervision are likely to be negligible.

Evaluation Research as Correctional Auditing

The last two chapters described much research conducted by the staff of California's Department of Corrections and Youth Authority, most of it in the 1960s and 1970s. Further studies could have been cited, for under McGee's leadership during this period, these two agencies probably completed more and better research evaluating correctional practices and policies than did the rest of the state and the federal governments combined.

Lay Initiation of Post-World War II Correctional Research

California participated in a post-World War II movement based on the general public demanding more use of science to guide sentencing and correctional practices. It was grounded in the increased public awareness of the social sciences, particularly psychology.

Clinical psychology, which burgeoned in the post-war decades, has had diverse applications in crime research. Psychoanalytic case studies, usually of notorious and bizarre offenders, infer that their subjects had unconscious motives and mechanisms that produced criminally deviant acts. Neo-Lombrosian biological studies (such as those of Hare and Mednick), correlate criminal conduct with sluggish autonomic nervous systems. Those who studied Skinner ascribe crime to the shaping of bad habits by differential reinforcement. All of these perspectives view lawbreaking as the product of learned or inherited deviant mentality, and insist that offenders must receive appropriate treatment rather than punishment alone.

Science courses in the schools also made people familiar with experimental research methods. Students' repeated subjection to intelligence tests, and attitude or personality questionnaires, exposed them to concepts of psychometrics. As Lee Cronbach pointed out in his 1957 presidential address to the American Psychological Association, experimentation and statistical analysis were "the two disciplines of scientific psychology" (1957).

Meanwhile, sociologists expanded research into delinquent gangs, neighborhood crime rate patterns, criminal subcultures, and parole prediction. Courses in criminology became popular at many colleges and universities.

These social science perspectives pervading public thought, combined with costs of rehabilitation programs for lawbreakers, prompted initiatives by lay persons to seek rigorous research on whether these programs worked. Their view of research as auditing such expenditures was illustrated in the preceding chapter's report that California's experiments with Special Intensive Parole Units (SIPU) were suggested to McGee by a legislative budget analyst. When asked to fund smaller parole agent caseloads, the analyst asked for experimental evaluation of a combination of smaller caseloads with earlier release on parole, so that the cost of closer parole supervision could be offset by reducing the length of incarceration.

McGee showed his alacrity in dealing with legislators when he recalled this experiment:

> By the end of the parole period, there was no significant difference between the experimentals and the controls. The experiment, however, could not be considered a failure. It added to the evidence that during the period of one year, shortening the time served in prison by 10 to 15 percent made no difference in subsequent criminal conduct of a random sample of inmates released on parole. More important, interest in this kind of experimentation within the system was aroused, and a long series of related experiments was launched.
>
> During the time of these early self-financed studies, an appetite for experimental methods was whetted not only within the department but also among the members of the state legislature and the staff of the state Department of Finance. They began to insist that we support our requests for new or expanded programs with detailed information that could be generated only by systematic research. In 1957, the legislative analyst, in his critique of the governor's budget, posed a series of questions about the programs in the Department of Corrections and the Youth Authority to which we did not have answers backed by solid data.

...we decided to tell the Department of Finance and the legislature that we agreed that they should have available such information but that to produce it we would need specialized personnel....We were already late in the budget cycle....We requested that funds be provided in the budget of each department to employ a qualified chief of research and a number of supporting aides...the Senate Finance Committee chairman agreed to introduce an amendment to the budget bill without objection from the fiscal staff specialists.... It should be noted...that the idea behind such a move had been fostered in the system for at least ten years (1981:143).

Similar tales were told in Britain, where it was reported that one Parliamentary reaction to correctional funding requests was to establish, as part of the Criminal Justice Act of 1948, the Home Office Research Unit, for evaluative assessments of correctional decision making (Mannheim and Wilkins, 1981). Also mentioned in the preceding chapter was the 1957 initiative of James V. Bennett, Director of the Federal Bureau of Prisons. To have his agency's correctional efforts evaluated by a university, he procured a Ford Foundation grant to the University of Illinois project, which I directed, to pay for such research. These efforts were suggested to Bennett by Dr. Francis B. Sayre, a retired Harvard law professor and Assistant Secretary of State, who earlier had been briefly Commissioner of Corrections in Massachusetts; when residing in Washington he continued his interest in penology by visiting with federal corrections officials (Glaser, 1964:7-8).

McGee led American corrections in the use of controlled experiments to test correctional practices, beginning in 1953 with the SIPU project. In 1957, he created what is said to have been the nation's first full-time correctional research unit (Simon, 1990:87). J. Douglas Grant headed the unit as Department of Corrections Research Director until 1964; John Conrad succeeded him for a brief period. In 1958, Keith Griffiths was made the Youth Authority's first Research Director, a post he retained until his retirement in 1983.

Each of these research agencies acquired staff, and initiated many studies, so that in 1973 McGee could say:

In 1953, the California correctional system employed two statisticians and no full-time professional researchers. Today, over 75 such persons are employed in the system (McGee, 1973).

When Grant became Research Director in 1957, he soon acquired as part of his staff the correctional statistics section of the Department of Justice's Bureau of Criminal Statistics. When Lawrence Bennett became Research Director in 1966, he had 120 employees, including twenty-four professional researchers and statisticians. His Research Division's budget was about $1 million.[1]

McGee's retirement ended this golden age for research:

> After 1968 the unit began to be whittled away. Its budget was severely cut and by the early 1970s it survived only by finding temporary assignments for its staff in other units and through occasional research grants. The Department continued to collect and publish statistics on its populations, but the experimental drive was largely eliminated. There is no question that the research unit's critical edge helped lead to its demise (Simon, 1990:123).

Early in the 1960s, the Federal Bureau of Prisons started a small research office under Benjamin Frank, previously its Director of Education. He retired a few years later, and was succeeded in this post by John Galvin, an innovative federal reformatory warden. The research movement spread slowly to other correctional systems, but has been significant in several states, notably Massachusetts, and in other nations, particularly the Netherlands, Britain, Sweden, and Australia.

McGee on Research

McGee was first and foremost a practical administrator, but he was a more profound and independent thinker than others in such positions. His singular dedication helping the public made him appreciate the need for both theoretical and applied science to evaluate correctional policies and practices. Don Gottfredson recalls:

> McGee's interest and support for research wasn't recognized much when he was in office. He was not a scientist by his own self concept, but he had the healthy skepticism, inquiring attitude, and respect for data that are the hallmarks of a scientist. When we began the Base Expectancy project, there was much more opposition to it in the statistics unit of the Department of Correction's research division, than you might have expected. People in this unit, which was entirely a population accounting section, firmly opposed almost every aspect of the project, and had a consistent

view that the work ought not to be done, that it was a waste of the taxpayer's money.

The controversy came to a head at a meeting of the Director's senior staff. I was soundly criticized by the California Department of Justice statistician who had developed the existing population accounting system, but I had Doug Grant as my defense attorney and McGee as judge. When this statistician argued that the project wouldn't result in even one percent of predictive gain in parole outcome, Doug offered to bet a hundred dollars that it would. (The bet was not accepted.) One senior staff member said that he didn't believe in statistics anyways, whereupon McGee responded: "That's just like not believing in arithmetic." McGee closed the discussion by giving a short lecture on the development of intelligence testing (a somewhat remote analogy, but an effective one), and announced that the project had his support.

The Base Expectancy studies' purpose was to develop a systematic record-keeping system in such a way that statistical designs similar to those we now call "quasi-experimental" could be used for repeated evaluations of correctional programs.

Due to McGee's support, and a grant from the National Institute of Mental Health to the Institute for the Study of Crime and Delinquency, I was able to create a research unit at the California Medical Facility at Vacaville, where we issued a number of reports through the Institute. This unit employed only me and Kelley Ballard as trained researchers, plus a life parolee I recruited as a secretary. The rest consisted entirely of inmates of the Medical Facility, a substantial group of capable research workers, ranging from 20 to 30 in number, who were organized into a coding section and a machine room section. Much statistical work was done by hand calculation, including a variety of complex multivariate statistics, as computer programs were not yet available for most of the work needed. The "machine room" readied punched cards for analyses, mostly at the Western Data Processing Center at UCLA. Without such a one as Richard McGee at the helm of the corrections system, I cannot imagine trying to conduct such an operation in a prison.

While at work in the basement office provided for the Base Expectancy work, I was surprised one day to receive a call from the Director. He said he was making some comparisons and had forgotten how to calculate a Chi Square. I refreshed his memory, he thanked me, and I never learned more about the question he sought to answer. But I remained impressed that he was taking this careful empirical approach to hypothesis testing on some management question on which he had to decide, and he was doing the analysis himself.[2]

McGee recognized the need for developing theory as well as gathering facts in science. He was also aware of the many impediments to research resulting from vested interests of staff and others, as well as from emotional public demands for hasty action concerning crime and criminals. Thus, he pointed out:

> ...centuries before Archimedes' birth, man had been making use of boats and ships without a precise knowledge of the laws of floating bodies....On the other hand, it would be difficult to conceive how marine engineers could design modern ocean-going craft displacing thousands of tons without making use of the basic principles involved....
>
> Research in the social sciences, just as in the physical sciences, ...is...extracting general principles, theories, laws or guides to assist in the improvement of practice. *Action research* makes use of the classical concepts and logic of scientific method but is carried on in conjunction with line operations involving a complex array of human beings, social systems, philosophical concepts, political constraints, legal barriers, moral biases and economic limitations....
>
> ...in the criminal justice field...the leader of the future...will look upon research and development as a function of his organization on a par with personnel training, fiscal management, and program development. He will realize that the research efforts of his agency must be planned, financed, and implemented in a manner similar to that used in all other functions....He... should...employ a qualified director of research as a member of his immediate staff....
>
> It is also important to note that the various elements of the administration of criminal justice are...routinized and institutionalized. The workers...feel secure and comfortable with things as they are....No matter what new direction is indicated by action research, it will not take place without strong leadership....
>
> ...risk taking by the policy makers and administrators represents one of the more serious obstacles to addressing many kinds of questions....Apprehension that the study might be looked upon

with disfavor by the public...or by relevant power figures is an ever present hazard....An action research project...must hold some promise of producing a useful result...in terms of effectiveness or of efficiency (1973)

Later he added:

Perhaps the most basic difficulty in addressing correctional problems by scientific methods derives from the fact that, historically, the two most influential professions in crime control and corrections have been...lawyers and the clergy. Both are respected and learned, but neither can be said to be devoted to the scientific method (1981).

On research results, and their dissemination to affect policy, McGee remarked:

Action research projects at their conclusion very often raise more questions than they answer. This is not necessarily bad nor to be unexpected....The long-term strategy in knowledge development should be analogous to building a wall with many articulated blocks.

...Public dissatisfaction with the high incidence of crime and delinquency is often accompanied by emotional responses based on fear, economics, and political opportunism. A few seeds of intelligent rationality do not take root easily....*What is needed in the crime prevention and crime control field are administrators and policymakers who have the optimism of the reformer tempered by the skepticism of the scientist....*

We should expect no absolutes from action research in criminal justice....We can expect to reduce the degree of our uncertainties and to narrow the gap between chance and certitude in our decisions (1976b).

Correctional research, especially in California, was bridging this gap in the 1960s and 1970s by building a vast wealth of new knowledge. But the optimism of that era that inspired such knowledge was largely canceled in the 1980s by the conservative skepticism of some social scientists, lawyers and politicians, who focused on holes and weak spots of the research. Indeed, research in the Department of Corrections declined quickly after McGee became Administrator of the Youth and

Adult Correctional Agency. Interviewed in 1982, after his retirement, McGee said:

> Had I stayed on I would have moved the whole research function into the Agency. To guide policy, research should be close to the top policy-making official.[3]

Research on convict reformation then declined, despite the evidence that it could greatly improve policy guidance.

The Delusion That "Nothing Works"

In 1966, a New York State Governor's Special Committee on Criminal Offenders decided that the state's prison programs were not adequately trying to rehabilitate their inmates. Two years later the state hired researchers Lipton, Martinson, and Wilks to survey what was known about the rehabilitation of criminals. When the study was completed in 1970, however, its conclusions so questioned the merits of programs then initiated or planned by the state, that publication of the study was suppressed by the sponsoring agency. In 1972, however, it became public when their 1,400-page report was subpoenaed for presentation as evidence in a court case.

The first publication from this study was Martinson's 1974 article "What works?," which summarized 231 studies deemed methodologically acceptable, all focusing on whether various correctional programs reduced recidivism rates. The book from this research also summarized studies on what programs work best for institutional adjustment, vocational success, educational achievement, alcohol- or drug-use control, attitude change, and community adjustment (Lipton, et al., 1975).

Martinson's article pointed out many problems in reaching conclusions even from the research deemed acceptable for this survey. He noted that:

> The studies differed in measures of recidivism; several compared outcomes for treatment and control groups that were not similar risks to begin with; some seemed to have different indicators of outcome for the treatment and control or comparison groups; there was little repetition of studies to check on how far one may generalize the findings from each.
>
>   Yet he concluded, "*with few and isolated exceptions, the rehabilitative efforts that have been reported so far have had no appreciable effect on recidivism*" (1974:24).

That "nothing works" in programs or services to reform criminals was a finding from this survey that many accepted unquestioningly. Conservatives still cite it as grounds for imposing punishments of a severity determined only by "just deserts"—penalties proportional in severity to the seriousness of the offense, and unaffected by the prior criminal record or estimated recidivism risk of the offender. They denounce making the duration of incarceration terms imposed by courts vary on the basis of subsequent evidence of reformation, and call for abandoning parole (von Hirsch and Hanrahan, 1978; von Hirsch, 1978; von Hirsch and Ashworth, 1992).

This "justice" approach is also supported by many former liberals, now often called "neo-conservatives," who state that improvement in corrections should focus primarily on making treatment of criminals more humane, not more rehabilitative. They point out much evidence of inconsistency and invalidity in predictions by judges, parole board members, and psychiatrists on the post-release conduct of allegedly dangerous and disturbed offenders, as well as the tendencies for humans to become cruel if even temporarily placed in guard roles (Rosenhahn, 1973; Zimbardo, et al., 1973; Cullen and Gilbert, 1982:112–25). Their influence led to marked reduction in use of indeterminate sentences and parole by the federal government and several states, including California (discussed in chapter 6).

The National Research Council appointed a "Panel on Research on Rehabilitative Techniques" which found that the Lipton, Martinson, and Wilks survey was too accepting of methodologically questionable studies, and should have reached even more damning conclusions. The panel asserted that the only reasonable finding is that research, thus far, is unable to determine what rehabilitates, and what does not. The panel seemed to imply that no knowledge is attained unless one gains absolute precision and certainty. Of course, one cannot challenge their conclusion that "research on offender rehabilitation should be pursued more vigorously, more systematically, more imaginatively,...and based upon strong theoretical rationales" (Sechrest et al., 1979:10; *see also* Logan, 1972; Halleck and Witte, 1977).

But other social scientists had different assessments. Ted Palmer (1975, 1978) pointed out that when he checked the studies covered by Martinson's article, he found some recidivism-reduction benefits from interventions in 48 percent of the cases, although only for particular types of offenders in most studies. Martinson (1976) responded only by criticizing Palmer's writing style, and questioning the value of trying to reduce recidivism rates, rather than overall crime rates.

A few years later, however, Martinson (1979) had somewhat reversed himself. He introduced the term "reprocessing rate," in place of recidivism rate, to refer to any new actions of any justice agency against an offender, including rearrests, parole or probation violations, or reconvictions. For each type of treatment, Martinson found, reprocessing rates vary greatly, but especially, *in different kinds of correctional settings*. For sentenced juveniles *in group homes*, all types of special interventions, but especially psychotherapy and job placement, contradicted expectations by increasing reprocessing rates. For sentenced juveniles incarcerated in institutions, however, most specialized services improved post-release conduct; intensive supervision, education, and individual help were most predictive of lower reprocessing rates after release. The rates were also lower for sentenced juveniles given *shock probation*, in which they are incarcerated briefly, usually in jail, before conditional release to supervision in the community; their reprocessing rates diminished further with volunteer help, psychotherapy, and education.

Unfortunately, Martinson did not attempt to explain these diverse findings, but he added:

> Perhaps the most extreme case of radical tinkering with the system of criminal justice is the nationwide movement to abolish parole release, and with it, parole supervision of released offenders. As part of our study, we were able to make eighty controlled comparisons between parolees and roughly comparable offenders released maxout [unconditional release at expiration of sentence]. In seventy-four of these eighty comparisons, parolees had lower reprocessing rates than those released without parole supervision (1979:257).[4]

This reassessment of correctional practices, like the Martinson group's earlier reports, did not control well for different types of offenders, and was largely atheoretical— it did not attempt to explain its findings.

The survey that most contradicted the negative conclusions of Lipton, Martinson, and Wilks came from a report on ninety-five correctional evaluation studies published between 1973 and early 1978. These were all the studies that authors Gendreau and Ross (1979) could find for these years that had at least six months follow up data on recidivism, had an experimental or quasi-experimental design, and provided detailed statistics. More than other surveys of evaluation studies, theirs classified reform efforts by the method of behavior change that was tested, placing the studies in four groups:

(1) *Behavior Modification for Juvenile Delinquents.* All these projects trained adults to apply behavior modification theory for changing specific behaviors of juveniles. The adults were in most cases parents, but some "community intervention" studies had adult "buddies" interact with misbehaving children. Three principles predicted the relative effectiveness of these efforts:

(A) The sooner the problem behavior is treated the better.

(B) ...the intervention should be within the child's community and involve his family and school experience.

(C) ...the less time the counselor is in actual contact with the family, the weaker the results.

Only one of thirteen studies in this category reported negative results, and these were largely ascribed by Gendreau and Ross (1979) to the clients' extremely disruptive initial behavior.

(2) *Contingency Management.* These were also applications of behavior modification psychology. Typically, courts had placed the offenders under the control of correctional agencies where they could accumulate tokens or points leading to a definite reward for desirable conduct, and often penalties or loss of tokens or points for misconduct. Some used "behavior contracts" whereby either offenders, or their parents or teachers, formally agreed to specific conduct patterns to eliminate targeted types of misconduct by the offender, with prospects of penalty for their non-compliance or rewards for compliance. These worked best where there were already good relationships between staff and subjects, and where the subjects were collectively supportive of the conduct-changing efforts.

(3) *Counseling.* These were all quite rigorous tests of counseling programs that were well planned, based on specific psychological theory, and targeting particular types of behavior, in sharp contrast to the non-directive group counseling by line staff in California prisons, described in chapter 3. Most were with juvenile delinquents, but one was for incarcerated adult heroin users. All reported distinct behavior improvements.

Sarason and Ganzer (1973), for example, randomly assigned incarcerated first offenders to modeling or group discussion counseling sessions, or to a control group. The focus of the counseling was on developing ability to apply for a job, delay gratification, and resist peer pressure. There were fourteen one-hour counseling sessions. Recidivism rates five years afterwards were 23 percent for each of the treatment groups, and 48 percent for the controls; there were similar but smaller advantages for the treatment over the control groups after three years.

In a California Youth Authority study, Jesness (1975) randomly assigned subjects to an institution run on a transactional analysis counseling system, an institution run with a behavioral modification system (included earlier under "Contingency Management"), and an institution without treatment. In this three-year project, recidivism rates for various types of inmates after two years out of prison were 10 to 25 percent lower for either of the treatment places than for the control group; the reduction was greatest for inmates classified earlier as "situational emotional offenders" and lowest for "manipulators."

(4) *Diversion.* These were programs to provide special treatment to juveniles in trouble with the law for incorrigibility, absconding, or other largely juvenile status offenses, as an alternative to sending them to juvenile court for formal court hearings and commitment to probation or to an institution. Treatments included behavior modification programs for their parents, as well as for the youths; the larger the variety of approaches employed, the greater the success rates. One very effective practice in Ohio was simply to bring the complainants and the accused together in the prosecutor's office for a night conference; apologies, penalties, and restitution were usually agreed upon without further court processing, with reduced recidivism rates, and at much less cost than formal court processing would generate (J. Palmer, 1975).

Gendreau and Ross (1979) also conclude that having an extensive *amount* of any of the kinds of treatment studied enhances effectiveness, and so does reliance on more than one type of treatment. Their data suggest that high recidivism rates of states or provinces are related to shortages of treatment programs in the communities to which offenders are released.

The Adams study of individual counseling (summarized in chapter 3), and the Community Treatment Project (summarized in chapter 4), both found recidivism reduction effects from individual counseling and instruction or other personal assistance only for unadvanced offenders of higher intelligence and verbal ability, who seemed to be concerned about reducing their criminality. But they found the "non-amenables" somewhat more recidivistic if placed in such permissive, assistance-oriented programs.

Similarly studying "non-amenables," Murray and Cox (1979) extensively analyzed the criminal records of serious delinquents (averaging thirteen prior arrests, eight for serious crimes) where commitment to a reformatory was legally warranted, but many were diverted to community-based programs. They found that for such cases, those sent to reformatories had lower rates of rearrest during subsequent periods of freedom than did the others. Furthermore, the more restrictive the controls placed on those in the community, the lower were their rates of rearrest.

Several other post-Martinson surveys, and more individual studies can be cited in support of the conclusions indicated by the foregoing literature summaries, which are:

(1) it is indeed a delusion to generalize that "nothing works" in efforts to reform offenders;
(2) many types of interventions have opposite effects on different kinds of lawbreakers;
(3) none have much effect if only done half-heartedly, or too briefly.

Opposite effects are most common when comparing the impact of any type of intervention on offenders who contrast greatly in extent of prior criminality, bonds with criminals, intelligence, or evident desire to achieve a non-criminal life.

Deficiencies of Research on Promoting Jobs for Ex-Prisoners

Evaluation studies in the Department of Corrections and Youth Authority were from the outset mostly oriented to assessing predominantly psychotherapeutic programs to reform offenders. This occurred, to a large extent, regardless of whether those conducting or supervising the research were trained primarily in psychology, or in sociology, social work, or other disciplines.

This focus on psychotherapy was largely due to the responsibilities delegated by McGee to two rather charismatic psychologists who were great salesmen: Norman Fenton, the promoter of group counseling, and J. Dougas Grant, the first Director of Research for the Department of Corrections, who (with others) created the Interpersonal Maturity (I-level) Scale, and promoted diverse types of psychotherapy.

John Conrad, commenting on California correctional research in a 1981 article, observed:

Our strategy committed our research division to the study of thin little programs that should have been regarded as the least likely to succeed. At the time, no one saw it that way. So sure were the clinicians that psychological interventions could redirect offenders that it did not occur to anyone that it would be more reasonable to test those programs in which a prisoner's full time was engaged. Legislative budget analysts, administrators, and program personnel wanted to know whether counseling and parole contacts made a difference when measured by the data of recidivism. No one wanted to known whether the State's much larger investment in prison education and vocational training was wisely spent. It should have been obvious that if any prison staff could positively influence prisoners, they were the teachers and work supervisors, not the psychiatrists and the counselors. The latter rarely saw any prisoner as often as once a week, and psychiatrists saw themselves as special consultants...and diagnosticians of prisoners whose behavior might be psychotic and justify hospitalization. If the prisoner could learn new ways to perceive himself and the world around him, the most likely avenue to his consciousness would run through the classroom or the factory floor. It would not be found in a weekly session with a half-trained counselor (1981b).

Pertinent to Conrad's remarks on the potential influence of vocational training in reducing recidivism is the fact that most felony arrests are of persons sixteen to twenty-five years old who are charged with crimes committed to secure money or other property. This is partly because youths are in a very volatile job market, and those prone to arrest are the least prepared for this market (Cook, 1975; Smith and Vanski, 1979; Orsagh and Witte, 1981).

Almost all persons require some years to make a clear transition from child to adult roles, and most get into some difficulties with adults while making this change. Of those who break the law in this period, some get little or no police intervention, while others are arrested, adjudicated, or even given a term of incarceration. Yet a majority of all of them eventually earn a legitimate livelihood, and cease serious law violations. In what ways may this ultimate change be facilitated and accelerated for convicts? Research on two types of programs for this purpose merit detailed comment.

Vocational Training in Prison

Early in the 1970s, I asked an official at the Chino prison if anyone had evaluated the reformative effects of the state's work and vocational training programs for prisoners. (At that time, neither of us was aware of the questionnaire survey—summarized in chapter 3—that asked parolees, their employers, and parole agents about the jobs parolees had procured, their performance rating, and their use of prison training on the job.) I was told that the department had never done such research, but that some years earlier they had granted permission to a Gilbert McKee to investigate this topic for a doctoral dissertation in economics at the Claremont Graduate School. No one knew if the dissertation was completed, or if so, what it found. My telephone call to Claremont revealed its completion, and that McKee was on the economics faculty of California State Polytechnic College, San Luis Obispo.

I purchased a copy of the dissertation from University Microfilms in Ann Arbor. About this time, Norman Johnston, a friend and colleague from former days of working together in the Illinois prisons, asked for suggestions for a new edition of the reader *Crime and Justice* that he co-edited. When I told him of McKee's (1972) study, Johnston asked that I suggest to McKee to contribute a summation of the dissertation. I phoned McKee; he said that he was too busy, and that he had other topical interests just then, but he allowed me to prepare a summary article to be published under his name in this volume (McKee, 1978). Later, when a new edition was also requested for the reader *Correctional Institutions*, that I co-edited, I prepared with his approval a somewhat briefer summation for publication (McKee, 1984). As far as I know, McKee's is the only rigorous evaluations by an economist of vocational training in prison, yet it is not cited, repeated, or extended.

McKee studied 1,010 men paroled between 1967–68 to the Los Angeles area, and he procured recidivism data from that area's parole files. He also had a larger statewide sample for which he lacked recidivism data, but from the prison files for all cases in both samples he recorded Social Security numbers, vocational training assignments, and for some vocational courses, the grades of the students. He then obtained data on the post-release earnings of each releasee from the California State Employment Service, based on Social Security payments. The earnings reported were zero whenever they either had jobs where Social Security was unpaid, were self-employed and not contributing to Social Security, were unemployed, or were incarcerated. Zero-earning periods greatly reduced the average of most recorded earnings that he compiled for these releasees, and summarized as average annual post-release income.

Releasees who had over two hundred hours of vocational training in prison had earned an average annual income of $2,749 (counting their zero income periods). This was $215 more than the $2,534 average for parolees without such training. Counting only those where some income was reported, two hundred hours or more of training was associated with incomes averaging $4,201 annually, and over one thousand hours with $4,580, while those without training earned $4,184. Clearly, earnings varied with the amount of training. Inmates in McKee's samples ranged in total vocational training from zero to over seven thousand hours, and his findings indicated that post-release earnings increased with training up to one thousand hours.

Average income, including zero-income cases, was $4,117 for machine shop training in prison, $3,344 for welding, $3,239 for offset printing, $3,214 for sheet metal, $3,177 for auto body repair, $3,139 for auto mechanics, and $3,077 for electronics. On the other hand, the annual rate of reported earnings for those with shoe repair training was only $708, and for dry cleaning it was $1,894; such training was favored by prison administrators for its service function to the institution, but had little financial benefit for releasees.

The strongest predictors of more post-release income included:

(1) more hours of training in welding, auto body, auto mechanics, electronics or general shop;
(2) recency of machine shop or bakery training at release;
(3) grades in electronics training.

For machine shop trainees, two-thirds obtained initial employment in this field, and the percentage doing machinist work was slightly higher six months and twelve months later, especially for those with no such employment or training before prison. Welding and auto mechanics had the next highest rates of job acquisition in the field of training, around 50 percent, both initially at release and thereafter. Work in their acquired trade was near zero for those given masonry training in prison, and was low for landscaping, dry cleaning, and shoe repair.

For all prison vocational training taken collectively, the percentage subsequently employed in the field of training varied directly with the number of hours of training received, and inversely with the duration of time between the end of training and date of release. These findings provide an argument against transferring trainees to outside trustee assignments when their release date nears, especially if this shortens trade training, yet staff seek "short timers" as they are presumed safe for outside work, and inmates want the outside jobs.

McKee also found, for Los Angeles County parolees, that recidivism rates were 12.4 percent for those receiving one thousand or more hours of training, and 17.9 percent for the untrained, but 16.5 percent if training totalled only 200 to 999 hours. He inferred from other labor economics data, that the average earnings advantage for those trained, compared with the untrained, rises at a compound interest rate of 20 percent annually for five post-release years. The greater the upfront investment, the results of less crime, less reimprisonment cost, and less welfare expense for the families of those advantaged by prison training, more than compensated for the cost of training.

It is especially regrettable that this type of research was not started sooner in the Department of Corrections, and developed continuously thereafter, since McGee was an expert on vocational education before he got into prison work. Statistics on the earnings of ex-prisoners would be invaluable to show net profits in dollars for specific types of training for particular kinds of inmates; proper precautions can be made to assure the privacy of such information on individuals. As chapter 3 shows, McGee was only partially successful in persuading legislators and the general public of the desirability of providing job-relevant work and education for prisoners to prepare them for post-release employment; he might have been more influential with better data on the cost effectiveness of this service for the public.

Unemployment Compensation for Newly-released Offenders

In my 1958–63 study of the federal prison and parole system, we interviewed about two hundred newly-released parolees from one to six times, at about monthly intervals. We also had one interview each with 250 releasees defined as "successful" on parole, when their median time out was forty-two months, and one interview each with 308 reimprisoned parole violators. Some of these subjects were "mandatory releasees," the term used then for federal prisoners denied regular parole, but let out of prison when they completed their sentences minus at least six months time off for good behavior. They were supervised in this time-off period as though on parole, and like parolees, could be reimprisoned on their old sentence for rule violations or new offenses. All will be called "parolees" here (Glaser, 1964, 1969).

These studies all showed high unemployment rates among parolees immediately or soon after release. This was often the case despite the rule that each had to show a job promise from someone before they could be granted parole. Promises were secured by many prisoners, through their families or friends, just to qualify for parole, but many promises were kept only briefly, if at all, after their release. About half the releasees got free room and board from parents or other relatives, but this seemed to foster family conflict if prolonged. There was a close correlation between unemployment and reconfinement for parole violations, including both serious rule breaking and new offenses.

Unemployment insurance is available in the U.S. only to persons who have had a specified minimum amount of job earnings in the free community during the preceding year, for which contributions are made by both the person and their employer to federal insurance funds. Newly released prisoners are ineligible for this insurance, even if they had worked regularly before their confinement, for they were in prison during the year preceding their release. Also, even the most destitute new releasees do not readily get welfare payments, especially if no one advises and assists them in applying for welfare. I suggested that if those who had pre-prison jobs that contributed to insurance funds were eligible for post-release unemployment insurance based on their contributions, their recidivism rates might be reduced. Several studies were done subsequently to test the impact of such unemployment compensation if based not on prior earnings, but on post-release needs.

In 1971, Kenneth Lenihan, with a U.S. Department of Labor grant, began a Baltimore project entitled "LIFE," or "Living Insurance For Ex-prisoners." He randomly divided about four hundred Maryland prison releasees under forty-five years old, with more than one prior conviction and less than $400 in savings, but not addicted to heroin or alcohol, into the following four groups:

(1) eligible for thirteen weeks of payments of up to $60 per week, for any week in which they earned under $40, and lesser amounts if they earned between $40 and $150, as well as job-placement services when they needed them;
(2) the same payment eligibility, but no job-placement services;
(3) job-placement services, but no payments;
(4) a control group with neither payments nor services.

During their first year out, the two groups getting payments had 8 percent lower arrest rates for theft than did the control group. Also, arrests of those insured did not occur so soon after release, and less often resulted in convictions, than arrests for the control group. Those not paid, but given job-placement services, had about the same recidivism rates as the control group. An analysis concluded that the unemployment compensation paid was more than repaid by the reduction in costs of crime and welfare (Lenihan, 1977; Rossi et al., 1980).

The U.S. Department of Labor then funded "TARP" (Transitional Aid Research Project), for urban areas of Georgia and Texas. About two thousand prison releasees in each state were randomly assigned to six groups that were differentiated in benefits during their first post-prison year, as follows:

(1) eligible for as many as twenty-six weekly payments when their earnings were low, in Georgia up to $70 payments for weeks with earnings no higher than $8, and in Texas up to $63 for weeks with earnings no higher than $15.75;

(2) up to thirteen weeks of eligibility for such payments;

(3) up to thirteen weeks of payments, but on a sliding scale so that they could get smaller payments if they earned somewhat more than the minimum figures above;

(4) no payments except for each of up to four interviews, at $15 each in Georgia and $10 in Texas, plus on request, job placement services and some payments, if needed, for work clothes, tools or books;

(5) interview payments only;

(6) control group with no payments or interviews.

In each state the control group had about one thousand releasees, the first group about 175, and the others about 200 each.

In both states, those getting unemployment insurance worked less, and if paid for the maximum of twenty-three weeks, worked half as much as the control group. Interviews indicated that the payments were deterrents to accepting low-paid jobs, but in the second half of the year out, the insurance recipients had higher-paying jobs than the others, most of whom grabbed the first job they could get. Therefore, all groups averaged about the same total individual earnings for the full year.

Interviews indicated that those paid when not working in their first half year out did more carousing than the others, that often led to arrests for drunkenness and other offenses. Idle hands seemed to be "the devil's workshop," as the saying suggests. The uncompensated, who worked at any job they could get, were more sober. But the compensated releasees had fewer arrests in the second half of the year, so that for the full first year, all groups had about a quarter of their members arrested one or more times. One might infer that the compensated releasees, who were earning more and recidivating less than the others by the end of the year, would in subsequent years have had lower recidivism rates than the others (Rossi et al., 1980). However, a recent fifteen-year follow up of the Texas cases shows little or no difference in subsequent crime rates or earnings for the various groups, but this study was hampered by very poor recordkeeping in Texas (Needels, 1993).

For a temporary period, beginning in 1978, California gave prisoners a post-release unemployment insurance credit of $2.30 per hour (then the U.S. minimum wage) for work at prison jobs or for participation in prison vocational training programs (although actual pay at prison jobs averaged only about 20 cents per hour, and there was no pay for being in training programs). If they were unemployed during their first year out, they could apply at state unemployment insurance offices for "FI" ("former inmate") insurance, provided their accumulated credits totaled at least $1,500, then the minimum prior year's earnings required for all unemployment insurance recipients. As with other unemployed persons, earnings of under $25 per week were not deducted from their compensation, but to be paid, they had to prove, by showing up for job interviews, that they were really looking for work.

A complex statistical analysis demonstrated that those paid under this state program had lower arrest rates than similar releasees who were unpaid (Rauma and Berk, 1987). How much of this reformation was due to the post-release payments, and how much to the work and training in prison, we do not know. Although the public benefited from these payments by having lower crime rates from the recipients, the legislature did not renew this program. It should be noted that this clearly effective compensation program differed from LIFE and TARP described earlier in that:

(1) It was administered through regular unemployment insurance offices for everyone in the community;
(2) payments would be cut off if recipients failed to show up to be interviewed for a job offered by these offices, or if they declined such a job.

In Britain and other western European countries, released prisoners who are unemployed go to the government welfare offices and are dealt with like any other needy persons. They are eligible for assistance with money and often with government-subsidized jobs. In the Scandinavian countries especially, many public works projects or services of lesser urgency are deferred or cut back in times of full employment, and automatically expanded when there are labor surpluses.

Such federal funding of jobs for the unemployed has been sought by the Clinton Administration, not always successfully, to alleviate the economic recession prevailing when he took office. Because it is not an institutionalized feature of our national economy as it is, for example, in Sweden, our unemployment rates are usually much higher. There has been bipartisan support for several rapidly-growing programs, which require that work-eligible persons receive job training or job placement as conditions for getting welfare payments. If such programs persist, expand, and are well administered, unemployment may become less extensive as an impediment to reforming offenders. Continued research is desirable on the anti-crime impacts of increases in job security, work relief, vocational training, and reduction of economic inequalities in our total society.

Summary and Conclusion

The Need to Routinize Evaluation Research

The public's advocacy and approval of research to evaluate correctional practices has been more continuous than the support of such research by politicians and correctional administrators. Yet among both the public and the government officials, blissful ignorance of criminological realities prevails at both extremes of the political spectrum. Harsher penalties are the sole reactions to crime advocated by arch conservatives, yet these measures alone usually have no effect on lawbreaking rates. Ultra-liberals call for abolishing imprisonment, but persons who have repeated success at getting income illegally, or at finding gratification in assaulting or sexually abusing others, do not usually diminish their crime rate unless they are first locked up.

McGee thought that evaluation research should be an institutionalized part of correctional administration, and won appropriations for such research to an extent that did not exist before, and has not persisted. Objective assessment of how well policies and programs work, and their cost effectiveness, were seen by him as ways by which governments could audit their activities. To operate a prison and parole system without such evaluations would be like operating a business without bookkeeping, hence without profit-and-loss statements.

Unfortunately, such evaluations have seldom been adequately maintained by criminal justice agencies. Those with in-house research staff, use them mainly to compile descriptive statistics on the number and attributes of clientele, personnel, and services, for budget justification, rather than to assess crime-control effectiveness. In fact, pursuing such long-range goals as recidivism reduction seem to be forgotten in favor simply of avoiding disorder or scandal, which can be more immediately damaging to the careers of agency administrators.

In assessing a correctional organization's accomplishments, it is well to measure separately its achievement of immediate, intermediate, and ultimate goals. The immediate goals are to provide on-going services, such as: admitting all persons committed to the agency by the courts; holding them in secure custody; giving them food, medical care, and academic and vocational education; recordkeeping; and legal releases. Attainment of these goals is measured by management information statistics on the organization's dimensions. These are the descriptive data required from government officials to account for money spent.

Intermediate goals are the direct purposes of the aforementioned services. For example, to measure attainment of intermediate goals by academic and vocational classes in a correctional agency, statistics are compiled on how much the students learn, using such indices as attainment test scores compared to those of students of the same grade in schools elsewhere, or student rates of improvement in these scores per unit of schooling completed. Diplomas or other certifications awarded may also be important. Similarly, medical services may be assessed by reduction of disease, or by comparing overall health ratings at admission and release. Provision of visiting and correspondence opportunities may be assessed by rates of change in relationship of inmates to spouses or others. By evaluating attainment of intermediate goals, correctional agencies can most quickly and validly show the efficiency of their activities. This kind of research is a check on management that McGee urged, but is not routinely done.

The ultimate goal of correctional agencies is to protect the public from crime, cost effectively, and justly. Evaluation of correctional achievements, therefore, requires linkage of intermediate goal attainment to such ultimate goals. For example, after an agency shows how successfully it has trained its wards, it should show how much this reduces the inmates subsequent crime rates, increases their post-release earnings, and provides other justifications for correctional budgets (elaborated in Glaser with Erez, 1988, ch. 8). This is the public policy need.

The claim that "nothing works" in pursuing the ultimate goal of reducing crime rates through correctional programs was widely ascribed to Martinson, but this is an erroneous ascription if one reads his later writings. These, and other research surveys, notably that of Gendreau and Ross, show clearly that programs of positive reinforcement, modeling, and counseling can reduce recidivism rates if provided extensively and soundly to those who desire them, and in appropriate places. Research also shows that highly criminalized offenders have lower recidivism rates if first given an appreciable term of confinement instead of *immediate* community correctional treatment.

Much of the best correctional evaluation was completed by research staff of the California Department of Corrections and Youth Authority while McGee was in office. Unfortunately, they did not present their findings clearly as validated general principles for reliable policy guidance. Even more regrettably, research budgets were slashed after McGee left, and the subsequent in-house studies completed were less often concerned with rigorously testing recidivism-reduction policies.

In his 1967 "Farewell Address," McGee urged Governor Reagan to continue some type of top control over both youth and adult correctional agencies, and to have:

(1) A closer relationship between...the directors of corrections and the paroling authorities.
(2) Broad scale planning and development involving *all* state and local correctional functions.
(3) Better coordination of *all* community-based correctional programs—state and local.
(4) ...a system-wide, computer-based information system which must not become the captive of a subordinate-level operating unit...[perhaps reflecting his statistical unit's opposition to Base Expectancy scales, described earlier in Gottfredson report].
(5) Top-level control of research studies and especially of those designated to evaluate on-going programs in the system.
(6) Top-level control of program budgets and key personnel policies.
(7) A single legislative relations program.
> These objectives can be achieved by retaining in modified form the present agency structure; or by creating a position such as "Deputy Executive Director" to assure oversight of the correctional system; or by enlarging and strengthening the role of the chairman of the Board of Corrections (McGee and Montilla, 1967:10–11).

Most of these goals were not achieved in McGee's time, or since.

Science will benefit the public most in guiding corrections if it is routinely applied to testing general principles on what alternatives are most reformative for specific kinds of offenders in various circumstances. This will yield dependable results most conclusively and quickly by controlled experiments.

When experimental research is not feasible, however, it can be replaced by multivariate statistical analysis of experience, supplemented by relevant case study and survey inquiries for illuminating and interpreting the statistics. Statistical data for multivariate analysis should include, for large and representative samples of offenders, information on their activities and achievements while in correctional custody or supervision, as well as their prior and post-release criminal records, earnings, health, area of residence, family status, and other variables. This would permit a full development of the quasi-experimental evaluations that Gottfredson and Wilkins sought in their Base Expectancy program, and what I repeatedly called for, last as "Routinizing Evaluation" (Glaser, 1955, 1957a, 1957b, 1973, and [with Erez] 1988). Such data are increasingly procurable from computerized public records, without labeling any individuals in violation of their privacy rights.

These types of studies, if well institutionalized and focused on cumulative formulation and testing of general principles, as well as regularly describing and assessing agency practices, can provide the scientific guidance and routine auditing of corrections that McGee sought.

6

Coordinating Total
Criminal Justice Systems

McGee, throughout most of his career, headed only correctional agencies, and was primarily concerned with prisons. Yet he regularly tried to coordinate all types of crime control efforts. In an address appropriately called "Doing the Job Together," he pointed out:

...Of the many thousands of offenses reported to the police, and the many thousands of persons coming to the attention of the police..., an amazingly small percentage ever comes under the jurisdiction of a correctional agency....Correctional agencies,... even if they were many times more effective than they are, could never hope to do more than take a relatively small place in the totality of society's efforts to deal with...crime and delinquency.

...delinquency...is a part of a larger group of maladjustments....Dependency, ill health, emotional maladjustment, mental deficiency and mental disease, child neglect, truancy, illegitimacy, and other handicapping conditions reside side by side, in varying proportions,...producing the grist for the welfare, police, and correctional mills.

After discussing the needs of such agencies, he concluded:

None of these problems—organizational patterns and relationships, jails, statutes, professional standards, budgets, research—is more important than the need for cooperation and coordination within and among correctional agencies and with other agencies of law enforcement and public welfare. We deal with the same clients, the same families, the same communities. In spite of shortcomings in our technical capacities or in the development of new knowledge in our special professional fields, we already know how to do a better job than we are doing—but we shall do it only if we find a way to do it together (1954b).

He also asserted, quite simply:

More emphasis needs to be placed on breaking through the barriers of misunderstanding between the various agencies that deal with specialized features of the total process of the administration of criminal justice. I am always distressed at the mutual criticism and lack of understanding that often takes place between probation and parole workers and institutional staff, between correctional workers and police, between the police and correctional workers and the courts, and so on around the circuit....We should be a unified, thoroughly coordinated, mutually supportive fabric of officialdom for dealing with one of the most perplexing problems of our times. Perhaps much of this could be overcome if we would get better acquainted (1958).

As detailed in chapters 3 and 4, McGee initiated much of the coordination between California's prison and parole agencies with other components of the criminal justice system. Notable, were the brief admissions of newly convicted felons to prison reception centers that prepared diagnostic reports to help judges with sentencing decisions, and the probation subsidy program to help counties try to reform more offenders in the community instead of sending them to institutions. McGee also spoke out frequently on many ways that agencies, other than those he headed, could improve society's total crime control efforts. During and just before retirement, he wrote a series of thoughtful and scholarly essays, published mainly in *Federal Probation*, in which he proposed a somewhat new division of functions among criminal justice agencies. His suggestions, if more fully heeded, could give us greater law, order, rationality, and efficiency in our criminal justice systems than prevail now.

Starting With Jails:
An Optimum Division of Criminal Justice Labor

Soon after he retired from state government, McGee published an article on problems of local jails that concludes with one of the best statements available on how to improve the division of labor among all of the different types of government agencies in the criminal justice field. This was his much too overlooked essay, "Our Sick Jails" (1971a).

In the introduction to this article, McGee notes that he opened New York City's Rikers Island Penitentiary, mainly intended to be a jail for sentenced misdemeanants, and that he later was responsible for administering all lockups and jails in that metropolis. He said that he had also "inspected scores of local jails." It will be recalled that while in the New York post he co-founded what has become today's American Jail Association. He continued:

> The total problem is not the jail alone, but the whole agglomeration of public services involved in the *management* of *law offenders* after *arrest.*
>
> The management problem involves all the parts of the criminal justice system—police, courts, prosecutors, defense attorneys, detention jails, probation services, and parole at the local level. Then there is the state government's correctional system; and overlapping these the federal system. The total so-called "system" must deal with the whole gamut of illegal acts, from minor traffic infractions to the most heinous of felonious crimes. The persons who commit offenses include every imaginable kind of human being in the society—murderers, drunk drivers, prostitutes, thieves, forgers, mental cases, alcoholics, drug addicts, muggers, juveniles out of control, rioters, beggars—everybody is eligible if he gives cause to be arrested.
>
> As a practical matter, however, we find the local jails being occupied principally by drunks, addicts, and petty thieves. And...if the prostitutes were eliminated...,most of the women's quarters would be virtually empty most of the time.
>
> Based on a very rough estimate, about 7 percent of the... millions...who pass through these jails each year are charged with or convicted of felonies, and 93 percent are misdemeanants. It can be seen...that the problem of jail administration, aside from holding a few felons awaiting disposition by the courts, is that of managing a miscellaneous array of persons charged with or convicted of offenses of a relatively minor nature....A study of two large counties in California revealed that about one-third of the sentenced prisoners on a given day were serving terms of 30 days or less, one-third of 1 month to 3 months, and one-third over 90 days up to and including a year.
>
> ...what can be accomplished toward treating, managing, or rehabilitating persons who receive sentences of 30 days or less?

The same...might be asked about those who receive sentences of 30 to 90 days. The group that we might well be most concerned about is the third that receive sentences of 3 months to 1 year. What, also, of the...untried defendants presumed innocent under our law who may wait in jail for periods of 3 months to a year or more while the judicial machinery unwinds....In some metro-politan jurisdictions 60 percent or more of the daily jail population is...unsentenced....One month in jail...to the prisoner may be the longest 720 hours in his life, and just one of those hours could include the most damaging experience in his lifetime. Contrari-wise, short stays in jail are a way of life for thousands of deteri-orated middle-aged alcoholics....Of some 7,000 inmates in New York...over 20 percent were serving a term which was their tenth or more (1971a).

He enumerated eight remedies, most of them fairly simple:

1. ...use of citations instead of jail booking for selected cases at the time of apprehension.
2. Release on "own recognizance" by the court at the time of arraignment of many of those unable to post money bail as a guaranty of appearance in court when ordered to do so.
3. ...courts giving priority in...disposition to those in jail as opposed to those waiting trial while out on bail.
4. The use of short form or "quicky" presentence probation reports in misdemeanor cases, so that the judge may have information about each defendant which might have relevance to his decision to choose among such alternative dispositions as suspended sentence, supervised probation, fine, and length and type of jail sentence.
5. ...payment of fines on the installment plan in cases wherein the defendant is employed but does not have enough ready cash... when the sentence is pronounced.
6. ...work-furlough releases for employable and reasonably reli-able jail inmates.
7. ...parole and post-institutional supervision for most jail inmates, especially for men with families who receive jail sentences of more than 60 days.
8. ...detoxification and rehabilitation programs outside the jail system for chronic alcoholics (1971a).

Unfortunately, his further assertions remain largely true:

> ...what is really startling to any taxpayer who is concerned about the effectiveness of his dollar is that the number of jurisdictions which exploit all of these practices to the fullest are almost non-existent.
>
> Assuming the same number of officers and the same degree of police vigilance and efficiency now existing, and assuming that the above practices were fully utilized, it is probable that the *daily populations of the Nation's local jails could be cut by as much as 50 percent without risk to the public safety* (1971a).

McGee blamed this jail "inefficiency and ineptitude" on administrative problems. He said that the country's approximately 3,500 local jails were very unevenly used:

> ...hundreds of jails are mere lockups for a dozen or so and many of these are completely empty part of the time....On the opposite end of the size distribution, we see great metropolitan facilities like those in Chicago, Los Angeles, and New York City, which number their inmates in the thousands. They are uniformly overcrowded, impersonal, undermanned, and underprogrammed.
>
> ...22 percent of all local jails are a part of city government, and with rare exceptions these are operated by the municipal police. Except for inertia and vested interest, there is no logical reason for the municipal police to run any jail where offenders are confined for more than 48 or 72 hours to permit delivery in court and transfer to a county or regional jail. This is especially obvious in a place like Sacramento, California, where the county detention jail and the police jail are located on the same city block, or in San Francisco, where the sheriff's jail and the city police jail are on the sixth and fifth floors respectively of the Hall of Justice.
>
> The most common practice is for local jails to be a part of county government and to be operated by the county sheriff....73.3 percent of all local jails are so managed. A few jurisdictions, like New York City and Denver, Colorado, have city-county governments, with the jails operated by an administrator appointed by the mayor or the board of supervisors....
>
> Municipal police forces have trouble enough enforcing the law and keeping the peace in the cities without expecting them also to be either expert or very much interested in managing local

jails, with all the challenges presented by their diverse inhabitants, and the ever present potentialities for crisis and scandal inherent even in the best of them....

Other patterns involve regional jail districts comprised of two or more counties, or contractual relations between adjoining jurisdictions, in which one county serves another for some kinds of prisoners on a cost reimbursement basis.

Most of these joint operations are fraught with real problems of transportation, funding for building construction, and petty political friction.

...institutions for the care and confinement of adult men and women...appear to have developed historically largely as un-wanted appendages of agencies charged with the jurisdiction's police power. However, with the movement of population to the cities, county sheriffs have been losing more and more of their direct enforcement functions to the city police. As a result, the county jails have tended to become a larger share of each sheriff's patronage empire, and hence a function he is unwilling to relin-quish. The prison systems of the state governments have been used...mostly for the more serious and more persistent convicted felons. In some states they may also accept sentenced misde-meanants of certain classes, especially women...the lion's share of the day-to-day prisoner traffic is still in the local jails (1971a).

A different pattern exists for juveniles, he noted:

...Just as confinement and treatment programs for adults have tended to grow out of the police function, the juvenile services have emerged from the judicial function. This is because probation services originated in the courts. Detention halls and probation supervision for wards of the juvenile courts are more often than not adjuncts of the judicial rather than the executive branch of government.

...in most counties, probation services for both adult and juvenile offenders are combined in the local probation depart-ments....Here again, we find every conceivable kind of variation....

...In California, each county has a probation department within the court system, serving both juveniles and adults, except in two counties. In Los Angeles County, the head of this largest county probation department in the State is appointed by and reports to the board of supervisors, not to the courts. Stranger still, in some counties he is appointed by the judge of the juvenile court, even though there are usually more adults than juveniles in the total caseload. In Wisconsin, probation and parole services are in the State Division of Corrections except in Milwaukee. In Washington State, adult probation is combined with the state parole system....

Viewed by anyone outside the correctional field...,the ways in which we...organize our resources to deal with millions of law breakers, from the point of arrest on, must look as if it were designed by a madman with the advice of Public Enemy No. 1 (1971a).

The solution, McGee thought, requires a new total system perspective:

If we would...think logically about...the "Justice System,"... we must start out...by calling to mind our doctrine of the separation of powers among the judicial, executive, and legislative branches. First, let us consider the role of the judiciary with particular reference to...the supervision of convicted persons placed on probation. It seemed sensible enough for the trial court judge in a one-man court with one or two probation officers, to appoint these persons as functionaries of his office to make presentence investigations and to report to him from time to time on how a handful of probationers were doing. But now, with most of our population concentrated in great metropolitan complexes, this arrangement is as archaic as a one-cow dairy. In Los Angeles County, for example, the Probation Department has some 4,000 employees, administers an annual budget of $53 million, runs 30 detention facilities for juveniles, and supervises a caseload of adults and juveniles of 41,000 persons.

The decision to grant or revoke probation is and should no doubt continue to be a judicial function, but the operation of the probation department is as clearly an executive function as is the city police department or the operation of the state prison system. Accordingly, except in those rural counties with one-man courts, we must conclude that the administration of probation should be an executive function and a unit of state or county government. Except for the historical development of the services, there is no more logic in having the judge administer the probation service than there is for him to run the jails and prisons to which he commits defendants....

Looking at the question in another way, one might inquire why the sheriff or other police official should not administer the probation services with just as much logic as supports the notion that he is best fitted to manage the jails....

A dispassionate view of the best possible way to organize the criminal justice system cannot but lead to the conclusion that there are three major groups of functions, each requiring different emphasis, different attitudes, and different professional training and occupational skills...as follows:

The Police
   Direct prevention and peace keeping
   Detection and apprehension

The Courts, including prosecution and defense
   Application of the law
   Judgmental disposition

The Correctional Agencies
   Presentence investigation and community supervision of probationers and parolees
   Management and control of defendants awaiting adjudication (jails and juvenile halls)
   Management of residential facilities and programs for all committed offenders (jails, prisons, correctional schools, and halfway houses)

If the preceding is a rational division of functions, it is clear that each political jurisdiction, be it a state or a county or a regional district within a state, should establish the equivalent of a department of corrections, which would be responsible for the management of all offenders under its jurisdiction, whether accused or convicted, and whether incarcerated or under community supervision.

This would mean: First, that the courts should relinquish administrative direction of probation services.

Second, that jails and camps for adult offenders must be removed from the administrative direction of police agencies.

Third, that in jurisdictions (usually counties) with too small a population to operate efficiently, they must either combine into regional districts or turn the functions over to state government.

Fourth, that the unrealistic administrative dichotomy between youth and adult correctional programs existing in many local jurisdictions be discontinued.

Fifth, that to encourage these changes and to ensure equality of treatment throughout the system, both the state governments and the Federal Government must provide financial assistance based upon adherence to decent standards.

"Equal Justice Under Law" are noble words....If we really believe in this...,we can hardly continue to tolerate...a mental case charged with disorderly conduct sitting naked on the concrete floor of a bare isolation cell at a local jail while in another jurisdiction he would be in a hospital.

It is equally incongruous for a minion of organized crime charged with felonious assault to be walking the streets free on bail while scores of minor but indigent offenders sit idly in over-crowded jails awaiting court disposition.

Finally, it is not enough to say that the local jail as we know it is a failure—it is a scandal! All the palliatives and all the unco-ordinated efforts at patching up the present system will continue to fail. Basic reorganization of the whole structure for managing offenders at the local levels of government is required. Nothing else will do! (1971a).

After his expression of concern that sheriffs tend to nurture their political patronage by clinging to control of jail administration, but have little interest or competence in improving the jail's quality, McGee might well have suggested taking the office of sheriff entirely out of politics. Oregon, for example, has eliminated election of sheriffs, making them merit system appointees of county governments, selected by competitive examination. Thus, some years ago, Lee P. Brown was made Sheriff of Multnomah County (Portland) after earning his Ph.D. in Criminology from the University of California at Berkeley and while also serving as a police officer. He may then have been the first sheriff with a Ph.D. , and one of the first black sheriffs. He became, successively, the police chief for Atlanta, Houston, and New York City, and then, President Clinton's "Drug Czar."

McGee's essay on jails complements other recommendations for optimum correctional functions that McGee made separately:

Provide for the diversion of as many persons as possible from the system who are more of a nuisance than a threat to the community. Chronic alcoholics, many drug abusers, and some others whose "crimes" are without victims are examples....

Establish as a legislative policy that those programs which provide substitute ways of dealing constructively and safely with offenders without incarceration are to be encouraged (1971b).

McGee's pioneering ideas for a more rational division of labor in our criminal justice systems could be providential. An overdue salvation may come from more completely following his ideas.

Probation—A Public Function in Trouble

McGee never administered a probation agency, but he seems to have been concerned about their activities throughout his many leadership roles. As noted in discussing the Probation Subsidy program in chapter 4, a study of this type of correctional service was an early project of the Board of Corrections that McGee chaired when he became Administrator of the Youth and Adult Corrections Agency. After noting that probation began in California in 1903, the study reported that, consistent with several much earlier surveys, it found great disparity in the use of this penalty from one county to another, and even among judges within the same county. The study also noted that probation had always been much more economical, and reduced recidivism rates more than did confinement, for most offenders, but that its protection of the public was diminished by recurrent increases in the average number of cases supervised per officer. The board recommended state subvention of county costs for better probation services, educating the public about probation, and conducting further research on probation (California Youth and Adult Corrections Agency, 1965).

McGee later remarked, on another aspect of probation work:

The closest thing we have in our nonsystem of criminal justice to an intake service is the probation service, usually attached to the courts. The presentence report and the recommendation to the judge, according to many studies, tend to be followed in more than nine cases out of ten. You may argue that the probation officer knows what the judge will accept, and is therefore influenced by the decision-maker, but it does not detract from the statement that the probation services provide the intake for corrections, state and local. This being the case, the probation officer is in an extraordinarily strategic position. I said "strategic," not "strong" position (1980a).

On the weakness of probation, another paper of the same date elaborated:

Probation in company with all correctional services is in trouble....Probation departments in California carry 70% of the adult caseload and 88% of the juveniles. These proportions may vary considerably from state to state, but the differences are not so dramatic as to refute the statement that the bulk of the task of controlling, managing, and servicing adjudicated human beings who pass through our judicial system year after year is handled by probation. These...workers are clearly the most important part of the correctional systems of our country.

Why, then, are they in trouble?

- They are the *newest* part of the Anglo-American system of criminal jurisprudence. They are still growing toward a mature and established role....
- Probation suffers from the image of "coddlers of criminals" and advocates of leniency, during a current popular trend toward more severity.
- They are in competition for public funds with old established associates in state and local government—the police, the prosecutor, the judges, the firemen, the health services, the schools, the hospitals.
- They have no effective constituency among the citizens. They have no PTA, no health association, no bar association, no medical association. To a large extent the workers in the system are their own constituency.
- They have no powerful national spokesmen, either political or professional. What senator or congressman takes a special interest in them or their professional mission? Where is the American Correctional Association or any similar body when their interests or their professional concerns are being eroded in county political chambers or in state capitols?
- They are submerged (in most jurisdictions) by the judiciary. They need strong and politically effective advocates. But judges by the very nature of their role in the system are and must be *judges*—not advocates.
- They, among all similar community services, are the most vulnerable to the effects of Proposition 13 and its counterparts in other states [enactments severely curtailing local taxing powers—dg]. Politicians are reluctant to cut back on police, fire pro-

tection, or health services. But they are not really convinced that probation services make their communities safer or better places to live.

- They are weakened as a political subdivision of government by jurisdictional fragmentation within a criminal justice "system" which itself suffers from parochialism, isolation, and even paranoia.
- They lack professional identity. There are no recognized professional schools to prepare for this profession. Currently practitioners come from a wide variety of educational and occupational backgrounds.
- There are no nationally recognized scholars, practitioners, or administrators who can truly be called eminent leaders in the probation profession.

There are current trends that exacerbate all of the above. To mention a few:

- The crime rates seem to grow in spite of increased expenditures on the criminal justice system.
- Reactionary forces in the legislative bodies have seized upon the lack of correctional leadership and the public anger at crime and violence to pass increasingly punitive laws without supplying the funds to deal with the consequences of such laws.
- Probation administrators and directors of corrections have become frequent and easy targets for political attack. The firing of Los Angeles County's chief probation officer,[1]...was a clear case of the "king killing the messenger who came bearing bad news."
- The continuing controversy about sentencing and rehabilitation has a negative effect on all correctional programs except those focused on simplistic concepts of punishment and rehabilitation. This arises out of a confusion...between the role of the judge and the correctional professional.

The judge should not, and probably never did, sentence defendants to programs or institutions for "rehabilitation." How could he when 8 out of 10 defendants plead guilty, usually under plea bargains, actual or inferred. It's the severity of the penalty which is bargained, not the opportunity for rehabilitation. Beyond this...,what judge would argue that judges are qualified as diagnosticians and prescribers...for the social reform of the diversity of clients who pass before the bench?

The correctional worker, be he in probation or in an institution, could maintain little respect for himself or his profession if he did not do what he could to help his wards to establish themselves as self-supporting and law-abiding citizens.

That at least two-thirds of those adults placed on probation successfully complete their terms, and that half of the highly selected few who go to state prison do not show up again within five years after discharge, is evidence that the system is not a total failure....

- The fact that it is difficult to prove why any of the alternative dispositions of defendant's case comes out well is another thorn in the side of professional probation leaders. Some of the research on the effectiveness of supervision tends to support the hypothesis that no matter what is done in the intensity or quality of probation supervision, the statistical results...show no significant difference.

It may be useful to mention some obvious points:

First, with massive caseloads it is probable that to compare intensive supervision with conventional supervision is much like comparing a round zero with a square one.

Second, it is possible that being on probation, even with minimal supervision, is a powerful deterrent because of the imminent threat of revocation and imprisonment.

Third, it may be that short periods of supervision, especially for adults with extensive criminal experience, may be just "too little too late."

Fourth, it is common knowledge to most practitioners that among probationers and parolees there is usually a substantial group who need no help and may do better just left alone. There is another group who regard the probation officer as the enemy and who will not respond positively to any outside officially oriented intervention. There is also a group probably smaller than either of the other two who can be reached and helped. Every agent has his success stories. These are what keep him going. But leaders and policy makers may be expecting too much. Rehabilitation is only one of the goals of probation—not necessarily its primary one.

So where do we go from here?

First, a reappraisal of probation's goals and purposes is needed. These...must be sold to the public and to policy makers in terms of what probation does and...can do—not idealistic and unrealistic promises.

Second, probation leaders need to examine their role and... position....Are they social caseworkers? Are they merely agents of the courts? What is their position in relation to police, prosecutor, public defender, and other public and private agencies? Should they be running institutions as well as court services, case analysis, and supervision? What should their relationship be with the executive branch of local and state government?

Third, who should pay for probation services? County government, special tax districts, state government? What are the consequences of shifting sources of fiscal support?

Finally, in spite of the truism that organizational change does not guarantee improved effectiveness, alternate organizational patterns should be examined (1980b).

As McGee summed up in another context:

...we might look at the work of a probation officer who is assigned exclusively to making pretrial and presentence investigations. He is really not a caseworker in the sense that he is a helping professional; he is basically a case investigator. Then let us look at some individual caseloads...that may run from 100 to 300 persons per officer....

...we have a group of people...who would like to be professionals and who in terms of education and background have more claim to that status than some of their counterparts... hampered by their placement in the "pecking order" of local government (1980a).

McGee's first major remedy for probation, more immediately feasible than most others, was the new division of labor in criminal justice proposed in the conclusion of his essay on jails. This would restrict judges to decisions on guilt and on penalties, or to the supervision of juries that make such decisions. Probation, along with jails, other residential institutions, and community supervision services, for both juvenile and adult offenders, would be administered by Departments of Correction. The departments could effectively be units of city, county, or state governments, depending mainly on population densities and crime rates. If these diverse services for dealing with arrested or convicted offenders were together in such departments of the executive branch of government, their staffs and leaders could enhance the public support and prestige for what they all have in common: membership in a single profession of corrections, unified despite its specializations.

McGee also anticipated some humorous consequences from such reorganization, recalling that when he was a Deputy Commissioner of Correction in New York City: "Our receptionist had trouble with a stream of citizens wanting their gas bills or their tax assessments 'corrected'" (1979).

Improving Penalty Determination

McGee was always concerned with and disturbed by "The most critical point in...administering criminal justice, the imposition of sentence," a phrase he quoted from Frankel's aptly titled book *Criminal Sentences—Law Without Order* (1973). In the State of Washington, and in California, McGee worked in two of the states that then had the most indeterminate sentencing systems in the nation. Most felons convicted in these states received prison sentences from the courts of one year to ten, one year to life, or five or ten years to life. The large gap between minimum and maximum penalties was stipulated by law for each offense, and gave the state parole board much discretion in deciding each inmate's release date.

These parole boards also ruled on revoking parole. With such indefinite sentences, several paroles often occurred before a prison penalty ended, if it ever did. For example, many young alcoholics given one year to life for armed robbery, as the law mandated, would persistently commit petty misdemeanors or rule violations—but no major new felonies—after each parole.

McGee, at first, seemed quite pleased with this sentencing system. It appeared to be compatible with his focus on trying to rehabilitate prisoners, since the parole date could depend upon the prisoner's good conduct and self-improvement while confined. Others argued for parole by claiming that the risk of recidivism is more evident after observing an inmate for a year or more in confinement than it is at sentencing, because the trial focuses on the offense rather than the offender. Toward the time of McGee's retirement in 1967, however, after watching how parole decisions were made in daily practice, he gradually shared widespread dissatisfaction with the indeterminate sentence. The result was his publishing, in 1974, in successive issues of *Federal Probation* a two-part article entitled "A New Look at Sentencing," with the second part a proposal for revising the California Penal Code. In 1978, in another article, he described the actual revision that went into effect in 1977, and only partially reflected his ideas.

McGee began his analysis by writing briefly on five main purposes in sentencing: Retribution, Deterrence, Incapacitation, Rehabilitation, and Maintenance of Respect for the Law:

(1) *Retributive Punishment*...satisfies the emotional need of the people to take some positive action...to prevent victims and citizens from taking the law into their own hands. Lynch mobs, tar-and-feather parties, beatings, and warnings out of town are all familiar examples of too recent a past....Most...commentators prefer to soft pedal the idea of retributive punishment in favor of more intellectual motivations but one would be politically insensitive...if he did not recognize that the average citizen thinks in these terms no matter how committed he may be to...ideas of reformation and forgiveness....

(2) *Deterrence*....The public knowledge that certain acts are defined by law as criminal and that at least some offenders are apprehended, convicted, and punished is thought to be... deterrent...on the assumption that potential criminals are rational beings who weigh their acts in terms of risk of penalties versus expected rewards. That this assumption is only partially sound is obvious....Why do so many...commit crimes...in which the probable penalty is so disproportionate to the possible gain? Also, why do so many who have been convicted and punished repeat? The imperfection...of the deterrent purpose leads to much debate...with respect to the usefulness of harsh sentences...on the relatively few who are caught and convicted.

Efforts to assess...deterrence by empirical studies have been inconclusive because of the...other factors which may affect crime rates.

(3) *Incapacitation*....One who is placed in a position where he cannot commit a crime obviously will not. Capital punishment is the ultimate in incapacitation. Prison terms are incapacitating for short periods. Other...measures include loss of professional and vocational licenses, deportation, and...confiscatory fines. Case supervision...under probationary sentences or parole is regarded...to a limited degree as incapacitative as well as deterrent.

That this purpose is limited and imperfect is also obvious. Some...commit crimes while in prison. It is also argued that the prison...makes some men worse risks after release...it is doubtful if the incapacitation function has much effect except for the few who serve extremely long sentences which cancel out the most crime prone years between ages 17 and 40. In...very short jail sentences what is gained in the process may be canceled out by its damaging effects.

(4) *Rehabilitation and Social Reintegration.* It is argued that while a convicted offender is under the control of...correctional authorities every effort should be made to change his attitudes, skills, and capacities to cope with life in a free society without committing criminal acts. No thoughtful person will ordinarily argue with this. The failure of so many to prepare constructively...would seem to rest first on the system's inability to provide effective training and treatment...and second, upon the unwillingness of substantial numbers of prison inmates to take advantage of such opportunities as the state does provide. Cohort studies...from California prisons...indicate that of those first released in a given year about 50 percent will have been in relatively serious trouble with the law sometime during the subsequent 5 years.

In view of the high selectivity of the more serious cases for prison...,this might be regarded as a good record....No consensus...has been arrived at as to what percentage...can be regarded as an acceptable minimum standard. As a consequence, anything less than 100 percent success tends to be regarded as failure. Many a good program has been condemned because of one sensational failure out of thousands of possibilities.

The consequence...is that the most punitive...and reactionary critics advocate abandonment of vocational training, general education, psychiatric treatment, counseling, recreation and similar programs, leaving the only alternative, simple warehousing, a little made-work and idleness. Conversely, the ultraliberals and the radical left want to tear down the prisons without offering an alternative which the public could or would accept.

Another kind of problem...has grown out of unrealistic expectations for rehabilitation. Many judges unfamiliar with the program limitations of prisons have...announced...that they are sending the defendant to prison "to be rehabilitated." This is as irrational as to send a person to prison to have his appendix removed or to learn the trade of his choice.

Rehabilitation does work for some offenders and should
be a principal objective of correctional programs, *but not the
reason for the imposition of the sentence....*

(5) *Maintenance of Respect for the Law.* The simple concept here is
that a rule (or law) must be enforced by some kind of sanctions...or the rule itself is largely nullified....The alternative is
either tyranny or anarchy. We have little tolerance for either.
Accordingly, the objective of the total society is to convince as
large a majority...as possible that it is to their own best interest
to obey the law....

...*Perhaps next to nonenforcement the factor which contributes
most to disrespect for law is the disparate or even whimsical
imposition of sanctions.* This is what gives rise to such pejorative
terms as "bargain basement justice," "judge shopping," and
"courthouse lotteries."...

A system needs to be devised...which will (a) protect the
public, (b) preserve the rights of individuals, and (c) satisfy
reasonable men that it is fair, consistent, intelligent, and incor-
ruptible (1974a).

McGee pointed out that the foregoing applies to all fifty states, but
that in suggesting remedies he would focus on California. He then
detailed some sources of dissatisfaction with the state's indeterminate
sentence law, enacted in 1917:

...It...is considered by many trial court judges as an executive
invasion of judicial prerogatives. It has been looked upon by others
as an unjustifiable delegation of broad discretionary power to a lay
executive board without the protections of due process or the right
of appeal to higher judicial authority. From another viewpoint,
those who espouse long periods of incapacitation...have often
been critical of parole boards for releasing...prisoners who later
commit new crimes.

...others contend that lay parole boards are so vulnerable to
political criticism that they tend to err in the direction of excessive
conservatism by keeping many prisoners longer than is just or
necessary. Some also argue that parole boards are inconsistent from
time to time, dependent upon instructions from the political
appointing power.

Prisoners and their families as well as prison administrators
complain that the uncertainty about release date...is damaging to

institution morale and also militates against job and family planning for the period after release to community living....

What then have been the historical arguments *for* prison sentence indeterminacy?

It has been contended...that trial court judges generally do not want the time fixing component of sentencing returned to them; first, because of the alleged workload, and second, because the opportunity to pass this onerous responsibility over to a State parole board relieves them of making this decision under public scrutiny and of dealing with an added set of pressures inherent in the sentence and plea negotiation process.

It has been held with some logic also that if a defendant is to be kept in prison for a substantial period of time, like 5 years or more, that it is virtually impossible for the sentencing authority to make a valid judgment so far in advance as to the person's readiness for release and the degree of tolerance the public might have at that time for his or her return to a free community. The trouble with this argument is twofold. More than half of all prison inmates released in any given year tend to have served from 6 to 30 months in California, and in some states half of them serve less than 18 months before first release. Furthermore, studies indicate that the capacity of a parole board to predict future behavior is no better after 5 years incarceration than it is after 5 weeks....

Another kind of argument for indeterminacy in sentencing was based on the now discredited medical analogy or "medical model"....This assumed that the sentenced criminal was "sick" and needed "treatment," and hence, should be turned over to professional "treaters" who would be empowered to release the "patient" when well enough to be returned, at least tentatively, to the free community. The assumption that the state of the art...has now advanced far enough to support this thesis is without scientific foundation. It is also common to overlook the fact that the parole authority is not the agency which does the "treating." Further, we have known for a long time that as a general rule "checkwriters" and "car thieves" are the worst backsliders and that murderers and armed robbers are least likely to repeat. Pursuing... the "medical model," since a bank robber is easier to "cure" than an NSF checkwriter, one should expect to release the robber earlier than the checkwriter. In terms of simple justice and concepts of public protection even the most irrational amongst us would be unlikely to accept such an idea.

...rehabilitation and education programs...should be applied within the framework of a criminal law which is intended primarily to protect the public by preventing crime and enhancing respect for the law, and...not be justified as itself a rehabilitative measure.

The only valid argument remaining for indeterminacy in sentencing felony defendants lies in the obvious injustices and inconsistencies growing out of excessive disparities in the sentencing practices of a multiplicity of judges in a jurisdiction administering the same laws and using common correctional institutions....The gross disparities in sentences...is a particularly difficult problem where the statutes permit discretion in length of sentence ranging sometimes from a few months to life....

On the other hand, flexibility and judicial discretion must be preserved within prescribed limits because the variables of personalities, intent, circumstances, and environment are simply too complex for statutory definition....The problem is not judicial discretion but the misuse or inconsistent use of it. A remedy must be sought which will provide for differences...while still observing...fairness and consistency.

...arguments for indeterminacy...have little appeal except as a means of counteracting the disparity problem....The whole sentencing and releasing function is in need of constant monitoring and judicial oversight. The judicial system is uniquely equipped to manage the decision-making process in accordance with law, if an appropriate system were established to control capriciousness in subjective sentencing judgments....

It seems abundantly clear that our lawmakers have been willing to allow sentencing judges to use their own discretion as long as they were not free to impose extremely long prison sentences. For example, jail sentences of less than a year for misdemeanants; probation with or without jail for most felons. But in the case of felons sent to State prison to serve statutory terms from 6 months to life, the sentencing judge loses jurisdiction to a politically appointed lay parole board which has tended to deliberate in private and far away in both time and space from the seat of the original trial.

The delegation of this extraordinary discretionary power to a lay administrative body (a parole board) in the executive branch of government is...open to question....Under American concepts of fairness and due process,...one can...predict more and more judicial intervention in a system that permits a nonjudicial board in the executive branch to exercise this...discretionary power over other human beings without judicial review (1974b).

McGee then proposed, as he did separately in his already cited works on jails and on probation, a new division of criminal justice labor:

Major Elements of a Revised Sentencing Plan for California

I. *All powers of sentencing convicted criminals, including length of confinement, release to community supervision, and revocation of such releases is placed by statute under the direct purview and control of the State's judicial system.*

II. *The management of State prisons and correctional schools is retained in the executive branch within the State Department of Correctional Services.*

III. *The management of agencies responsible for the supervision and control of persons placed on probation or conditionally released from State penal or correctional institutions is placed in the executive branch,* but this group of functions would be unified at the local level. Whether the organizational structure is State, county, or regional is irrelevant to the basic plan except that if administered by local governments the State would set standards and contribute to fiscal support.

IV. *All sentencing, term fixing, releasing, discharging, and revoking of releases is done by trial court judges subject to law and to standards, guidelines and review by a special division of the State Court of Appeal.* (See Section X.)

V. *The sentencing structure or table of sanctions in the statutes is revised by the Legislature...*into a limited number of categories or degrees on an ascending scale of severity....There are *infractions* for which the penalties do not include the possibility of imprisonment, but are punishable by fines and other sanctions, such as cancellation of licenses. *Misdemeanors* are of two degrees. The maximum penalty for a second degree misdemeanor is 6 months in jail and 1 year in jail for those of the first degree. Felonies are divided into five degrees with minimum and maximum penalties as follows:

 5th degree—3 months to 3 years. These in most cases may be reduced to misdemeanors of the first degree in the discretion of the court.

4th degree—6 months to 5 years.

3rd degree—12 months to 12 years.

2nd degree—18 months to 20 years.

1st degree—7 years to life, or death if the law permits.

The statutory maximums are left relatively high to provide considerable latitude to the court to deal with demonstrably dangerous persons and professional criminals.

Only the most heinous crimes, such as first degree murder, kidnapping with bodily harm, airplane hijacking, and treason would be included in the first degree classification.

Other felonies…would be classified in the other four degrees, depending upon the Legislature's judgment….

Probation would be permitted in the discretion of the court in all felonies except those of the first degree.

…The administration of good conduct credits is the responsibility of the director of correctional services.

VI. *The trial court judge will fix each defendant's sentence subject to conditions set forth below.*

In the case of 5th degree felons treated as misdemeanants commitment to the county jail shall be only as a condition of probation so that the court can retain jurisdiction to (a) insure postrelease supervision and (b) to eliminate the need for local parole boards which have proven generally ineffective and are wholly inoperative in some counties.

In those cases in which the judge chooses to commit the defendant to the custody of the State Department of Corrections this decision would be subject to certain limitations, including guidelines, reporting, and appellate review….

VII. *All legal sentences providing for commitment to the State Department of Corrections are divided into three classes.*

Class A sentences are those in which the prescribed period of incarceration in a State facility is in excess of 24 months. These would be subject to *automatic* review by the Sentence Review Division of the Court of Appeals.

Class B sentences are those in which the time prescribed is 24 months or less. These sentences would not be reviewable except in very exceptional cases and solely at the discretion of the Sentence Review Court.

Class C sentences are those in which the trial court judge chooses to place the defendant on probation, but provides that as one of the conditions of that sentence he would spend not less than 6 months nor more than 12 months in the custody of the State Department of Corrections. This alternative is suggested to relieve the county jails and to discourage long periods of confinement in such facilities.

VIII. *Post-institutional supervision is automatic as provided by law.*

Since under this system there would be no discretionary parole, and since most releasees from prison and similar correctional facilities require the kind of guidance and supervision conventionally provided for probationers and parolees, the following provisions are made:

(1) At the expiration of any sentence described above as Classes A, B, or C less good conduct credits, the offender would be released from custody mandatorily and referred to the probation department in the jurisdiction in which he (or she) expects to live. He would be treated thereafter just as if he were on probation from the superior court in that county. Such release would be mandatory but continued probationery freedom would be conditional upon good behavior.

(2) In case of Class A sentence the offender would be subject to 3 years of probationer supervision unless the sentence was life, in which case he would be subject to supervision for life, unless discharged sooner by the SRDCA.

(3) In Class B sentences the offender would be on probation for 18 months.

(4) In Class C sentences the period of postinstitutional supervision would be determined by the court at the time of sentence.

IX. *Revocation of mandatory release and discharge from sentence are functions of superior court judges.*

In the event the releasee should violate the conditions of his release, the court would be empowered after a hearing to recommit him to the Department of Corrections to serve out all or any part of the unexpired sentence.

Should the releasee be convicted of a new crime during the period of postinstitutional supervision, his instant sentence would stop running and the sentencing court could decide whether the unexpired part of the original sentence should be served concurrently or consecutively and whether if consecutively, that portion of the old sentence should be served in an institution or under probationary supervision....

The probation department having supervision of any releasee who is serving a Class A sentence should also be empowered to recommend to the court a reduction in the statutory period of postinstitutional supervision after 2 years of clean conduct and if the judge concurs, he could issue a final discharge after 24 months following release from the Department of Corrections facility.

X. *A State Sentence Review Court is established as a special division of the present State Court of Appeal.*

It will have five members who will be assigned from time to time by the Chief Justice of the State Supreme Court. It will have general and specific powers of oversight over the sentencing function of all courts with criminal jurisdiction in the State as set forth in the statute (1974b).

In addition, McGee's proposed new code specified details of selection and tenure for the proposed Appeal Court. He assigned the court the duties of establishing and regularly reviewing sentencing guidelines, and provided for the court to receive data on all felony sentencing in the state. He required that the court consider for review all sentences of over 24-months confinement, and had it advise the governor on all applications for Executive Clemency.

McGee's proposed new California sentencing plan, in my opinion, would achieve his goal of "maximum justice with minimum capriciousness" more fully than any alternative ever enacted, or to my knowledge, ever proposed. He concluded:

> The proposed system...overcomes the problem of lack of representation; it addresses...disparity in the imposition of long sentences. It also provides for revocation hearings to take place in the communities where the violations occur. *Perhaps most important of all it provides for continuing judicial supervision of the sentencing function by a higher court operating on a Statewide basis....*
>
> ...the entire system avoids...parole decision-making as an administrative function, and even discards...the word "parole." Confusion between..."parole" and "probation" has been annoying to both professionals and laymen, and..."parole" and "parolee" are more pejorative in the public mind than "probation" and "probationers." Under the new system all offenders under community supervision are simply *probationers....*
>
> ...The struggle between State and county governments over who should pay for what portions of the costs of the correctional system should be faced and settled by the Legislature....The question of financing correctional services...is not more insolvable than the financing of the public schools, mental health services, or any other set of related functions for which both State and local governments have a responsibility....
>
> The proposal...will...not...make the system either more punitive or more lenient. Its prime purpose is to bring order where

there is no order and...sentencing which can more nearly approximate the ideal of "Equal Justice under the Law" (1974b:10-11).

From 1970 on, the California legislature repeatedly attempted to
revise the state's sentencing system, and finally compromised disparate
viewpoints to pass the Determinate Sentencing Act of 1976, effective July
1, 1977. This new law, also in my opinion, much improves prior law, but
is grossly inferior to McGee's proposal. Yet several of its changes may
reflect his influence as one of the drafting committee's many consultants,
and it has other interesting innovations. As McGee summarized:

It repeals the old indeterminate sentences which provided a
minimum and a maximum term of imprisonment for each of some
300 offenses which were defined as felonies and for which
commitment to state prison was possible but not...mandatory.

The new law retains the essential features of the indeterminate sentence for all sentences of natural life and parolable at a
minimum term of imprisonment of seven calendar years or more.
In terms of numbers of cases, these sentences are proportionately
few and are chiefly those which are alternatives to the death
penalty (1978).

In other felony crimes, he noted:

...the court has a choice of three definite sentences. The expectation
is that the judge will choose the middle term unless mitigating
factors argue for the lower term or aggravating factors suggest...
the highest of the three. Either party to the proceedings may
present arguments in support of mitigation or aggravation, but the
judge may also take into considerations facts presented in the
probation officer's report. If he elects any of the three prison terms,
he must set forth his reasons in writing and inform the defendant.

Each definite sentence may be reduced not by discretionary
parole but by the reinstatement of the older concept of "good time"
credits....For each eight months served without forfeiture of time
for disciplinary infractions, the prisoner earns three months credit
and one month more for participation in required programs of
work and self-improvement. Thus, by good conduct and participation in...programs, a prisoner with a 3-year sentence will be
released in 2 years.(1978).

He also pointed out that the new law creates a Community Release Board (CRB), and added:

> After the automatic release, there is a period of 1 year of post-institutional supervision in all cases irrespective of the length of time served in prison, excepting those with natural life sentences; for the latter, the parole...period is 3 years. The CRB may in its discretion waive the postinstitutional parole....
>
> In...furtherance of the reduction of disparity, the (CRB) is required to review each case and to refer back to the court those it considers...disparate. The court may reduce but not increase the sentence....
>
> This board is not a parole board in the sense that it sets prison terms and grants paroles. It does have the duty to review each case to determine all actions and procedures affecting the forefeiture of good-time credits. This is the only sense in which it can affect parole releases, except in cases with natural life sentences with 7-year minimums....
>
> ...If the releasee's parole is revoked for cause other than conviction for a new crime, he or she may not be reimprisoned for longer than 6 months. This provision is more significant than it may appear...for it acts as a countermeasure to prevent prose-cutors with weak cases or crowded calendars from encouraging the substitution of parole violations for court conviction and sentence. Under the old law, it was not uncommon for a prisoner to serve more time for a series of parole violations than he had before his first parole release (1978).

McGee's proposal for a State Sentence Review Court as a special division of the Court of Appeals was not accepted, partly because, as he put it, "...the justices of the Court of Appeal, were naturally wary of the added workload and the unpredictable costs of such appellate reviews" (1978). Four compromises with his ideas went into the Act:

> First,...the legislature narrowed the range of imprisonment options for any one offense far more than many would have wished. Second, the sentencing judge is required to state the reasons for his sentencing choice on the record of the proceedings. Third, the Community Release Board was created in the executive branch...to serve as a monitor of the good-time credit system administered by the Department of Corrections, and to call to the attention of judges

it is commonly exercised on the basis of less information than judges possess; and, indeed, its exercise may depend less upon considerations of desert, deterrence, and reformation than upon a desire to avoid the hard work of preparing and trying cases. The discretion of American prosecutors, in short, has the same faults as the discretion of American judges and more (1978:69).

Noting that California's code revision was designed to stop judges m encouraging pleas of guilty in exchange for reduced penalties, but moted charge bargaining, Alschuler added:

The persistence of plea bargaining would yield the same disparity of outcomes, the same racism and classism, the same games-manship, and the same uncertainty (1978:71).

The California Judicial Council confirms that Alschuler's predic-n was valid:

After the operative date of the determinate sentencing law, July 1, 1977, dispositions by trial began to decrease and guilty pleas to increase relative to total dispositions in superior courts. This trend...continued after the adoption in June 1982 of Proposition 8, which included...new penalties.
    While it is impossible to say with any certainty that either statutory change is the cause of the increase in guilty pleas and decrease in trials, that conclusion is suggested by the stability of the trial percentage during the years before these changes (1989).

The quadrupling of California's prison population during 1980–92 ected many factors, but one of these, noted within a year of the new tencing system's 1978 start, was that the parole board was no longer ailable as a "safety valve" to alleviate overcrowding, as well as to uce patently excessive terms (Brewer et al., 1981; Clarke, 1983).
    John Conrad (1978) observed that under the old indeterminate tence law, "good time"—time off the sentence for good behavior in son—was "redundant"; its impact was negligible because the parole rd had so much power to fix the duration of confinement. Under the v law, since there is no parole discretion, good time may cancel up to f of the court's penalty: one-third off for good conduct plus one sixth self-improvement activities. This potentially major incentive, Conrad nplained, would only benefit society if the inmates could "sweat for

those cases which seem to the board not to have been ;
accordance with the intent of the law. The fourth
resolution introduced another wholly new element. Tl
"The Judicial Council of California is a constitutional b
by the chief justice of the Supreme Court. It is a prestig
with 21 members, most of whom are judges from
judicial levels....

California has devised an alternative to the...in
sentence....It is not, in the opinion of this observer, th(
wisest alternative that could have been devised, but
the temper of the times it came out better than migh
expected (1978:5–9).

As McGee predicted, the new law has been much
mainly by the enhancement of penalties, including more
mandatory minimums. Most notable was the passage o:
on the June 1982 ballot, which especially increased th(
repeat offenders. The revised code was enacted in 1976
cratic Governor Edmund G. (Jerry) Brown, Jr.; but pris(
rose mainly from the longer and more often mandatory
conservative Republican Governor George Deukmejian,
1983. He advocated longer prison terms, construction of
and capital punishment.

In commenting on this code revision, Professor Al
pointed out that it shifted sentencing power most of all to
although it purports to transfer the power from the jud;
board to the legislature by having the law specify the p(
type of offense. Alschuler predicted that the revised c
increasingly evaded by plea bargains occurring before fo
with the defendant informally agreeing to plead guilty if
does not use charges that fit the crime, but finds other cha
the law specifies lesser penalties. He added:

The exercise of prosecutorial discretion is more frequ
judicial discretion] made contingent upon a waive
tutional rights; it is generally exercised less openly; it is
to be influenced by consideration of friendship [w
lawyers—dg] and of reciprocal favors of a dubious ch
commonly exercised for the purpose of obtaining co
cases in which guilt could not be proven at trial; it is u
cised by people of less experience and less objectivity

it," by having opportunities to work hard at meaningful labor and beneficial studies. Such opportunities for self-improvement have too often been unavailable, he claimed, especially for the increasingly large proportion of prisoners placed in segregation due to either their own alleged danger to others, or the threats of others to them.

Robert Dickover reports that the Department, because of crowding of its institutions, is now constrained to maximize the number getting full good-time credits, but cannot give most inmates a realistic work schedule.[2] Ideally, with indeterminate sentencing, good time is applied only to the maximum sentence for just desert, allowing a parole decision on the minimum before release to be based more on prior criminality and on any evidence of self-improvement during imprisonment (Griset, 1991:16–17).

Capital Punishment as Seen by a Prison Administrator

California has always had the death penalty, and as head of the state's prison system, McGee repeatedly had to assure that such sentences were carried out. Yet even before his retirement from state employment, he wrote one of the most persuasive, profound, and original essays against capital punishment. The following quotations abbreviate his presentation:

> The basic arguments advanced for the death penalty are retribution, deterrence, and rehabilitation, with the latter stated negatively—that efforts at rehabilitation are largely fruitless....
>
> It is the unique deterrent value capital punishment is assumed to possess that provides the mainstay of the arguments for retention of the death penalty....
>
> ...studies...comparing homicide rates between jurisdictions with and without capital punishment...must inevitably bring any person who is more influenced by facts than by emotion to the conclusion that the argument for the death penalty as a deterrent is without merit....
>
> Then the argument turns slightly. The public must be protected from known killers....The killer must be exterminated because otherwise he will be released to kill again. Even life without possibility of parole is not certain....
>
> A damaging side effect has been, in the words of the California Supreme Court, that "the jury sometimes lamentably has 'tried' the Adult Authority" [then the California parole board for

adult males] because zealous prosecutors have heavily stressed the possibilities of parole. While...there have been instances when a paroled murderer killed again,...the rate of parole violation for the homicide group is the lowest of any offense category.

California annually has some 600 homicides. There are about 100 convictions...for which the defendant...could be sentenced to death. Approximately one-fifth are sentenced to death and...a tenth are ultimately executed....Minority race members are over-represented among those executed. The wealthy never reach Death Row.

This is more like Russian Roulette than the even hand of Justice.

A corollary set of arguments proclaim that the death penalty is necessary for the protection of prison personnel. All of them conveniently ignore the experience of states and countries without capital punishment.

...There are innumerable sanctions...short of death that... provide...effective control....

Experience shows that it is not the life-term prisoner who kills prison officers or inmates....

A review of all California prison homicides during the past two years shows that of the known killers, 50 percent had a maximum term of 10 years or less. Only one had a definite life sentence....

Perhaps the most dangerous person held in a California prison in modern times—a man who was known to have killed four persons and anxious to add to his score—wasn't sentenced to prison at all, but was being held for the Department of Mental Hygiene.

But perhaps the biggest fallacy of the argument that the death penalty protects prison officers is the implicit assumption that either those to be executed do not come to prison or are executed immediately upon arrival. Nothing could be further from the truth....

...One man spent more than 11 years on condemned row....The median is 15 months for those executed.

These long periods of confinement under sentence of death... create a whole series of management problems, but also certainly reduce any possible deterrent effect of the death penalty....

...proponents of capital punishment present two side approaches: capital punishment would be effective if we had but used it more, and what they call the "common sense" approach.

The first conveniently ignores thousands of years of bloody history and the second is actually nonsense.

Society *has* used the death penalty extensively. Only 150 years ago when the population of England and Wales totaled half that of California's population today there were more than 100 public executions in the London and Middlesex district alone. It has been stated that during the reign of Henry VIII...72,000 were executed in England....

...Furthermore, the death penalty was carried out in a variety of hideous ways well into the 19th century—...drawing and quartering, removal of the bowel and heart while the condemned was yet alive....

Capital punishment tried in enormous volume, in the most terrifying ways and as publicly as possible, failed.

The..."common sense" argument is epitomized in the following quotation of a...District Attorney...: "...the universal experience of mankind is that death is the most fearsome thing a human being can face and it, therefore, theoretically, logically, historically, and, as a matter of common sense, is the greatest deterrent."...

Yes, it's "common sense" to ignore history while citing it,....

One of the problems...is that great weight is given...the opinion of judges and lawyers who, because of the rigorous demands of their own specialty, have had little, if any, opportunity to study human behavior formally....

There is also the argument of cost. Why support some murderer for the rest of his life when we could execute him and save all that money....

...The actual costs of execution, the cost of operating the super-maximum security condemned unit, the years spent by some inmates in condemned status, and a pro-rata share of top level prison official's time spent in administering the unit add up to a cost substantially greater than the cost to retain them in prison the rest of their lives....

Thus, our studies indicate that just on the basis of prison costs alone, it would actually be cheaper to do away with the death penalty. When the other costs of death penalty cases are added— the longer trials, the sanity proceedings, the automatic and other appeals, the time of the Governor and his staff—then there seems no question but that economy is on the side of abolition.

Those favoring abolition also have their subsidiary arguments.

One is the ugly possibility of executing an innocent man. I don't know that this has...happened in California. We had one homicide case in 1959 where the convicted man...was later found unquestionably to be innocent. [There have been several in recent years—dg] Furthermore, death sentences have...been reduced to life by the courts on appeal. In at least two cases in the past 10 years acquittals resulted from appeals.

...in a number of cases stays of execution have come too late—the execution was underway...further proceedings might have resulted in a lesser sentence or even freedom.

These last-second stays are...harrowing aspects of administering the death penalty for both staff and condemned. It has become...almost a standard operating procedure for attorneys to rush into court, any court, five or 10 minutes before the scheduled execution, with a writ or an appeal, many of them without merit.... Sometimes this results in months of delay. Other times it produces an off-again, on-again situation that inflicts a frightful emotional strain on the prisoner.

...Why then, if these arguments are so persuasive has the California Legislature repeatedly refused to abolish capital punishment?

...There have been close votes. I think there have been a number of reasons for the "no" votes: Frequently some sensational...case has beclouded the broader issue; complex testimony concerning human motivation has been difficult to understand; the solid stand of peace officers and district attorneys *is* impressive; the press and bar largely favor retention; and many of the Legislators are accurately reflecting the attitude of their districts.

Unfortunately, the public view reflects far more of the cave man than the space man.

And, inevitably, as the witnesses defending capital punishment...proceed, they fall back on the argument of retribution although they deny this.

But these excerpts are fair samples of their testimony:

"...the murderer who has deliberately, wantonly, killed another man, woman or child, brutally, sadistically, in cold blood...men who have seen the... victims and their battered, mutilated bodies...men who have talked...to the loved ones left behind to grieve."

...Some crimes are so horrifying, so shocking to the human conscience that there seems to be no answer short of the death penalty. Indeed, some feel that even death...is too slight a penalty....

I have not been a stranger to violence or violent men. I have walked through the cooling blood of murdered men on more than one occasion. These experiences arouse in me, and I believe, in most normal men,...an elemental desire to take retributive action.

I've been physically assaulted in the course of my work and I know how it feels to want to return violence with violence. But, I knew too, that as a warden, my example might have profound effects on several hundred subordinates. It would be easy to turn loose a veritable storm of violence and brutality.

If my personal example might do this, of how much greater influence is the law itself? Unless the penal law itself provides restraint...,how can we be sure that the very measures we adopt to prevent violent crime may not, in fact, be contributing to it?

I believe that capital punishment is brutalizing and meets needs in the minds of men which are among their basest instincts....

We tend to be quite irrational about punishment. When punishment does not work, we cry for harsher punishment. This generally is even less effective....

Punishment...works best on the persons who need it least and frequently, not at all on the disordered personalities to whom it is most often directed....

I believe the basic problem is that having accepted punishment as the basic tool of the criminal law, the exceptions from punishment must be few. In efforts to define who these...exceptions should be...,the lawmakers become enmeshed in the concept of criminal responsibility....

The debate over free will...not only poses an insoluble problem, it may be a problem that we do not need to solve.... Punishment will be had in any event. The arrest, the trial, the notoriety, loss of reputation, the costs in money, are all punishment. Certainly any loss of liberty, the enforced separation from family and friends through institutionalization is a high penalty no matter how therapeutic the program. The practical question is, perhaps, how much more punishment do we need and what price should we pay for it?

The price we are paying for...excessive punishment is a continuing high rate of crime and a continuing high rate of failure by our correctional apparatus....

In selecting punishment as the basis for our criminal law, we not only yielded to an...atavistic emotion but...we picked an indirect method of accomplishing our objective...

What we really want to do is control human behavior. If we can do this through prevention, excellent. If we can do it through reforming the offender, fine. If we can't reform him, we can at least manage him. Manage him in an institution or out. Manage him by substituting external controls for the ones he lacks. Manage him by manipulating his environment....

...Punishment, whether it be the ultimate or the most minor penalty, should be a by-product of society's systems of control and not its central purpose. In this context capital punishment is both unnecessary and irrational (1964b).

Summary and Conclusion

An optimum division of criminal justice labor, McGee contended, would eliminate the distinctions between organizations concerned only with juveniles and those limiting their attention to adults. Also, all would be more consistently guided by the "separation of powers" as stated in the Constitution, that the legislative, judicial, and executive functions of government be assigned to independent persons or agencies. This separation of branches of power helps to maximize the check and balance system.

McGee wanted judges to make all decisions on the liberty of persons charged with crimes, including not only determination of guilt and penalties, but also decisions on parole and its revocation. He suggested that the term "probation" be broadened to include what is now called "parole," since decisions on granting, revoking, and administering the two are so similar. He would also have the same officials overseeing both. He also proposed that city, county, state, or federal departments of correction be part of the executive branch of government. They would administer all pre- and post-sentencing custodial facilities, as well as the supervision of probationers; instead, many detention places are now run by police, and others by judges. Some judges also administer large probation staffs, while cities, counties, states, and the federal executives control still other places and agencies.

Although such a division of labor was in the new sentencing code that McGee proposed to replace California's indeterminate sentencing system, the legislature's 1976 law had only a few of his specific proposals. It did include other innovations of similar orientation, but due to prosecutors' charge bargaining, some have had effects contrary to the legislators' intent.

Finally, McGee's opposition to death sentences was distinctive not only for his astute formulation of traditional arguments, but also for his perspectives based on problems of prison administration in a capital-punishment state.

7

McGee's Forecasts, and the Future of Corrections

In an article appropriately called "What's Past is Prologue," McGee presented a history of human reactions to criminals, and then made twelve forecasts, with the comment:

> Predictions of things to come are, of necessity, a combination of hard-headed logic and hopeful expectation. Those which follow are no exception (1969)[1].

A discussion of these 1969 anticipations or wishes (whatever they were), and of some trends that McGee did not mention, can usefully serve as a summary and conclusion for this book. It should be noted that many of these predictions were foreshadowed in McGee's "Farewell Address," the fifteen-page letter and over two hundred-page volume (written with Montilla) that he sent, about six weeks before his retirement, to newly elected Governor Ronald Reagan.

Reduced Confinement

The first of McGee's dozen predictions for corrections was:

> Fewer offenders, and especially the younger ones, will be confined for long periods in custodial institutions (1969).

He realized that when lawbreakers are confined together they tend to be preoccupied with adjusting to each other, and thereby, they increasingly share habits of speech and thought, including rationalizations for crime and derogations of law-abiders. This results from the most fundamental law of sociology and social anthropology, that I call the Law of Socio-cultural Relativity: **Social separation differentiates cultures.**

In diverse ways and at different rates, all cultures and subcultures change. Persons in an isolated group do not assimilate changes that occur among persons who are not isolated. That is how languages and shared beliefs become different among humans. That is also why, when prisoners adjust and assimilate into an inmate society, their thoughts and speech differ from those in law-abiding outside social circles. These differences handicap them in their post-release pursuits of a legitimate livelihood.

But McGee's anticipation of less confinement seems to have been only a wish. It contrasted sharply with what actually happened in subsequent years, especially during 1980–92, when the number of persons imprisoned more than doubled nationally, and quadrupled in California. (See Table 3.1).

The state's incarceration splurge partly reflected its growth in population, but it was mainly due to its conservative political leaders during this period. The leadership emphasized severe penalties, and a futile "war on drugs." California did little to offset growth of extreme poverty, broken homes, and homelessness during the economic recession of the late 1980s and early 1990s.

Although total national production grew during 1980–92 due to a hike in military expenditure, this growth was achieved by quadrupling the national debt, and reducing appropriations for education, health care, and aid to the poor. These trends increase economic inequality in both the short- and long-term (Mattera, 1990). Indeed, between 1973 and 1987 the median income of the poorest tenth of U.S. families with children declined 22 percent, while that of the richest tenth rose 23 percent (Karoly, 1993). Economic inequality, especially when associated with family breakup, is highly correlated with violent crime rates (Krahn et al., 1986; Sampson, 1987; Messner, 1989).

About one third of U.S. households now consist of one parent with one or more children. One quarter of U.S. children now live in poverty, and make up 40 percent of all persons below the poverty level. In urban areas, welfare payments hardly cover the cost of rent plus utilities, and food stamps cover only about three-fourths of food costs. This leaves nothing at all for clothing, health care, transportation, or entertainment. These situations foster homelessness, and a lack of a residential address makes one ineligible for routine welfare payments (Jencks, 1992:ch. 6).

About half of Aid for Dependent Children (AFDC) and general relief payments come from state and local, rather than federal funds, but some states and counties with the highest unemployment rates have made the most severe cuts. Los Angeles County slashed welfare payments for single adults from $341 per month in 1992 to $293 at the beginning of 1993, and to $212 in September of the same year. Los Angeles has high rents—even skid-row rentals for one room exceed $212. Homelessness in the county, estimated at 75,000 before the cut, rose as a consequence.

As a result of government payments being inadequate to meet their needs, or their other desires, practically all welfare recipients in our country have unauthorized non-welfare income. Although the social workers who supervise the distribution of welfare aid are supposed to prohibit this practice, they know that much extra income is essential, so they only intervene in extreme cases. Most of the non-welfare income is obtained from unofficial part-time jobs, or consists of gifts from friends or relatives, but some income is from criminal activities. Even those urban residents who work at today's minimum wage rate earn little more than they would receive from welfare aid (Jencks, 1992; Corbet,1993). These conditions promote welfare dependency, delinquency, and crime.

Perhaps even more conducive to crime than the economic and social handicaps of the so-called "underclass," especially for many blacks, has been their continued segregation from the rest of society. The cultural consequences of this segregation in slum-like ghettos are suggested by the Law of Sociocultural Relativity, and are well stated in a book aptly called *American Apartheid*:

Although poor black neighborhoods still contain many people who lead conventional, productive lives, their example has been overshadowed in recent years by a growing concentration of poor, welfare-dependent families that is an inevitable result of residential segregation....

By building physical decay, crime, and social disorder into the residential structure of black communities, segregation...also concentrates conditions such as drug use, joblessness, welfare dependency, teenage childbearing, and unwed parenthood, producing a social context where these conditions are not only common but the norm....

As a direct result of the high degree of racial and class isolation created by segregation, for example, Black English has become progressively more distant from Standard American English, and its speakers are at a clear disadvantage in U.S. schools and labor markets. Moreover, the isolation and intense poverty of the ghetto provides a...niche for the emergence of an "oppositional culture" that inverts the values of middle-class society. Anthropologists have found that young people in the ghetto experience strong peer pressure not to succeed in school, which severely limits their prospects for social mobility in the larger society. Quantitative research shows that growing up in a ghetto neighborhood increases the likelihood of dropping out of high school, reduces the probability of attending college, lowers the likelihood of employment, reduces income earned as an adult,...

Moreover, segregation confines these unpleasant byproducts of racial oppression to an isolated portion of the urban geography far removed from most whites (Massey and Denton, 1993:8–16).

Such segregation and its handicaps has also occurred extensively for other poor people of diverse ethnicity in many areas. McGee recognized its effects in the 1960s when he wrote of the "new ghettos" in his state's metropolitan areas:

> The new ghetto is a trap....
>
> The families that live there have a much lower income than those outside and a rate of unemployment that is two or three times as high. The proportion of adults that have finished school is 50 percent or more below that of the rest of California.
>
> The present school reflects the residential pattern so there is no leavening effect of pupils of other social and economic backgrounds....School attendance is less and studies have indicated that school achievement is less. The drop-out rate is much higher. Employment opportunities are lower.
>
> The difficulty of escape from this trap breeds a sense of alienation, of bitterness, and hopelessness.
>
> The lack of contact with the larger community means that minority views are solidified, that negative views of the social system and particularly law enforcement persist, and that they do not feel themselves part of the larger community.
>
> Unfortunately, this is compounded because the larger community scarcely knows the ghetto exists. We in the field of law enforcement and those in social welfare have a much better idea than most as to how the "other quarter" lives. But the suburban dweller who travels the freeway to his office and then home again has no idea (1963).

The effects on youth thought patterns from such isolation in a ghetto, with no job opportunities for those out of school, are especially criminalizing for youths in one-parent households, or where one or more parents have addiction problems or criminal records. The most attractive and readily available opportunities for many such youngsters are in the lawbreaking cliques and street gangs. Incarceration with more advanced offenders, intensifies their criminality. The resultant subculture among the most persistent and aggressive offenders, and its relationship to their typically diverse types of crimes, are well depicted by Jack Katz:

> "Career" robbers recall adolescent years dedicated to the perfection of "badass" identities, the key to which is the portrayal of a personal character that is committed to violence beyond calculations of legal, material, or even physical costs to oneself. They learn that what wins in a showdown...is not so much superiority in fighting skill or firepower but escaping the ghost of reason and continuing to attack when an opponent...will back off....
>
> Violent predators typically reside near other violent predators, on ghetto streets and in state confinement....In order to defend against surprise attacks, violent predators maintain a constant readiness for violence, often literally sleeping with a weapon under the pillow and driving with a gun in the glove compartment. In the context of this lifestyle, there are so many good reasons for anticipating situationally unprovoked attacks that a complementary, nonrational commitment to violence would itself be rational....
>
> Persistent offenders structure their sexual involvements along lines analogous to those governing their drug and alcohol use, in intense and episodic relationships....The biographies and autobiographies of especially hard-core, repeat offenders are full of accounts of "partying," a general celebratory, multiday episode involving illegal drugs and short-term understandings with prostitutes or girlfriends interested in sharing the fruits of some recent crime....
>
> To some commentators, the heavy alcohol and illicit drug use of serious offenders will seem causally crucial; to others, the offenders' transient sexual partnerships and their extreme "macho" style in posture and culture will stand out. But both lifestyle patterns help to maintain an adventuresome, sensually emphatic quality throughout the offender's life, and this appears to be more fundamental motivationally than either considered alone....[There] is a parallel relevance for the gambling metaphor...suggested by the interchangeability of terms among drug use, sexual practice,

and gambling events (e.g., drug dealers, craps players, and sexual partners seek "action," trying to "score" when they "go down"...); by evidence in the biographies of persistent robbers of gambling in their lives and in the lives of older men who were significant models for them...; and by the magical power of gambling to make a stretch of life into "action," something more fully embodied and more intensely realized than ordinary, mundane life (Katz, 1991; *see also* Katz, 1988).

Appreciation of the difficulties of reducing this criminal enculturation once it becomes advanced, as well as the research summarized in chapters 3 and 4, motivated McGee to stress:

(1) the classification of prisoners and parolees by pertinent differences among them;
(2) consequentially diverse types of programs for those differing in criminality, but helping all to build bonds with conventional persons and to prepare for legitimate employment;
(3) emphasis on community treatment as exclusively as possible for unadvanced offenders, but initial confinement, and remedial education and work for hardened offenders.

A policy begun in the U.S. during the 1930s of building public housing in huge projects that accepted only the very poor, and evicted residents whose income increased even moderately, tended to concentrate and segregate multi-problem families in these abodes. This led to delinquency and vandalism so extensive that many of the buildings were damaged to the point where they had to be prematurely abandoned and destroyed.

Much less conducive to crime are the "Section 8 subsidies," developed during the 1970s, whereby the government pays developers to set aside some units in apartment buildings, and in many neighborhoods, to lease to low-income tenants. The occupants then pay rent not in excess of 30 percent of their certified income, as in public housing, and the landlord receives a certificate to redeem for the additional payment by the government. Most Chicago welfare recipients are reported to get a Section 8 apartment within a year of applying, the same time delay as occurs in applying for a unit of a large public housing development in a much less desirable setting, and less time than is required with the longer waiting lists for small public housing developments (Jencks, 1992:219).

During the Bush Administration, with Under-secretary of Housing and Urban Development Jack F. Kemp, public housing construction was limited to smaller and more scattered projects, eviction of residents for becoming more prosperous ceased, and purchase of individual residences by the occupants was facilitated, as well as home improvement financing thereafter. These policies have been continued not only in public housing, but also in privately constructed residences developed with federal subsidies for the poor. In addition, there have been numerous efforts under the Clinton Administration to reverse the growth in the prior twelve years of extreme inequalities in family income, and to promote remedial education programs. But requested funds for such measures are sometimes curtailed by Congress.

Some places have reduced the confinement of criminals. This has been most dramatic for juveniles, with Massachusetts pioneering this practice, followed by Vermont, Utah, and other states, but not California. In 1972, social worker Jerry Miller, as head of the Massachusetts Department of Youth Services, closed all of its institutions. He sent the inmates either to their family homes, to foster homes, or to secure custody houses holding no more than fifteen youths, but gave all a higher quantity and quality of adult contacts (Coates et al., 1978; J. Miller, 1991; Krisberg and Austin, 1993: ch.5).

The consequences in Massachusetts, after some initial adjustments, has been lower recidivism rates and less costs than are experienced by other states. A recent comparison reports:

> Only 55 of every 100,000 youngsters in Massachusetts are in custody, contrasted with more than 450 of every 100,000 in California....
> The result is that in Massachusetts only 23% of those committed to the state's youth services programs are incarcerated as repeat offenders—contrasted with 63% for the California Youth Authority. And, despite the salaries required for intensive supervision of delinquents, the cost of running the system is nearly half the national average (Harris, 1993).

Increasingly established for young adult offenders in recent years are "boot camps," modeled on basic training for new recruits in the military forces. The inmates in these camps are very intensively worked, drilled, and trained for a few months in lieu of a longer term of incarceration. Such places have not proven clearly more reformative than traditional institutions for similar lawbreakers, but they seem promising if appreciable training is provided of a type that contributes to the offenders' post-release employment prospects. Also, they usually confine the offenders for shorter periods of time than prisons without greater recidivism rates; despite somewhat greater cost per month than prisons, the boot camps prove less costly per stay (MacKenzie, 1991; MacKenzie and Paren, 1992; Austin et al., 1993).

Growing rapidly as a substitute for jailing is a more restraining form of probation: house arrest with electronic monitoring. Used primarily for adults, each probationer is required to wear a device that signals a supervising office if he or she departs from home at times when it is not permitted.

Such monitoring usually costs the government much less than jailing, particularly if the offender must pay for all, or some, of the cost of this type of surveillance. Especially for alcoholic or drug-abusing lawbreakers who have poor employment records but no professional criminality, electronic monitoring is followed by lower recidivism rates than similar offenders have if either jailed or given less supervised ordinary probation. When electronically monitored, such probationers work more, carouse less, are likely to improve their family relationships, and build bank accounts more than do comparable probationers who are not monitored (Glaser and Watts, 1991; Jolin and Stipak, 1992; Lilly et al., 1992).

Electronic interlock devices, mentioned while discussing alcoholism in chapter 3, attach to an automobile's ignition to prevent the engine from starting unless an alcohol-free breath is blown into its breath analyzer. These have already been proven more effective than license suspension in reducing recidivism for drunken driving (Morse and Elliott, 1992). Electronic interlock devices will probably be imposed more often for driving offenses, as a condition of probation in lieu of jail or with a reduced jail sentence.

Also expanding, and reducing confinement slightly, is use of fines instead of incarceration, or as supplements to shorter than customary jail or prison terms. Especially promising for this purpose is the day fine, long used in Scandinavia and some other nations, to reduce the unequal financial burden that fines impose when the same fixed amount is demanded by the court from anyone who breaks a particular law, regardless of differences in income among the lawbreakers. With a day fine, the judge requires that each offender pay a specified number of days' earnings. Then deductions are made for minimum necessities and for support of dependents, if any. Thus, a richer offender pays more than a poorer one, but their burden from the fines is more equal than it would be otherwise. Day fines reduce recidivism rates more than do either traditional fines or confinement penalties for similar offenders (Albrecht, 1984; Hillsman, 1990; Winterfield and Hillsman, 1993).

These sentencing trends may promote the ultimate realization of McGee's initially very erroneous prediction of diminished confinement. This is likely only if crime rates are also reduced by more motivation and facilitation of schooling for youth, better family conditions, and aid for the poor that reduces their segregation, and increases their employment.

Increased Preparation of Prisoners for Post-release Life

The second of McGee's predictions for the future of corrections was:

> The programs of custodial institutions will place greater emphasis on preparation for release and reintegration into normal society and less on the prevention of escapes and on economic production, unless the latter contributes to occupational competence (1969).

He had recognized the tendency for both prison staff and inmates to be preoccupied with their own immediate prospects, and to be unconcerned about the long-term societal consequences of their activities. The most immediate dangers to the job security of wardens and other prison officials are inmate disorder, violence, or escape; not post-release recidivism rates. Indeed, little effort is made to keep track of such rates.

I believe that most top officials in prisons today would, if candid, agree with the 1934 assertion of Court Smith, then warden of Folsom Prison: "Probably the time will never come when discipline is not the most important concern of any prison."[2] Although punishments for rule violations persist, reliance on individual and group counseling as a means of getting prisoners to conform to disciplinary requirements is perhaps greater today than in the 1930s, primarily because officials have learned that these programs create order in the institution.

John DiIulio points out that because prison officials have mostly an "institutional perspective," they "evaluate programs not mainly in terms of what they do to reduce the likelihood of recidivism or otherwise affect inmates' post-release behavior but as institutional management tools" (DiIulio, 1991:114). He asserts, persuasively, that when conservative political leaders during the 1980s declared that prisons were for punishment, not treatment, most prison officials agreed, but the prisons retained the treatment programs as a means of keeping inmates manageable.

In addition, legislators, deciding on correctional budget appropriations, are more impressed by thrifty production of goods or services that the state needs than by work or other programs to reform inmates. On the other hand, the inmates, as indicated by citations of Toch's research in chapter 3, tend to be more preoccupied with finding a safe niche in prison than with long-term self-improvement. Chapter 3 details how McGee was preoccupied with promoting education, work experience, and beneficial visits to prepare prisoners for post-release integration into law-abiding society, but he was especially stymied by political pressures of business and union interests from providing adequate work for inmates.

The preparation of prisoners for a legitimate post-release life does not seem to be currently growing. Indeed, it has been recently contended that: "It is the duty of prisons to govern fairly and well within their own walls. It is not their duty to reform, rehabilitate, or reintegrate offenders into society" (Logan and Gaes, 1993). This perspective is epitomized in the slogan, now popular among prison officials, and credited by McGee to James V. Bennett, long the Director of federal prisons: "Criminals are sent to prison as punishment, not for punishment."[3] This slogan is uttered by many officials as an excuse for abandoning interest in conforming to research findings on what works best for reforming inmates, and for not maintaining research on this issue. Contrary to viewpoints presented in chapter 5, some academic criminologists support this view by perpetuating Martinson's initial failure to note salient contrasts in evaluation results for diverse kinds of offenders (see Glaser, 1994).

Small Size and Urban Locations for Correctional Institutions

McGee's third prediction for the future of corrections was:

> The new correctional institutions for both youths and adults will be much smaller, perhaps less than a hundred residents each, and will be located in cities, not on farms as has been our tradition (1969).

In the 1920s and 1930s, when a bigger-is-better perspective led cities to compete to have the tallest skyscrapers, state prisons were also expanded to record size. Michigan's Jackson and Illinois' Joliet-Stateville penitentiaries ultimately exceeded 5,000 inmates for normal housing capacity, while Missouri's Jefferson City and California's San Quentin were near 4,000 (McKelvey, 1977:282–83). Since 1980 especially, all have frequently been filled well above these normal capacities.

But as indicated in chapter 3, McGee sought smallness. When he could not get it, he divided larger institutions into distinct sections that could be run as though separate prisons. Smallness makes it easier to separate prisoners for either reformation or managerial purposes (for example, by dispersing gangs, keeping aggressors away from potential victims, or simply grouping inmates by work or school assignments). Smallness also makes it easier for staff to communicate with prisoners individually, and thus to know them personally. For these reasons, smallness can aid in control, reformation, and efficiency.

McGee also expanded the number of small "halfway houses" in California, most of which he called "work furlough centers." Prevailing resistance to having convicts reside in neighborhoods prevented or slowed the opening of many halfway houses, and completely blocked most efforts to construct larger urban prisons, even in industrial areas.

McGee's prediction that newly constructed correctional institutions would be smaller than old ones has been validated in most states. However, the only location where construction of a new facility is politically feasible is usually either a remote area anxious for more job opportunities, or most often, on state-owned land adjacent to older institutions.

Federal prisons have a larger number of halfway houses in big cities, often as segments of a larger establishment, such as a YMCA hotel. These halfway houses are often made places for serving short sentences, conditional on good conduct, so that they are essentially urban extension of state and federal prisons that are almost all in more rural locations. However, the residents of halfway houses have considerable freedom to depart during the day and sometimes at night to work, visit families, or for other legitimate reasons.

Many elderly prisoners serve most of their multi-year sentences in California's urban work furlough centers. Some have incomes from pensions or social security from which they are expected to pay for all or part of their room and board, as do the employed occupants of the halfway houses serving the last few months of their prison sentences. There are also many residential places in our cities for delinquents committed to county or state custody by juvenile courts, although they are more often in probation camps located in outlying rural areas. However, I know of no clear evidence that traditional types of prisons that confine inmates for nearly all of their pre-parole terms are increasingly in urban locations, as McGee seems to have forecast in his earlier-quoted third prediction.

Blurring of Distinctions Between
Institutional and Community Corrections

One reason for difficulty in seeing a clear shift of correctional institutions to urban locations is the growing validity of McGee's fourth prediction:

> There will be less and less of the sharp dichotomy between incarceration and parole or probation supervision. Offenders will move in and out among varying degrees of restraint. Work and training furloughs, week-end sentences, halfway houses, and similar community-based programs will become more common and more varied (1969).

This account of the future closely fits the foregoing discussion of small size and urban location of correctional institutions. Much of the Youth Authority's Community Treatment Project, described in chapter 4, which maintained both confinement facilities and community supervision offices, fits McGee's prediction. The parole agents were given leeway to return their wards to custody for a few days while they counseled the wards and investigated alleged serious violations, without having them formally charged as violators and terminating their release. This flexibility is approximated in many halfway houses that gradually grant more and more home leave to their residents if they behave properly, before finally releasing them completely, but this process may be reversed if the wards return late, drunk, or under the influence of drugs, or seriously misbehave.

Weekend sentences in jail have been tried in some jurisdictions, but sheriffs running the jails object because of difficulties in staffing for large day-to-day fluctuations of inmate population. House arrest with electronic monitoring permits maximum blurring of the distinction between imposing restrictions on liberty and permitting freedom for legitimate activities. I know of a 1993 case in Massachusetts where the judge permitted such monitored house arrest as a substitute for legally mandated confinement traditionally served in a house of correction.[4] This surveillance technology was not available when McGee was alive, and he did not anticipate it, but it seems to fulfill his fourth prediction.

McGee's fifth and sixth predictions largely overlap the fourth one, on blurring of distinctions between institutional and community corrections. The fifth was:

Probation services will expand, but they will be better supported and will include a much wider variety of programs, including hostels, group homes, training programs, job placements, sheltered workshops, psychiatric services, and special counseling (1969).

The sixth made such a forecast for parole:

Post-institutional supervision (parole) will also exhibit changes in variety and character similar to those in the community programs for probationers (1969).

McGee, in his 1967 "Farewell Address" to Reagan, said that 83 percent of offenders serving county penalties and 48 percent of those under state sentences were then in community programs, rather than in institutions; he advocated raising these figures by 1975 to 90 and 66 percent, respectively (McGee and Montilla, 1967). But neither probation nor parole have experienced the expansion and improvement that he advocated and predicted. The supervisory staffs have larger caseloads, and fewer resources for assistance other than those that replace and reduce the cost of confinement, such as work furlough centers and halfway houses. Most of these programs, however, are not run by probation or parole offices, but by agencies that also administer traditional confinement institutions.

McGee's recommended Model Code for sentencing reform in California, presented in chapter 6, would largely eliminate the distinction between probation and parole by making the courts responsible for granting or revoking either one. He would then call all supervision of conditionally released offenders "probation," whether in lieu of a confinement term, or only for the last portion of it. Departments of correction, state or local, would supervise the releasees, rather than the courts. The releasees would all be called "probationers"; the terms "parole" and "parolee" would become obsolete.

Replacement of Parole Boards by More Professional Release Tribunals

The foregoing forecasts of changes in probation and parole supervision were linked to McGee's seventh prediction, on parole boards:

The character, composition, and function of parole boards will change. These boards, made up largely of lay persons appointed by state governors, are seldom well qualified for their decision-making tasks, and, to compound the problem, they are peculiarly vulnerable to the most reactionary influences in the society, which do not support the majority concept of rehabilitation as opposed to retribution (1969).

He followed this prediction by a somewhat vague eighth forecast, on parole board replacements:

New forms of disposition tribunals, as substitutes for the conventional "sentencing" by judges and the term-fixing and paroling functions of lay parole boards will be developed (1969).

What seems to be involved here is McGee's concern that there be more "equal justice under law," the slogan on the U.S. Supreme Court Building that he liked to quote. He was troubled by the limited competence of any single category of persons to make optimum release or confinement decisions, and the need for checks and balances on their authority to decree or alter penalties.

McGee expressed his respect for the training of lawyers, and for their consequent commitment to due process, careful weighing of evidence, and fairness. This respect is the foundation for the proposal, in his Model Code (presented in chapter 6), that courts be the agencies to grant or revoke probation or parole, rather than having this done either by boards of lay persons or by correctional executives.

Yet McGee's concern about the diversity of judges, and their frequent inconsistencies, led to his code calling for:

(1) development of sentencing guidelines that limit judicial discretion to deviate from standard penalties;
(2) a sentencing review division of the state Court of Appeal, to monitor sentencing and release decisions for evidence of gross irregularities, and to rule on complaints about them.

Court of Appeal members declined this role in 1977, but the Judicial Council of California was created partially to fulfill it.

There is now, to my knowledge, no clear evidence that the changes in sentencing and parole that McGee predicted are materializing. Several states and the federal government have eliminated or reduced parole boards, and have commissions to issue sentencing guidelines, and monitor sentencing, but none have a clearly different new type of tribunal for sentencing. The parole boards that survive are not clearly different from their predecessors. Many courts may sentence criminals to life confinement without parole, but they do not make other parole decisions.

Consolidation of Community-based Correctional Programs

McGee's ninth prediction is another that seems desirable, and that he greatly emphasized in his "Farewell Address," but it is not rapidly being realized:

Community-based programs must make more and more use of related community resources, both public and private. To do this, the organization and management of the correctional services must be consolidated and co-ordinated in each community. It is now the rule rather than the exception in major cities, in an area, say, ten miles square, to find from five to ten separate governmental agencies (federal, state, county, and city) supervising several thousand probationers and parolees of all ages and both sexes. There is no valid excuse for the cost, confusion, and inefficiency of this arrangement (1969).

While there has been some local consolidation in several metropolitan areas, one must conclude that McGee's complaints here are still warranted.

More Computerized Criminal Justice Information Systems

As chapter 3 indicated, soon after McGee came to California he gave the criminal justice system leadership in the quality and efficiency of its criminal justice records and statistics. He repeatedly stressed their importance, and their growth was his tenth prediction:

More and more attention will be given to the development of information systems making use of modern computer technology so that decision-makers throughout the justice system can operate on a basis of facts instead of opinion and guesswork (1969).

McGee wrote this when computerized records and statistics compilation were quite primitive compared to their present development. These systems are still rapidly growing and improving, but for many, empirical generalizations made in discussing the qualities of criminal justice agencies, one must still rely heavily on subjective "opinion and guesswork."

To some extent, probably all states now employ computers for collecting and tabulating criminal justice data. The Bureau of Criminal Justice Statistics in the U.S. Department of Justice helps to improve this activity not only by its advisory publications, but also through cash grants to state and local criminal justice agencies in response to their applications for specific types of assistance (Bureau of Justice Statistics, 1992a, 1992b). The federal government and some states are much more advanced than others in this development.

Increased Guidance by Empirical Research

McGee had high hopes for research, on which he focused in his eleventh prediction:

Empirical research methods will be employed more and more as the means of defining and refining the problems of crime and delinquency and of evaluating and testing the effectiveness of programs (1969).

As chapters 3, 4, and 5 detailed, McGee pioneered in the promotion of experimental methods for testing correctional practices and policies. He also appreciated the functions of theory in the development of science, and therefore, most of California's experimental innovations were guided by explicit theories. This was especially true of studies conducted by the research staff of the Youth Authority and the Department of Correction.

In recent years there has been an effort by the federal Bureau of Justice Statistics to make knowledge from criminological research more cumulative by having data from prior studies available for re-analysis by other scholars. This has been done because of a requirement that all federally-funded studies submit computerized data files to the National Archive of Criminal Justice Data, operated under contract by the Inter-university Consortium for Political and Social Research of Ann Arbor, Michigan. These archives also have data from sources that were not federally funded. This information covers almost every topic in criminology, and ranges from very limited studies by academicians and others, to routinely collected police, court, and correctional statistics. It is too early to assess the utility of this compiled information for testing theory or practice, but it should become increasingly evident (Bureau of Justice Statistics, 1993).

Chapter 5 indicated that what is especially needed is routine compilation of evaluation statistics on correctional programs for different types of offenders, using for this purpose the increasingly computerized criminal justice information on attributes and recidivism rates of individual cases. This must include:

(1) compiling statistics on the extent to which programs achieve their immediate service goals, for example, providing academic and vocational education;
(2) measuring attainment of intermediate goals by these services, such as the scholastic attainment scores, skills and diplomas that offenders of different types achieve;
(3) relating these data to the ultimate goals of reducing recidivism rates and increasing lawful employment, for various types of offenders.

Studies summarized in chapters 3, 4 and 5 indicate that the most "amenable" offenders, those seeking help to change their lifestyles, will have less recidivism if given good programs of individual counseling, training, and various types of positive reinforcement, often more effective if provided only in community treatment programs. The studies also show, however, that the "unamenable," those most criminalized and resistant to change, have lower recidivism rates if the above types of programs occur during and after a term of confinement.

The "New Corrections" as Less Elusive for Offenders and More Protective of the Public

In his final prediction, McGee envisioned corrections of the future as still imperfect, but as much more consistent and infallible than that prevailing in his day. He asserted:

From the standpoint of the offender who would seek to escape the consequences of his behavior, the "New Corrections" will be far more difficult to evade than is the case under our present system; conversely, for those who need help, professionally competent assistance will be provided, and the long-term needs for public protection will be better served (1969).

By the "New Corrections," McGee seemed to be referring to what might exist if and when all the changes he forecast are achieved. By an offender escaping "the consequences of his behavior," McGee was perhaps concerned with the high rates of non-arrest, non-conviction, too-lenient sentencing, and inappropriate parole for some advanced law-breakers, especially for leaders of organized crime and major white-collar criminals, of whose non-prosecution or mild sentences he some-times complained. Yet the major focus of all his work was on protecting the public by trying to manage ordinary offenders and their circum-stances, both to foster their reformation, and to control them quickly if they did not reform.

Changes that McGee Failed to Foresee

McGee, of course, did not anticipate all the important develop-ments in corrections that occurred after his 1969 predictions. Electronic monitoring and interlock devices, already mentioned as significant inventions, post-date his predictions. Yet as they reduce use of institu-tional confinement, and blur its distinction from community corrections, they promote many changes that he did forecast.

Another growing development which McGee did not include in his predictions is the operation of many county and state prisons, as well as other correctional facilities, by private firms. As reported in chapter 1, soon after California gained statehood in 1850, its first prison, which became San Quentin, was begun by a private individual under contract with the state to build and run it. This practice was then customary throughout the nation, but because of the consequent inhumane con-ditions and corruption, California, in 1879, became the first state to terminate such arrangements. Eventually, all states did likewise. Yet today, many states have come full circle to reestablish private prisons, with predictions that it will become the norm everywhere.

Correctional institutions operated by private parties are still contro-versial, but objective and rigorous evaluations indicate that they often save money for governments, while providing services as good or better than those by the public agencies they replace. Economy, however, seems to be their main attraction to policy makers. They also can be built quickly because private contractors are not obligated to the time-consuming and often costly bidding procedures normally required for government buildings. These factors explain their strong footholds in many locations (*see*, Logan, 1990; McDonald, 1990; Logan, 1992; Bow-man, et al., 1993; Ethridge and Marquart, 1993).

Corrections Corporation of America, founded in Nashville, Tennessee in 1983 by the same group of investors who own Kentucky Fried Chicken, is now the largest firm in this field. In 1993, the corporation was reported to own or operate four county jails, two juvenile detention centers, two penal work camps, two alien detention units, and two minimum-security state prisons. The corporation makes a profit despite the fact that it does run all of Tennessee's prison system. Several other firms operate one or more state prisons, including two penitentiaries in Texas. Collectively, private facilities incarcerate over 20,000 prisoners, but they comprise only about 2 percent of the nation's total incarceration capacity (McCrie, 1993).

Some critics of private prisons have expressed fear of "lowballing," the practice of submitting a low-price bid to receive a contract, then steadily raising charges as the government becomes dependent on the private firm and cannot readily replace its services. Thus far, this does not seem to have occurred in modern times, although it can be alleged whenever higher rates are requested at contract renewal time.

Some warn of government monetary liability for wrongdoing by private prison operators—such as denying inmates their legal rights, recklessly killing an inmate, or other offenses. But this can be covered in well-drafted contracts that make the prison operators liable for any of their wrongdoings, and requires that they buy insurance that guarantees payment if liabilities arise (Joel, 1993; Cooper, 1993).

Perhaps the most persuasive argument for expansion of privately run prisons is that they can provide a "yardstick of economy and efficiency" for assessing publicly operated facilities (Cikins, 1993). This implies that maintaining a mixture of public and private prisons provides what in the health-care field has been called "managed competition." This competition keeps each facility striving to operate more satisfactorily than the others. Such competitive mixing now seems likely to be the "wave of the future" in all types of correctional administration, and in many other traditionally government functions.

Still another trend post-dating McGee's retirement, and not mentioned by him, is the employment of more women in all staff positions of prisons for men. Currently, they comprise 15 to 20 percent of employees in such institutions in California. There has been, as could be expected, much resistance to this change by many of the male staff. Situations occurred where male staff have harassed female officers, sometimes in front of inmates, with the prisoners encouraged to join in. Law suits brought by women employees against the state for sexual harassment cite many such allegations, but the potential economic cost of these suits to the state has prompted efforts to eliminate these offenses. I know of no rigorous evaluation of the effects of female staff in men's prisons, but impressions of many that they improve the language prevailing among both employees and inmates may mean that they help prepare the prisoners for better post-release adjustment in law-abiding circles.

Somewhat related is the development of "co-ed prisons," officially called "co-correctional facilities." These facilities allow men and women inmates to mingle for many activities. Although female prisoners in many states had previously been held in structures within the walls of institutions for males, the women were kept completely apart from the men at all times. Only a few facilities for juvenile delinquents, mostly in the South, had long housed boys and girls in separate quarters, but allowed them to mingle in classrooms and workplaces.

Co-ed arrangements for adult prisoners were pioneered by the federal prison system in 1971, starting at its Correctional Institution at Morgantown, West Virginia. The practice was then rapidly expanded in the same year after a riot at the Alderson, West Virginia federal prison for women; 45 alleged leaders of the disturbance were transferred to the newly opened federal correctional institution at Fort Worth, Texas, which was only partially filled, and held only men (Keve, 1991:227–78).

I happened to visit this institution twice, first in 1972, and again a year or two later. On both occasions, staff and inmates with whom I talked were quite supportive of the co-ed arrangements, agreeing that it improved the language and conduct of everyone there. Threat of transfer of any inmate who severely misbehaved to a one-sex institution helped to promote good conduct. Co-ed activities included not only work and school, but also dances and other recreational activities, with no greater intimacy than hand-holding allowed. The Fort Worth correctional institution experienced its first pregnancy about a year after opening, but the prospective mother was transferred to a prison for women, where many inmates arrive already pregnant; the babies, born either in the prison or under guard at a nearby hospital, are soon released to relatives of the mother, or placed in homes by welfare agencies. However, there has been a movement to keep the babies with their mothers even if imprisoned for a year or more.

At one time the federal system had three co-ed prisons, then claimed that segregation by gender was inefficient; they now retain co-corrections only at Fort Worth. Massachusetts and a few other states have also tried this system, but California has not. Criminologist Edith Flynn concludes:

When we examine the various studies…,it can be said unequivocally that co-educational institutions seem to be more manageable than traditional institutions. They have less inmate and staff violence, fewer problems of homosexuality, better living conditions, more internal freedom, substantially reduced tensions, fewer grievances, and more "normalcy," than any other institutional modality in corrections" (1980).

There are several other possible developments in corrections that McGee hoped for, and assessed as highly desirable, but did not include in his predictions. For example, as chapter 3 explained, he wanted very much to provide work to keep all prisoners fully occupied at tasks that would prepare them for employment in their post-release lives. He also wanted to make it possible for all inmates to further their education, both academic and vocational, during their confinement.

McGee tried, with only partial success, to give all prisoners incentives for work and study, especially wages at a level that would increase over time if they worked well, and if they gained academic diplomas or vocational certifications. Perhaps he did not venture to forecast such developments because he deemed them improbable in the political settings of his time, despite his viewing them as investments that if pursued well, could yield public benefits in excess of their cost.

Although McGee advocated a period of supervision in the community after release from prison, he shared with John Conrad misgivings about traditional supervision methods in parole and probation. The basic problem, well set forth in Conrad's 1979 essay "Who Needs a Doorbell Pusher?", is the difficulty of one person combining surveillance and assistance concerns. The rapport needed for assistance to released offenders is impaired by the fact that the assister is pressured to check that the releasee is not breaking rules or committing new crimes. The development of relationships of mutual trust needed to assist a releasee effectively is impeded by the detective-like continuous suspicion needed for effective surveillance.

Accordingly, few supervision officers do both jobs well. Conrad proposed a separation of these two roles. Agents of a social work type would check to see which parolees or probationers need help, and try to build good relationships with them while giving feasible aid when warranted, but also teaching the releasees how to meet their needs themselves. Detective-type agents would check to see which probationers and parolees were reverting to crime, and incidentally, be less concerned with minor rule violations than with serious lawbreaking.

Conrad credits McGee with ultimately sharing his negative reaction to traditional parole, but the dual type of supervision was not an explicit McGee prediction.

Before concluding, it should also be noted that McGee repeatedly asserted that crime reduction would not come primarily from improving corrections or other components of the criminal justice system, but from more fundamental changes in our total society. He liked to make statements that were roughly like the following more recent ones, which are more precise than his earlier "guestimates" because they are based on recently improved statistics of crime victimization:

> ...with every 1,000...burglaries: More than 600 are never reported to the police, 960 do not result in arrest, 987 do not lead to conviction for burglary, and some 990 are never sentenced to jail or prison. Of those who are sentenced, not all are actually locked up, because of jail and prison overcrowding....
>
> The fallout...is even greater for some other crimes. For example, the National Crime Survey estimates 21 million larcenies nationally in 1990, but only 61,918 were sentenced to incarceration for larceny (3 per 1,000) (Felson, 1993:9).

In McGee's Presidential Address to the American Prisons Association in 1943, before he had even begun employment in California, he advocated classification of prisoners to permit individualized programs and casework for them, but added:

> The family doctor at the bedside or the surgeon at the operating table represents individual treatment, but far more lives have been saved by the less dramatic work of the public health doctor who ensures the safety of our water and our milk, and concerns himself with the elimination of the germ-bearing hosts of epidemic disease (1943:109).[5]

He repeatedly told general audiences, throughout his career, not only that very small proportions of actual lawbreakers are sent to correctional agencies, and that at this stage it is most difficult to change them, but that offense rates can be more effectively reduced by altering the home and community conditions that evoke crime.

McGee's pioneering did not fully achieve all of his objectives or wishes, either those explicitly specified in his predictions or the others that he stated elsewhere or only implied. Yet he left his accomplishments, especially in research, as a model to repeat, and to surpass. His main goals are a legacy and a challenge for his successors: Benefit all of humanity by combating the causes of crime, and by preparing convicts for law-abiding lives.

Notes

Chapter 1

1. Testimony by Kenyon J. Scudder, October 19, 1957, at a hearing of the State Personnel Board, on salary increases for group supervisors and other prison staff. Scudder was then retired from California state employment, but was Director of Field Services for the Osborne Association, a correctional reform organization. *See* Scudder, 1952, for his account of his prior career, and his viewpoints on many correctional issues.

Chapter 2

1. From letter by R. A. McGee Jr. to Glaser, September 8, 1993.

2. Most of the biographical material on McGee in this book is from McGee's (1976a) contribution to the Earl Warren Oral History Project. It is a transcript of lengthy interviews with McGee, done on three separate days in 1971, 1972, and 1973. The transcriptions were reviewed by the participants. McGee's son, Richard A. McGee Jr., has checked and supplemented the biographical material in this chapter.

3. From letter by Richard A. McGee Jr. to Glaser, August 14, 1993.

4. Transcribed from K. Nelson's June 15, 1993 tape-recorded communication to Glaser.

5. Transcribed from D. Brewer's September 8, 1980 tape-recorded interview of Moore.

6. This is from an undated fourteen-page manuscript, *A New Force in the War on Crime*, issued by the Institute for the Study of Crime and Delinquency, several copies of which were in McGee's papers. This document not only states plans for the institute, but also details the additions and departures of prominent individuals such as board or staff members, since the Institute's founding in 1959.

Chapter 3

1. The quotations designated "McGee 1953a" are from *Proceedings of the 1953 Annual Congress of Corrections*, reprinted with permission of the American Correctional Association, Laurel, MD.

2. From letter by J. W. L. Park to Glaser, May 31, 1993.

3. From letter by J. W. L. Park to D. Halley, dated January 21. 1992, copy sent to Glaser in 1993.

4. From undated correspondence by K. Nelson to Glaser, received July 6, 1993.

5. For an excellent account of Black Muslim prison groups' changing their emphasis from what initially seemed to be militant rebellion against whites into effective inculcation of conventional non-criminal values, that I also observed in Illinois and Federal prisons. *See* J. Jacobs, 1979.

6. From letter by J. W. L. Park to Glaser, May 31, 1993.

7. From letter by L. Bennett to Glaser, July 21, 1993.

8. From notes sent by N. Holt to Glaser, August 4, 1993.

9. The quotations designated "McGee 1939," are from Richard McGee, *Correctional Education Today*, reprinted with permission of the American Correctional Association, Laurel, MD.

10. Transcribed from the June 15, 1993 tape-recorded comments sent by K. Nelson to Glaser.

11. From notes sent by N. Holt to Glaser, August 4, 1993.

12. From letter by L. Bennett to Glaser, July 21, 1993.

13. A July 14, 1993 *Los Angeles Times* article on the twenty-four year follow-up by Anglin's UCLA group (Hser, et al., 1993), reports that the interviewers frequently found that those who persisted in heroin use also regularly shared needles, despite their awareness of the risk from AIDS. The newspaper adds that in a telephone interview, Professor Herbert Kleber of Columbia University estimated that nationally there were then 600,000 to 750,000 persons who use heroin "frequently."

14. From R. Dickover's marginal comments, in August 1993, on a draft of this book.

15. *Ibid*.

16. From letter by L. Bennett to Glaser, July 21, 1993.

17. From letter by L. Wilkins to Glaser, May 22, 1993.

18. From letter by J. W. L. Park to Glaser, May 31, 1993.

19. From letter by L. Bennett to Glaser, July 21, 1993.

20. Transcribed from D. Brewer's May 11, 1981 tape-recorded interview of Oberhauser.

21. Transcribed from D. Brewer's March 30, 1982 tape-recorded interview of McGee.

22. From copy of letter by J. W. L. Park to D. Halley dated January 21, 1992, sent to Glaser in 1993.

23. This is the American Law Institute definition, that combines language of M'Naghten, Durham, and "control" rules, but adds the requirement that justifications for acquittal on grounds of insanity include evidence of mentally disturbed behavior other than that of the crime. *See* A. Goldstein, 1983.

24. Described in numerous articles in the *New York Times* October 21, November 8, 9, 10, and 11, 1973.

25. Since this writing, an institution for offenders requiring medical care, similar to that at Vacaville, has been established adjoining the Chino prison for prisoners from the southern part of the state.

26. From letter by L. Bennett to Glaser, July 21, 1993.

27. Transcribed from D. Brewer's March 4, 1982 tape-recorded interview of McGee.

Chapter 4

1. From letter by J. W. L. Park to Glaser, May 31, 1993. The transfer of parole supervision to the Department of Corrections, and the tensions among personnel, are well described in Takagi, 1967.

2. Percentages on types and outcomes presented are only for 1961–69 cases in the Sacramento-Stockton area; San Francisco data were unavailable for the project publications, but were reported to be similar to those for Sacramento-Stockton. The description here, including all the quotations, are from T. Palmer, 1974. To make it easier to read, however, this presentation rearranges the sequence of details presented in the text, the footnotes and appendices of that article, and reduces the use of acronyms.

3. From letter by L. Bennett to Glaser, July 21, 1993.

4. From R. Dickover's marginal comments, in August 1933, on a draft of this book, and from his letter to Glaser, September 13, 1993.

5. From letter by R. Dickover to Glaser, September 17, 1993.

6. From letter by R. Dickover to Glaser, September 25, 1993.

7. From notes sent by N. Holt to Glaser, based on Holt's report for the Little Hoover Commission, June 23, 1993.

8. From phone conversation, Glaser to Holt, September 25, 1993, and from Bass, 1975, 6–7.

9. From letter by L. Bennett to Glaser, July 21, 1993.

10. From letter by D. Gottfredson to Glaser, August 2, 1993.

11. Transcribed from D. Brewer's March 30, 1982 tape-recorded interview of McGee.

12. From letter by R. Dickover to Glaser, October 8, 1993.

13. From phone conversation, Glaser to R. Polakow, Program Services Officer, Los Angeles County Department of Probation, September 1, 1993.

Chapter 5

1. From letter by L. Bennett to Glaser, July 21, 1993, and letter from R. Dickover to Glaser, September 25, 1993.

2. From letter by D. Gottfredson to Glaser, August 2, 1993.

3. Transcribed from D. Brewer's March 30, 1982 tape-recorded interview of McGee.

4. This quotation from Robert Martinson, *New Findings, New Views: A Note of Caution Regarding Sentencing Reform*, 7 HOFSTRA L. REV. 243, 257(1979) is reprinted with the permission of Hofstra Law Review.

Chapter 6

1. Kenneth Kirkpatrick, who was eventually reinstated.

2. From R. Dickerson's marginal comments, in August 1993, on a draft of this book.

Chapter 7

1. The quotations in this chapter from Richard A. McGee, "The Past is Prologue," ANNALS OF THE AMERICAN ACADEMY OF POLITICAL AND SOCIAL SCIENCE Vol. 381 (January 1969), 1–10, copyright 1969, by the American Academy of Political and Social Science, reprinted by permission of Sage Publications, Inc.

2. This quotation is the opening of Messinger, 1969.

3. Transcribed from D. Brewer's March 30, 1982 tape-recorded interview of McGee.

4. Fitchburg District Court (Massachusetts) No.9016/JC/1490 (A)(B) Commonwealth v. Sinethorne Manisy.

5. The quotation designated "McGee, 1943" is from *Proceedings of the 1943 Annual Congress of Correction* reprinted with permission of the American Correctional Association, Laurel, MD.

References

Abramson, H. 1983. "State's First Corrections Chief, Richard McGee, Sr., is Dead at 86." *Sacramento Bee*, October 31.

Adams, S. 1962. "The PICO Project." In N. Johnston, et al., (eds.) *The Sociology of Punishment and Corrections*. 1st Ed. New York: Wiley (also in 2nd ed., 1970).

Albrecht, H. 1984. "Recidivism After Fines, Suspended Sentences, and Imprisonment." *Journal of Comparative and Applied Criminal Justice* 8(2):199–207.

Alschuler, A. 1978. "Sentencing Reform and Prosecutorial Power." In National Institute of Law Enforcement and Criminal Justice, *Determinate Sentencing: Reform or Regression?* Washington, D.C.: U.S. Department of Justice.

Anglin, M. 1988. "The Efficacy of Civil Commitment in Treating Narcotics Addiction." *Journal of Drug Issues* 18(3):527–45.

Auerbach, B. 1993. "Federal Government Involvement in Private Sector Partnerships With Prison Industries." In G. Bowman et al., *Privatizing Correctional Institutions*. New Brunswick: Transaction Publishers.

Austin, J., et al., 1993. *The Growing Use of Jail Boot Camps: The Current State of the Art*. Washington, D.C.: National Institute of Justice, Research in Brief.

Austin, R. L. 1975. "Construct Validity of I–Level Classification." *Criminal Justice and Behavior* 2(2):113–29.

Baird, S., and Austin, J. 1985. *Current State of the Art in Prison Classification Models*. San Francisco: National Council on Crime and Delinquency.

Bakalar, J., and Grinspoon, L. 1984. *Drug Control in a Free Society*. Cambridge: Cambridge University Press.

Barnes, H., and Teeters, N. 1959. *New Horizons in Criminology*. 3rd Ed. Englewood Cliffs: Prentice–Hall.

Bass, R. 1975. *An Analysis of the California Department of Corrections Work Furlough Program in Fiscal Year 1969–70*. Sacramento: California Department of Correction, Research Report No.57.

Bookspan, R. 1987. "'A Germ of Goodness': Labor and Penal Policy in California, 1849–1944." Unpublished Ph.D. Dissertation in History, University of California, Santa Barbara.

Bowman, G., et al., (eds.) 1993. *Privatizing Correctional Institutions*. New Brunswick: Transaction Publishers.

Braithwaite, J. 1989. *Crime, Shame and Reintegration*. Cambridge, England: Cambridge University Press.

Bramford, P. 1973. *Fighting Ships and Prisons*. Minneapolis: University of Minnesota Press.

Brewer, D., et al., 1981. "Determinate Sentencing in California: The First Year's Experience." *Journal of Research in Crime and Delinquency* 18(2):200–31.

Bureau of Justice Statistics. 1992a. *Attorney General's Program for Improving the Nation's Criminal History Records*. Washington, D.C.: Department of Justice, NCJ–134722.

———. 1992b. *Bureau of Justice Statistics Statistical Programs, Fiscal Year 1993*. Washington, D.C.: Department of Justice, NCJ 139373.

———. 1993a. *Survey of State Prison Inmates, 1991*. Washington, D.C.: Department of Justice, NCJ–136949.

———. 1993b. *Data Available From the National Archive of Criminal Justice Data, Update Summer 1992*. Ann Arbor: ICPSR, Institute for Social Research.

Burkhart, W. 1969. "The Parole Work Unit Programme." *British Journal of Criminology* 9(2):125–57.

———. 1977. "The Great Parole Experiment." In E. Miller and M. Montilla, (eds.), *Corrections in the Community*. Reston: Reston Publishing Company.

California Youth and Adult Corrections Agency, Board of Corrections. 1965. *Probation Study*. Sacramento: The Agency.

California Youth Authority. 1980. *Institutional Violence Reduction Project: The Impact of Changes in Living Unit Size and Staffing*. Sacramento: California Youth Authority.

Cikins, W. 1933. "Partial Privatization of Prison Operations: Let's Give it a Chance." in G. Bowman et al.

Clarke, S. 1983. "Sentencing: Determinate Sentencing." In *Encyclopedia of Crime and Justice*. New York: Free Press.

Coates, R., et al., 1978. *Diversity in a Youth Correctional System: Handling Delinquents in Massachusetts*. Cambridge: Ballinger.

Cohen, R. L. 1992. *Drunk Driving*. Washington, DC: Bureau of Justice Statistics.

Conrad, J. 1977. "News of the Future: Research and Development in Corrections." *Federal Probation* 41(4):51–54.

———. 1978. "The Law and Its Promises: Flat Terms, Good Time, and Flexible Incarceration." In National Institute of Law and Justice, *Determinate Sentencing: Reform or Regression?* Washington, D.C.: U.S. Department of Justice.

———. 1979. "Who Needs a Doorbell Pusher?" Prison Journal 59(2):17–26 (Reprinted in Conrad, *Justice and Consequences*. 1981. Boston: Lexington Books)

———. 1981a. "Foreword," in G. McGee, 1981.

———. 1981b. "A Lost Ideal, a New Hope: The Way Toward Effective Correctional Treatment." *Journal of Criminal Law and Criminology* 72(4):1699–1734.

———. 1984. "Administrative Craftsman." *Corrections Today* 46(2):81.

Cook, P. 1975. "The Correctional Carrot: Better Jobs for Parolees." *Policy Sciences* 1(4):11–53.

Cooper, L. 1993. "Minimizing Liability With Private Management of Correctional Facilities." In G. Bowman, et al.

Corbet, T. 1993. "Child Poverty and Welfare Reform." *Focus (University of Wisconsin–Madison Institute for Research on Poverty)* 15(1):1–17.

Cronbach, L. 1957. "The Two Disciplines of Scientific Psychology." *American Psychologist* 12(6):671–84.

Cullen, F., and Gilbert, K. 1982. *Reaffirming Rehabilitation*. Cincinnati: Anderson.

DeWitt, C. 1986. "California Tests New Construction Concepts." *National Institute of Justice Construction Bulletin*. Washington, D.C.: National Institute of Justice.

Dickover, R., et al., 1971. *A Study of Vocational Training in the California Department of Corrections*. Sacramento: California Department of Corrections Research Report No.40.

Dickover, R., and Durkee, K. 1974. *Guidance in Sentencing: The Pre–Sentence Diagnostic Observation Program*. Sacramento: California Department of Correction, Research Report No.53.

DiIulio, J. 1991. *No Escape: The Future of American Corrections*. New York: Basic Books.

Dorris, M. 1989. *The Broken Chord*. New York: Harper and Row.

Dwyer, D., and McNally, R. 1993. "Public policy, prison industries, and business: An equitable balance for the 1990s." *Federal Probation* 57(2):30–36.

Ethridge, P., and Marquart, J. "Private Prisons in Texas: The New Penology for Profit." *Justice Quarterly* 10(1):29–48.

Feeney, F. 1978. "Foreword." In Lemert and Dill, 1978.

Felson, M. 1993. Crime and Everyday Life. Thousand Oaks: Pine Forge Press.

Finn, P. and Newlyn, A. 1993. *Dade County Diverts Drug Defendants to Court–Run Rehabilitation Program.* Washington, D.C.: U.S. Department of Justice, Program Focus NCJ 142412.

Flynn, E. 1980. "Foreword." In J. O. Smykla, (ed.) *Co-ed Prison.* New York: Human Sciences Press.

Frankel, M. 1973. *Criminal Sentences—Law Without Order.* New York: Hill and Wang.

Garland, D. 1986. "Foucault's Discipline and Punish: An Exposition and Critique." *American Bar Foundation Research Journal* 1986(4):847–80.

Gendreau, P., and Ross, B. 1979. Effective Correctional Treatment: Bibliotherapy for Cynics." *Crime and Delinquency* 25(4)463–89.

Gilbreth, F., and Carey, E. 1948. *Cheaper by the Dozen.* New York: Crowell.

Glaser, D. 1955. "Testing Correctional Decisions." *Journal of Criminal Law, Criminology, and Police Science* 14(3):679–84.

———. 1957a. "Criminal Career Statistics." In: *Proceedings, American Correctional Association, 1956.* Laurel: The Association, 103–06..

———. 1957b. "Released Offender Statistics: A Proposal for a National Program." *American Journal of Correction* 19(2):15–17, 25.

———. 1961. "Correctional Research in California: An Outsider's View." Unpublished Consultant's Report to California Department of Corrections.

———. 1964. *The Effectiveness of a Prison and Parole System.* Indianapolis: Bobbs-Merrill.

———. 1969. *Ibid.* Abridged Edition.

———. 1973. *Routinizing Evaluation.* Washington, D.C.: National Institute of Mental Health.

———. 1982. "Social Science Perspectives on Classification Decisions." In *Classification as a Management Tool.* College Park: American Correctional Association.

————. 1994. "What Works and Why it is Important: A Response to Logan and Gaes." *Justice Quarterly* 11(4):711–23.

Glaser, D., with Erez, E. 1988. *Evaluation Research and Decision Guidance*. New Brunswick: Transaction Publishers.

Glaser, D., and Gordon, M. 1990. "Profitable Penalties for Lower Level Courts." *Judicature* 73(5):248–52.

Glaser, D., and Watts, R. 1991. "Electronic Monitoring of Drug Offenders on Probation." *Judicature* 76(3):112–17.

Glaser, L. 1992. "What Do Urine Tests Test?" *Massachusetts Bar Association/ Criminal Justice Section News*. July:3,7.

Goldstein, A. 1983. "Excuse: Insanity." In *Encyclopedia of Crime and Justice*. New York: Free Press.

Gordon, M., and Glaser, D. 1991. "The Use and Effects of Financial Penalties in Municipal Courts." *Criminology* 29(4):651–76.

Gottfredson, D., and Gottfredson, M. 1982. "Risk Assessment: An Evaluation of Statistical Classification Methods. In *Classification as a Management Tool*. College Park: American Correctional Association.

Griset, P. 1991. *Determinate Sentencing: The Promise and the Reality of Retributive Justice*. Albany: State University of New York Press.

Halleck, S., and Witte, A. 1977. "Is Rehabilitation Dead?" *Crime and Delinquency* 23(4):372–82.

Halley, D. 1992. "Richard A. McGee—Profile of a Criminal Justice Pioneer," Unpublished Master of Science Dissertation in Criminal Justice, California State University, Sacramento.

Harris, R. 1993. "One State Gives Juveniles a Hand Instead of a Cell." *Los Angeles Times*. August 25. 1993.

Harrison, R., and Mueller, P. 1964. *Clue Hunting About Group Counseling and Parole Outcome*. Sacramento: California Department of Corrections, Research Report No. 11.

Havel, J. 1965. *Special Intensive Parole Unit, Phase Four*. Sacramento: California Department of Correction, Research Report No. 13.

Havel, J., and Sulka, E. 1962. *Special Intensive Parole Unit: Phase Three*. Sacramento: California Department of Correction, Research Report No. 3.

Hillsman, S. 1990. "Fines and Day Fines." In M. Tonry and N. Morris, (eds.) *Crime and Justice: A review of Research*. Vol. 12. Chicago: University of Chicago Press.

Himelson, A. 1968. "When Treatment Failed: A Study of the Attempt of a Public Service Organization to Change the Behavior of an Intransigent Population." Unpublished Ph.D. Dissertation in Sociology, University of California, Los Angeles.

Holt, N., et al., 1982. "California's New Inmate Classification system." In *Classification as a Management Tool*. College Park: American Correctional Association.

Holt, N., and Miller, D. 1972. *Explorations in Inmate–Family Relationships*. Sacramento: California Department of Corrections, Research Report No. 46.

Hser, Y., et al., 1993 "A 24–Year Follow–up of California Narcotics Addicts." *Archives of General Psychiatry* 50(7):577–84.

Jacobs, J. 1977. *Stateville: The Penitentiary in Mass Society*. Chicago: University of Chicago Press.

———. 1979. "Race Relations and the Prisoner Subculture." In N. Morris and M. Tonry, (eds.) *Crime and Justice: An Annual Review of Research*. Vol. I. Chicago: University of Chicago Press.

Jencks, C. 1992. *Rethinking Social Policy: Race, Poverty and the Underclass*. Cambridge: Harvard University Press.

Jessness, C. 1972. "Comparative Effectiveness of Two Institutional Treatment Programs for Delinquents." *Childcare Quarterly* 1972:119–30.

———. 1975. "Comparative Effectiveness of Behavior Modification and Transactional Analysis Programs for Delinquents." *Journal of Consulting and Clinical Psychology* 43(6):758–79.

Jew, C., et al., 1975. *Effectiveness of Group Psychotherapy With Character Disordered Prisoners*. Sacramento: California Department of Corrections, Research Report No. 56.

Joel, D. 1933. "The Privatization of Secure Adult Prisons: Issues and Evidence." In G. Bowman, et al.

Johns, D. A., et al., 1974. *California's Probation Subsidy Program: A Progress Report to the Legislature*. Sacramento: California Youth Authority.

Joint Committee on New York's Drug Law. 1977. *The Nation's Toughest Drug Law: Evaluating New York's Experience*. New York: Association of the Bar of the City of New York.

Jolin, A., and Stipak, D. 1992. "Drug Treatment and Electronically Monitored Home Confinement." *Crime and Delinquency* 38(2):159–70.

Jones, M. 1953. *The Therapeutic Community*. New York: Basic Books.

Judicial Council of California. 1989. *1989 Annual Report*. Sacramento: The Council.

Karoly, L. 1993. "The Trend in Inequality Among Families, Individuals and Workers in the U.S." In S. Danziger and P. Gottschalk, (eds.) *Uneven Tides: Rising Inequality in America*. New York: Russell Sage Foundation.

Kassebaum, G., et al., 1971. *Prison Treatment and Parole Survival*. New York: Wiley.

Katcher, L. 1967. *Earl Warren: A Political Biography*. New York: McGraw–Hill.

Katz, J. 1988. *Seductions of Crime*. New York: Basic Books.

———. 1991. "The Motivation of the Persistent Robber." In M. Tonry, (ed.) *Crime and Justice: A Review of Research*. Vol. 14. Chicago: University of Chicago Press.

Keve, P. 1991. *Prisons and the American Conscience: A History of U.S. Federal Corrections*. Carbondale: Southern Illinois University Press.

Kinkade, P., et al. 1992. "Probation and the Drunk Driver: The Cost of Being MADD." *Federal Probation* 56(2):6–15.

Kinkade, P., and Leone, C. 1992. "The Effects of 'Tough' Drunk Driving Laws on Policing: A Case Study." *Crime and Delinquency* 38(2):239–57.

Knight, D. 1971. *The Impact of Living-Unit Size in Youth Training Schools*. Sacramento: California Youth Authority.

Krahn, H., et al., 1986. "Income Inequality and Homicide Rates." *Criminology* 24(2):269–95.

Kramer, J., and Bass, R. 1969. "Institutionalization Patterns Among Civilly Committed Addicts." *Journal of the American Medical Association* 208 (June 23, 1969):2297–2301.

Krisberg, B., and Austin, J. 1993. *Reinventing Juvenile Justice*. Newbury Park: Sage.

Laub, J., and Sampson, R. 1993. "Turning Points in the Life Course: Why Change Matters to the Study of Crime." *Criminology* 31(3):301–25.

Lemert, E. 1967. *Human Deviance, Social Problems, and Social Control*. Englewood Cliffs, N.J.: Prentice-Hall.

Lemert, E., and Dill, F. 1978. *Offenders in the Community: The Probation Subsidy in California*. Boston: Lexington Books.

Lenihan, K. 1977. *Unlocking the Second Gate*. Washington, D.C.: U.S. Department of Labor, R. & D. Monograph No. 45

Leopold, N. 1958. *Life Plus 99 Years*. New York: Doubleday.

Lerman, P. 1968. "Evaluative Studies of Institutions for Delinquents: Implications for Research and Social Policy." *Social Work* 13(3)55–65.

Lewis, R. 1976. *M–2 Project Evaluation: Final Parole Follow–Up of Wards in the M–2 Program.* Sacramento: Department of the Youth Authority.

Liberman, R., et al., 1993. "A Plan for Rescuing the Mentally Ill: These Californians Face a Terrible Fate as the State Shifts Responsibility to Financially Strapped Counties." *Los Angeles Times*, Commentary Section, September 6, 1993.

Lilly, J., et al., 1992. "The Pride, Inc., Program: An Evaluation of 5 Years of Electronic Monitoring." *Federal Probation* 56(4):42–47.

Lindesmith, A. 1965. *The Addict and the Law.* Bloomington: Indiana University Press.

Lipton, D., et al., 1975. *The Effectiveness of Correctional Treatment.* New York: Praeger.

Logan, C. 1972. "Evaluation Research in Crime and Delinquency: A Reappraisal." *Journal of Criminal Law, Criminology and Police Science* 63(3):378–87.

———. 1990. *Pros and Cons.* New York: Oxford University Press.

———. 1992. "Well Kept: Comparing Quality of Confinement in Private and Public Prisons." *Journal of Criminal Law and Criminology* 83(3):577–613.

Logan, C., and Gaes, G. 1993. "Meta-Analysis and the Rehabilitation of Punishment." *Justice Quarterly* 10(2):245–63.

Los Angeles Times. 1933. "Bill to Limit Conjugal Visits is Defeated." May 19, 1993.

MacKenzie, D. 1991. "The Parole Performance of Offenders Released From Shock Incarceration (Boot Camp Prisons): A Survival Time Analysis." *Journal of Quantitative Criminology* 7(3):213–36.

MacKenzie, D., and Paren, D. 1992. "Boot Camp Prisons for Young Offenders." In J. Byrne, et al., (eds.) *Smart Sentencing.* Newbury Park: Sage.

Mannheim, H., and Wilkins, L. 1955. *Prediction Methods in Relation to Borstal Training.* London: H. M. Stationery Office.

Martinson, R. 1974. "What Works?—Questions and Answers About Prison Reform." *The Public Interest* 35:22–54.

———. 1976. "California Research at the Crossroads." *Crime and Delinquency* 22(2):180–91.

———. 1979. "New Findings, New Views: A Note of Caution Regarding Sentencing Reform." *Hofstra Law Review* 7(2):243–58.

Massey, D., and Denton, N. 1993. *American Apartheid: Segregation and the Making of the Underclass.* Cambridge: Harvard University Press.

Mattera, P. 1990. *Prosperity Lost*. Reading: Addison–Wesley.

McAfee, W. 1990a. "A History of Convict Labor in California." *Southern California Quarterly* 72(1):19–40.

———. 1990b. "San Quentin: The Forgotten Issue of California's Political History in the 1850s." *Southern California Quarterly* 72(3):235–54.

McCrie, R. 1933. "Private Correction: The Delicate Balance." In G. Bowman et al., 1933.

McDonald, D. 1990. *Private Prisons and the Public Interest*. New Brunswick: Rutgers University Press.

McGee, R. 1937. *The Problem of the Petty Offender of the City of New York*. New York: Penitentiary of the City of New York, Rikers Island (Pamphlet printed for the Regional Conference on Social Hygiene of the Social Hygiene Council of Greater New York, at New York City's Pennsylvania Hotel, February 3).

———. 1939. "Institutional Maintenance Work and Industries as Educational Agencies." In *Correctional Education Today*. Laurel: American Prisons Association.

———. 1943. "Presidential Address: Correctional Administration in a Changing World." *Proceedings of the 73rd Annual Congrees of Correction of the American Prison Association*. Laurel: The Association.

———. 1947a. *Panel Discussion of General Administrative Problems*. (Mimeographed document identifying McGee as discussant, but not indicating where or exactly when discussion occurred.)

———. 1947b. *Public Aspects of Alcoholism*. Presented at Institute on Alcoholic Studies, UCLA, October 1947.

———. 1949. "Correctional Administration in California." *Canadian Bar Review*. 27(9):1127–1139.

———. 1951. "A Quarter Century of Progress in the Treatment of the Offender." Speech at 13th Annual Conference, Western Probation and Parole Officers Association, Vancouver, B.C., August 1951.

———. 1952. *Establishing Nationwide Standards for Prison Administration*. Speech at Western Governmental Research Association, October 24, 1952.

———. 1953a. "Prisons at the Crossroads." *Proceedings of the Annual Congress of Correction*, Toronto, Canada, October 12, 1953.

———. 1953b. "California's Prison Program." *Tax Digest* 31(11):373–76, 388–94.

———. 1953c. *The Role of Labor and Management in the Rehabilitation of Prisoners.* Paper presented to North American Conference on Apprenticeship, Balboa Park, California, August 4, 1953.

———. 1954a. "Saving Prison Waste." *Annals of the American Academy of Political and Social Science* 293:59–69.

———. 1954b. "Doing the Job Together." *Focus (National Probation and Parole Association)* 33(6):179–84.

———. 1957. Statement on Group Supervision (Institutions) for Hearing of the State Personnel Board, October 19, 1957, Item 13.

———. 1958. *The Administration of Justice—The Correctional Process.* Presentation at the Police–Community Relations Institute, Michigan State University, May 21, 1958.

———. 1962. *Statement to Senate Committee on Judiciary, Public Hearing on Senate Resolution No. 87.* March 8 and 9, 1962. (Distributed by California Youth and Adult Corrections Agency).

———. 1963. "Correction Faces Social Change." *Correctional Review* 1(3):19–24. (This journal was briefly published by the California Department of Correction, and is in few libraries.)

———. 1964a. *Treatment and Management of the Criminally Insane.* Paper for Interstate Workshop on the Criminally Insane, Midwestern Governors; Conference, Minneapolis, Minnesota, July 29.

———. 1964b. "Capital Punishment as Seen by a Correctional Administrator." *Federal Probation* 28(2):11–16.

———. 1965. "New Approaches to the Control and Treatment of Drug Abusers in California." In D. Wilner and G. Kassebaum, (eds.) *Narcotics.* New York: McGraw–Hill.

———. 1969. "What's Past is Prologue." *Annals of the American Academy of Political and Social Science* 381:1–10.

———. 1971a. "Our Sick Jails." *Federal Probation* 35(1):3–8.

———. 1971b. "The Organizational Structure of State and Local Correctional Services." *Public Administration Review* 31(6):616–21.

———. 1973. *Research in Crime Prevention and the Administration of Criminal Justice.* Presentation to United Nations Interregional Seminar, Copenhagen, August 27, 1973.

———. 1974a. "A New Look at Sentencing: Part I." *Federal Probation* 38(2):3–8.

————. 1974b. "A New Look at Sentencing: Part II." *Federal Probation* 38(3):3–11.

————. 1976a. *Participant in the Evolution of American Corrections: 1931–1973*. Berkeley: University of California, Bancroft Library, Earl Warren Oral History Project, MS# 12011.

————. 1976b. *Research and Development in Criminal Justice*. Presentation at Institute of Contemporary Corrections and the Behavioral Sciences, Sam Houston State University, Huntsville, Texas, June 11, 1976.

————. 1978. "California's New Determinate Sentencing Act." *Federal Probation* 42(1):3–10.

————. 1979. *Where Does Probation Fit Into California's Correctional Plan?* Presentation at Chief Probation Officers Meeting, San Jose, September 17, 1979.

————. 1980a. *Notes Concerning Probation as a Part of the Criminal Justice System, and Some of the Problems Confronting it in the 1980s.* (A draft dated July 23, 1980 and labeled "Unedited transcript from a tape"; slightly edited here by Glaser.)

————. 1980b. *Probation—An Occupation and a Public Function in Trouble.* (a draft dated July 23, 1980).

————. 1981. *Prisons and Politics*. Boston: Lexington Books.

McGee, R., and Montilla, M. 1967. *The Organization of State Correctional Services in the Control and Treatment of Crime and Delinquency*. Sacramento: State of California Youth and Adult Corrections Agency.

McKee, G. 1972. "A Cost–Benefit Analysis of Vocational Training in the California Prison System." Unpublished Ph.D. Dissertation in Economics. Claremont Graduate School.

————. 1978. "Cost–Effectiveness and Vocational Training." In N. Johnston and L. Savitz, *Crime and Justice*. New York: Wiley.

————. 1984. "Cost–Benefit Analysis of Vocational Training." In R. Carter, D. Glaser, and L. Wilkins, *Correctional Institutions*. 3rd ed. New York: Harper & Row.

McKelvey, B. 1977. *American Prisons: A History of Good Intentions*. Montclair: Patterson Smith.

McKenna, C., 1987. "The Origins of San Quentin." *California History* 66(1):49–54.

Messinger, S. 1969. "Strategies of Control." Ph.D. Dissertation in Sociology. University of California, Los Angeles.

Messinger, S., Berecochea, J., Rauma, D., and Berk, R. 1985. "The Foundations of Parole in California." *Law and Society Review* 19(1):69–106.

Messner, S. 1989. "Economic Discrimination and Societal Homicide Rates." *American Sociological Review* 53(4):597–611.

Miller, D. 1980. "Alternatives to Incarceration: From Total Institutions to Total Systems." Unpublished Doctor of Criminology Dissertation, University of California, Berkeley.

Miller, J. 1991. *Last One Over the Wall.* Columbus: Ohio State University Press.

Molof, M. 1967. *Forestry Camp Study.* Sacramento: California Youth Authority Research Report No. 53.

Morales, R. 1980. "History of the California Institution for Women, 1927–1960: A Woman's Regime." Unpublished Ph.D. Dissertation in History, University of California, Riverside.

Morse, B., and Elliott, D. 1992. "Effects of Ignition Interlock Devices on DUI Recidivism." *Crime and Delinquency* 38(2):131–57.

Murray, C., and Cox, L. 1979. *Beyond Probation.* Newbury Park: Sage.

Needels, K. 1993. "The Long–term Effects of the Transitional Aid Research Project in Texas: Recidivism and Employment Results." Unpublished Draft Report. Princeton: Princeton University Industrial Relations Section.

Orsagh, T., and Witte, A. 1981. "Economic Status and Crime: Implications for Offender Rehabilitation." *Journal of Criminal Law and Criminology* 72(3):1055–71.

Palmer, J. 1975. "Pre–arrest Diversion: The Night Prosecutors' Program in Columbus, Ohio." *Crime and Delinquency* 21(4):100–108.

Palmer, T. 1974. "The Youth Authority's Community Treatment Project." *Federal Probation* 38(1):3–14.

———. 1975. "Martinson Revisited." *Journal of Research in Crime and Delinquency* 12:133–52.

———. 1978. *Correctional Intervention and Research.* Boston: Lexington Books.

Petersilia, J. 1979. "Which Inmates Participate in Prison Treatment Programs?" *Journal of Offender Counseling, Services and Rehabilitation* 4(4):121–35.

Pollack, J. 1979. *Earl Warren: The Judge Who Changed America.* Englewood Cliffs: Prentice–Hall.

Quay, H. 1977. "The Three Faces of Evaluation: What Can be Expected to Work?" *Criminal Justice and Behavior* 4(6):341–54.

Rauma, D., and Berk, R. 1987. "Remuneration and Recidivism." *Journal of Quantitative Criminology* 14(3):3–27.

Reimer, E., and Warren, M. 1957. "Special Intensive Parole Unit." *National Probation and Parole Association Journal* 3(3):222–29.

Robison, J., and Takagi, P. 1968. *Case Decisions in a State Parole System.* Sacramento: California Department of Corrections, Research Report No. 31.

Robison, J. et al., 1971. *By the Standard of His Rehabilitation: Information, Decision, and Outcome in Terminations From Parole: The Implementation of Penal Code Section 2943.* Sacramento: California Department of Correction, Research Report No. 39.

Rosenhahn, D. 1973. "On Being Sane in Insane Places." *Science* 179(4070):250–58.

Ross, H. 1992. *Confronting Drunken Drivers.* New Haven: Yale University Press.

Rossi, P., et al., 1980. *Money, Work, and Crime.* New York: Academic Press.

Rusche, G., and Kirchheimer, O. 1939. *Punishment and Social Structure.* New York: Columbia University Press.

Sampson, R. 1987. "Urban Black Violence: The Effect of Male Joblessness and Family Disruption." *American Journal of Sociology* 93(2):348–82.

Sampson, R., and Laub, J. 1992. *Crime in the Making.* Cambridge, Mass.: Harvard University Press.

Sarason, I., and Ganzer, V. 1973. "Modeling and Group Discussion in the Rehabilitation of Juvenile Delinquents." *Journal of Counseling Psychology* 20:(3)442–49.

Scudder, K. 1952. *Prisoners are People.* Garden City: Doubleday.

Sechrest, L., et al., (eds.) 1979. *The Rehabilitation of Criminal Offenders: Problems and Prospects.* Washington, D.C.: National Academy of Sciences.

Seckel, J. 1965. *Experiments in Group Counseling at Two Youth Authority Institutions.* Sacramento: California Youth Authority, Research Report No. 11.

Seckel, J., et al., 1973. *A Comparative Study of the Community Parole Center Program.* Sacramento: California Youth Authority, Research Report No. 63.

Simon. J. 1990. "From Discipline to Management: Strategies of Control in Parole Supervision, 1890–1990." Unpublished Ph.D. Dissertation in Jurisprudence and Social Policy, University of California, Berkeley.

Smith, R. 1972. *A Quiet Revolution.* Washington, D.C.: U.S. Department of Health, Education, and Welfare, Publication No.72–26011.

Smith, R., and Vanski, J. 1979. "The Volatile Teenage Labor Market: Labor Force Entry, Exit, and Unemployment Flows." *Youth and Society* 11(9):3–31.

Spencer, C., and Berecochea, J. 1972. *Recidivism Among Women Parolees: A Long Term-Survey*. Sacramento: California Department of Corrections, Research Report No. 47.

Spindler, R., et al., 1986. *Inmate Classification System Study: Final Report*. Sacramento: California Department of Corrections.

Star, D. 1979. *Summary Parole: A Six and Twelve Month Follow-up Evaluation*. Sacramento: California Department of Correction, Research Report No. 60.

————. 1981. *Investigation and Surveillance in Parole Supervision*. Sacramento: California Department of Correction, Research Report No. 63.

Studt, E., et al., 1968. *C-Unit: Search for Community in Prison*. New York: Russell Sage Foundation.

Sullivan, C., et al., 1957. "The Development of Interpersonal Maturity: Applications to Delinquency." *Psychiatry* 20(4):373–85.

Takagi, P. 1967. "Evaluation Systems and Adaptations in a Formal Organization: A Case Study of a Parole Agency." Unpublished Ph.D. Dissertation in Sociology, Stanford University.

Toch, H. 1977. *Living in Prison: The Ecology of Survival*. New York: Free Press.

Vaillant, G. 1983. *The Natural History of Alcoholism*. Cambridge, Mass.: Harvard University Press.

Visher, C., and McFadden, K. 1991. *A Comparison of Urinalysis Technologies for Drug Testing in Criminal Justice*. Washington, D.C.: National Institute of Justice, Research in Action. June 1991.

Voigt, L. 1949. *History of California State Correctional Administration From 1930 to 1948*. San Francisco. (Publisher not indicated; appears to be privately printed and distributed to libraries, but text indicates it is an update of a 1929 Master's thesis in Political Science by Milton Chernin at University of California, Berkeley.)

von Hirsch, A., 1978. *Past or Future Crimes: Deservedness and Dangerousness in the Sentencing of Criminals*. New Brunswick: Rutgers University Press.

von Hirsch, A., and Hanrahan, K. 1978. *Abolish Parole?* Washington, D.C.: U.S. Department of Justice.

————. 1992. "Prediction and False Positives." In A. von Hirsch and Ashworth, A. (eds.) *Principled Sentencing*. Boston: Northeastern University Press.

Warren, E. 1977. *The Memoirs of Chief Justice Earl Warren*. Garden City: Doubleday.

Weaver, J. 1967. *Warren: The Man, the Court, the Era.* Boston: Little Brown.

Weber, M. 1978. *Economy and Society.* Edited by G. Roth and C. Wittich. Berkeley: University of California Press, Vol. II.

Wedge, R., et al., 1980. "I–Level and the Treatment of Delinquents." *Youth Authority Quarterly* 33(4):26–37.

Wilkins, L., andGottfredson, D. 1969. *Research, Demonstration, and Social Action.* Davis, Calif., NCCD Research Center (Now archived at Criminal Justice/ NCCD Collection, Center for Law and Justice, Rutgers University at Newark).

Wilson, J. 1980. "'What Works?' Revisited." *The Public Interest* 61:3–17.

Winterfield, L., and Hillsman, S. 1993. *The Staten Island Day Fine Project.* Washington, D.C.: National Institute of Justice: Research in Brief Series.

Yaley, B. 1980. "Habits of Industry: Labor and Penal Policy in California, 1849–1940." Unpublished Ph.D. Dissertation in History of Consciousness, University of California, Santa Cruz.

Zimbardo, G., et al., 1973. "A Pirandellian Prison: The Mind is a Formidable Jailer." *New York Times Magazine* (April 8, 1973):38–40.

Index